A History of Income Tax

A History of
INCOME TAX

B. E. V. SABINE

London

GEORGE ALLEN & UNWIN LTD

RUSKIN HOUSE MUSEUM STREET

PRINTED IN GREAT BRITAIN
in 10 point Times Roman type
BY HAZELL WATSON AND VINEY LTD
AYLESBURY, BUCKS

Foreword

To understand all is to forgive all – perhaps; though it is hard to think of any circumstances in which the taxpayer can wholly forgive his taxmasters. But if taxation is the scourge of the twentieth century – the civilised evil, as it were – we must learn to live with it. And we may hope that our masters will also learn, at least humility, from this brilliant work by Mr Sabine on the history of income tax.

It is the first history of its kind ever to be written, and – deservedly – it will long remain a standard work. Like all historical works of real value (they are fewer than might be imagined from the bookshelves), it illuminates more than its own subject. Without departing from his clinical detachment, or losing the main thread of his history, Mr Sabine traces the development of a whole range of social thinking. 'Of all the dangerous doctrines that could possibly be held out in a legislative assembly, there was not one that could be more mischievous in its tendency than that of equalising all ranks of society by reducing the higher orders to a level with those of a different class, and depriving them of every comfort which they had a right to expect from their exalted situation.' That was Lord Henry Petty, introducing the Income Tax Act of 1806, and pouring scorn on those who suggested that the tax might be graduated, so that the rich paid at a higher rate than the poor. 'Right to expect . . .!' – it is inconceivable that such a sentiment could be expressed in the Commons today. Yet in 1806 the majority agreed with Lord Henry.

We have changed all that, and income tax has been an important instrument of change. But its use as an instrument of social reform was not accidental; it was bitterly contested, and the fact that Chancellors do not raise an eyebrow now by regarding their budgets as instruments of social planning as well as fiscal policy owes everything to the campaigns of individual reformers. Political memories are short, and it is good to be reminded by Mr Sabine of the high place in English social history of Sir William Harcourt and Sir Charles Dilke.

The mechanics of reform are seldom regarded as sharing in importance with the ideals of reformers, but without human mechanism no human purpose could ever be achieved. It is an accepted national tradition that our Civil Service 'is wonderful,' but the devoted (and often ill-paid) work of the Revenue staffs in enabling the assessment and collection of income tax to be done at all is almost beyond belief. What is more, it is done fairly. We may complain of unfairness in the incidence of tax, but that is a complaint against Governments: no one in Britain can complain of unfairness in the administration of tax collection by the Board of Inland Revenue and its officials. The integrity of the inspectorate is a national honour. So, I think, is the behaviour of taxpayers, in spite of the evasions that we hear so much about in Parliament from time to time. There may be grouse moors on some expense sheets locked in Somerset House, but certainly there are not many.

Mr Sabine is concerned to record, not to criticise. From his important record – put together for the first time – there will emerge, I hope, a new body of constructive criticism, an approach towards a philosophy of income tax. For all its untold blessings, the harnessing of atomic energy may lead to the destruction of man's physical world; so perfecting the instrument of income tax may destroy the structure of human society. For many God has been all-but argued out of existence, and mammon taxed out of existence: in a world without God or mammon, what is left? Talk of incentives is the small change of modern politics, but man *does* need incentive to break out of the common rut of existence. The First Elizabethans whom we are so often told to emulate made Britain great: they did so in a spirit of independence, knowing that they worked for themselves as well as for the State. There are limits to healthy public spending, strict limits to the idea of 'The State owes me an upbringing, a university education, a living – let the State look after me.' The machine of income tax in its modern efficiency has levers that are already, perhaps, too tempting to some political theorists. Mr Sabine has not asked political questions, but his work invites them. That is its special importance, for it enables questioning to be based on accurate, historical fact. In this, it seems to me, Mr Sabine has done a unique service to our society.

J. R. L. ANDERSON

Contents

Introduction

My thanks are due, in the first place, to the Board of Inland Revenue for permission to write this book while still a member of the Chief Inspector's Branch on the understanding that it was to be a purely historical account. I must thank my colleagues both in the Association of Inspectors of Taxes and in the Inland Revenue Staff Federation, too, for opinions, anecdotes and explanations, some of which they may recognize; in particular, I should mention Victor Grout, H.M. Senior Principal Inspector of Taxes, who has read each chapter in typescript and made many valuable suggestions and amendments, while leaving the whole still my own responsibility.

I am most grateful to the staff of the Board's Library, especially Miss Williams and Mr Berry, for unlimited help and trouble. The local libraries of Stalybridge and Stockport, too, have given notable assistance, along with the Manchester Central Reference Library. I am also indebted to the British Museum and the Public Record Office.

My typist, Mrs D. Sockett, must also be included in grateful acknowledgment of her unfailing patience and ability to decipher my handwriting, and John Anderson of the *Guardian* for constant encouragement.

Finally, I must thank my family for their encouragement, criticism, help in the inevitable chores of composition and their understanding of a temporary withdrawal from some of the pleasures of family life.

B. E. V. SABINE
Mottram-in-Longdendale
Cheshire
May, 1965

CHAPTER I

Life Without Income Tax

DIRECT taxation in Britain before 1799 had a very spasmodic history and was usually associated with some sort of national emergency.[1] The chief and the oldest type of direct land taxation was the Danegeld, which had been levied and paid to buy off the Danes; indeed, direct taxation began in this somewhat humiliating form. Canute, the Danish invader, continued the tax, in spite of the extinction of its original purpose, as a war tax for the defence of the realm. William the Conqueror regarded this source of revenue as so important that the first great enquiry into landed property, later known as the *Domesday Book*, was made for the purpose of assessing Danegeld and it continued to be levied until the reign of Henry II.

A further source of income, since 1066, was the various feudal dues, which soon became commuted for money. Scutage, for example, or 'shield money', was made payable, if the King approved, to the Exchequer from lands in lieu of the military service of their knights by virtue of which their lands had originally been granted to them. This emphasis on hard cash was intensified by such dramatic events as the demanding by the Emperor Henry VI of ransom for Richard I when he was captured returning from one of his Crusades. A tax on movables, as opposed to land, had been levied by Henry II to finance the Third Crusade. The experiment was made again in the agonizing attempt to raise the Lionheart's ransom and henceforward personal property became a regular subject of assessment.

Taxing personal property required a different form of survey from that which had been undertaken in the time of Domesday and many such investigations were carried out during the thirteenth century.

---

[1] The early history of taxation in England is still probably best approached by way of W. Kennedy's *English Taxation 1640–1799* and Stephen Dowell's *History of English Taxation* (vol. I). There have, of course, been many highly specialized studies of various aspects of taxation, but no recent general histories. There is much material in economic histories, for instance E. Lipson's *Economic History of England* or that of J. H. Clapham; it is, however, often necessary to search for it and it is rarely segregated in specific chapters or sections. The classic study is still E. R. A. Seligman's *The Income Tax*. An excellent modern study on one particular aspect is F. Shehab's *Progressive Taxation*.

But early in the fourteenth century, these came to a halt and the system of tenths or fifteenths was set up, which was in effect the grant to the King of a parliamentary subsidy based on a tenth or a fifteenth of the value of certain personal property in each area. It was clearly easier to levy fixed sums or multiples of fixed sums in this way and to leave the various local authorities to settle the incidence among themselves.

But national expenditure, even during the Middle Ages, often outpaced national income; an example of this was the beginning of the reign of Richard II when a combination of bad finance and military extravagance led to the imposition of the poll taxes of 1377, 1379 and 1380. These failed for three main reasons: the populace was either hostile or reluctant; the type of survey required was really a census, which had never before been attempted; and the officials found practical difficulties in its administration.

The poll tax of 1380 was a graduated tax – the highest amount to be paid by any individual being 20s and the lowest 4d. 'The poor were to aid the rich' but the individual contributions were governed by rank. This worked out most inequitably; in a poor village the full amount would be exacted from the poorest labourer, but in a more prosperous community the less wealthy would pay the minimum amount. The money was obtained, it is recorded, '*non sine diris maledictionibus*', but there was widespread evasion. When the returns came in it appeared that the population had fallen since the poll tax of 1377, by nearly half a million. Early in 1387 a writ was issued in the name of the King to the Barons of the Exchequer demanding immediate efforts to collect the rest of the tax and fresh Commissioners were set up who found ample justification for the Crown's allegations of wholesale fraud. But in some areas the hated Commissioners were set upon and stoned. The Chief Justice of the Common Pleas was met at Brentwood by an armed mob, three of his clerks seized and executed and their heads mounted on poles. The unhappy Judge was lucky to escape with his life. This was, in fact, the beginning of the great rebellion of 1387. The story that the rebellion was provoked by a collector of taxes insulting Wat Tyler's daughter seems to be a legend since the first uprising was not in Kent, but in Essex, but no doubt it was excellent anti-government propaganda.

The fate of the poll tax well illustrates the more complicated issues arising in the later Middle Ages as compared with the unsophisticated times of the Conqueror. Then a comparatively primitive community could be surveyed by the techniques of an efficient and clearheaded ruler. Three hundred years had changed both the personality of the state and of the people. It was still possible to make reasonably accurate surveys, assessments and records. But a competent and reliable staff to execute a tax based on these instruments did not exist. Still less was there any administrative machinery to make possible the drawing up of an annual income and expenditure account, or any sort of annual budget.

For this is the curious anomaly in the financial history of England during the later Middle Ages. On the one hand there is the elaborate organization of the Exchequer and the other household departments which it controlled; and on the other hand the haphazard and wasteful expenditure which it carefully recorded, but could not control. The King was expected to be a good housekeeper and 'live off his own'; additional revenue should only be raised for extraordinary purposes. Thus it was that the King was continually forced into the position of having to justify his need for additional revenue, a process which came to a head in the constitutional struggles of the seventeenth century.

Direct taxation is not a prominent feature of Tudor finance. For one thing, Henry VII and Elizabeth were magnificent housekeepers; and Henry VIII, for all his extravagance, had his father's resources at the beginning of his reign and the spoils of the monasteries at the end. Taxation was still not a normal, but an abnormal, incidence on the country and over Elizabeth's whole reign, for example, parliamentary taxation averaged rather less than £80,000 a year, and for the first thirty years little more than £50,000.[2]

The subsidy was one of the normal ways of raising money granted by Parliament. The sum named was divided between the counties for collection and administrative machinery was set up to bring in the required amount. In 1541, for instance, the rate was at one shilling in the pound for land and sixpence in the pound for goods, so combining the two different taxes of the Middle Ages on land and movables.

The Stuarts and their Judges used the magic phrase 'the defence of the realm' to cover a system of direct taxation which included ship-money, a seventeenth century throw-back to the old Danegeld. But the nation realized as well as Strafford that 'the debts of the Crown taken off, you may govern as you please'.[3] Resistance, instigated by Hampden, was followed by London; very few local officials could be persuaded to collect the tax; and the Scottish war in 1639 dissipated the surplus so painfully achieved the year before.

Cromwell developed a variant of direct taxation in the 'Monthly Assessment', based on a specific quota from each district, although it could be varied at will. But central control was so weak that it had

---

[2] J. E. Neale's *Queen Elizabeth*, p. 284.
[3] *The English Revolution* by Idris Deane Jones, p. 44.

to permit 'concessions to practicability' which left its view of 'equitable distribution little more than a statement of opinion'.[4] It became, in fact, a stereotyped land tax, but it should be noted that, like the subsidy, the assessing body was composed of local Commissioners. They were appointed by a 'Names' clause in the 1656 Act for instance. The lists are not long and that for Huntingdon shows the Protector had not neglected his own family. The other officials were the Surveyors, who are mentioned three times in the Act and then ignored,[5] the assessors, whose duty it was to draft the assessments, and the various collectors. All these were appointed by the Commissioners and were paid one penny in the pound on completing their tasks, except the unfortunate Surveyor. Absentees from the realm paid double duty, a final clause probably aimed at the exiled Cavaliers.

The question whether the numbers of Commissioners should be increased was debated in the Lords in 1666, but it was argued that the greater the number, the less tax would be raised 'for many Commissioners encumber one another and rather preserve the case of themselves and their many friends than the advance of the King's service and the public benefit'. In 1660 the Monthly Assessment produced £70,000 and a poll tax, in the same year, was estimated to produce £40,000.[6]

By the end of the seventeenth century, the Commons had taken from the King his prerogative of economic regulation and the new political leaders, men like Montague, Godolphin, Walpole and Pitt, gained and held power on the ground of financial genius. But taxation was still a surprisingly haphazard affair, despite the need for reliable sources of revenue, aggravated by the expense of carrying on the various military and naval campaigns of the period. The experiment of aides was the latest in a long series of extemporizations and here again, the important point is not so much the yield of the tax, but the fact that as with the Monthly Assessment before it, it relied for its administration on the local Commissioners.[7]

But in the England without income tax in the last years of the seventeenth century, two of the elements necessary for such a sophisticated tax were already present. Supervision by Parliament over the collection and expenditure of additional revenue needed by the Crown

---

[4] Kennedy (*op. cit.*), *English Taxation*, p. 41.

[5] A good deal of the information on pre-1799 direct taxation and its administration is derived from E. V. Adams's article 'The Early History of Surveyors of Taxes' published in the *Quarterly Record of the Association of H.M. Inspectors of Taxes* (July, 1956). His research had been on documents in the possession of the Board of Inland Revenue now held at the Heyes Repository.

[6] Dowell (*op. cit.*), *English Taxation*, vol. III, p. 81.

[7] The aide of 1692 is dealt with in more detail by Dowell (*op. cit.*), vol. III, p. 93.

had now been established, and although the expedients adopted – subsidies, poll taxes, monthly assessments and aides – usually foundered on the rocks of insufficient administration, they did a great deal to create that intelligent interest in national finance which has always been a feature of English political life. The safety and welfare of England was bound up with sound finance and this became a tradition of English political criticism which has lasted to the present day.

The second element was the emergence of the local Commissioners to form the administrative framework by which the latest direct taxes such as the aides were to be assessed and paid. These Commissioners were, in effect, the local gentry, as can be seen from the list of Commissioners which may be found in many local histories. Their administrative unit was the division and they met twice a year. On the first occasion, the various officials were appointed – clerk, assessors and collectors. At the second meeting they made the actual assessments and signed the duplicates, one of which was sent to the Exchequer by the Receiver of the town or county. Central control was vested in the Agents for the Bringing in of Taxes.

This control was directly exercised. The Agents corresponded with the local Commissioners encouraging them in the performance of their official duties in general and advising them on points of law, or matters in dispute in particular. Normally, however, the Commissioners were left to get on with the day to day administration of the aides without interference from the central government unless their advice was requested, or an Act for a new aide was brought in which might require fresh instructions.

But the tradition of evasion continued. From the disappearing population of the fourteenth century poll tax, the complaints of the Elizabethan Commissioners that 'many be twenty times, some thirty and some much more worth than they be set down at', to Bacon's 'The Englishman is most master of his own valuation and the least bitten in purse of any nation in Europe', such current criticisms from the Agents as 'there is strange neglect and omission in the Assessor's returns' have an all too familiar ring.

The Commissioners themselves had considerable difficulty in making the complex machinery of assessment and collection work efficiently, judging by the number of complaints by the Agents. There were delays in holding meetings, delays in appointing officials, delays in delivering the duplicates of their assessments; but even more important to the Exchequer, delays by the local collector in making his payment to the central receiver for the particular county or town or, as seems most common, delays by the receiver in making final payments to the Treasury. But it is hard to see how the Agents could exercise any supervision in the strict sense; their instructions tended to become exhortations and the Commissioners executed the functions of their office as best they could rather than as the Acts intended they should.

The last decade of the seventeenth century, which saw many fiscal experiments, was notable for the aide of 1692 which granted a levy of 4s in the pound for one year 'for carrying on a vigorous war against France'. The tax was imposed on the annual value of land, on the income from various offices (not naval or military) and an income from merchandise and goods on the assumption that they would yield six per cent – the rate of interest then usual – on their capital value. Once again administrative difficulties proved insuperable, especially that of assessing intangible property. Returns were made in the most casual fashion, and while partisans of William and the revolution were generous in their estimates, those who still looked to the king over the water were guided by their political sympathies in judging their income. To begin with, the yield was close on £2,000,000, but this began to diminish and within six years the tax had become an apportioned tax, that is, each county was allocated its share of the amount which it was desired to raise. It also became almost exclusively a land tax, being first called by that name in 1697. During the eighteenth century the fact that this tax was a land tax became the basis of the squires' complaints that they and not the merchants of the towns made the greatest contribution to the Treasury. The tax lived on until a few years ago, although it was being gradually extinguished by a system of compulsory redemption; it was finally abolished by Section 68, Finance Act, 1963. The tax on offices, incidentally, which was, as mentioned, part of the original 1692 Act, could be and was avoided from the beginning by simply changing the title of any particular office liable; however, it remained on the statute book until 1876, when it was repealed; in 1866 it had yielded £823.

There was probably more direct taxation in the seventeenth century than in the eighteenth, which believed more in indirect taxation on luxuries with a return to the Tudor and Stuart tradition of exempting the poor. Direct taxation needed an efficient bureaucracy and a more searching method of ascertaining an individual's income, both of which factors had yet to come. It was much easier to raise money by customs and excise. In 1715, for instance, customs and excise yielded £4,000,000 out of a total revenue of £5,500,000; in 1755 the figure was nearly £5,500,000 out of a total of about £6,750,000.[8] This pattern continued until 1793 when, in Pitt's words 'the happy result of ten years of economy, of labour, of firmness and of wisdom on the part of parliament in their endeavours to cultivate the arts of peace, to augment the revenue and to ameliorate the condition of the

[8] Dowell (*op. cit.*), vol. II.

people of the country'[9] was shattered as Louis Capet mounted the scaffold on that wet and dreary morning of January 21st.

So despite the intense national concern with all forms of taxation, and the long-standing existence of a system of assessment and collection by Commissioners and their officials going back at least to the fourteenth century, it was becoming clear that no type of direct taxation could succeed with amateur interest only and an intrinsically amateur organization. The solution was to appoint reliable local representatives of the central government, but it was not to be expected that this solution would either occur or commend itself to contemporary economists and politicians. This reform came gradually, almost clandestinely. Like the office of Commissioner itself, the Surveyor, who entered direct taxation very much by the back door, acquired duties and responsibilities almost by a process of organic growth than conscious legislation.

The Surveyor, as previously mentioned, first occurs in the Taxing Act of 1656, which required the Commissioners to appoint 'two at least of the honest and able inhabitants within each parish, township or other distinct place to be surveyors and assessors'. But it was the assessors who were to do all the work of drafting the assessments; the Surveyors may have had some personal survey work since there is nothing to show that forms of any kind were to be issued, but no specific duties were laid down and, what is more important, no remuneration, so the office must have been supernumerary.

Forty years later, in 1696, there was an 'Act for Making Good the Deficiency of the Clipped Money' by which 'the hearth of the Englishman was darkened by the appearance of the tax gatherer at his window' and the duty of the Surveyor under that Act was to count the number of windows in houses.[10] The tax was progressive – a house with less than ten windows paid two shillings; from ten to twenty windows, two shillings, plus an additional four shillings; twenty windows, or more, two shillings and eight shillings additional. Administration was in the hands of the Land Tax Commissioners who appointed the Surveyors and collectors.

The first record of the establishment of the Surveyors is one fixed by the Treasury in 1719 and also by the same instrument, the central Commissioners' salaries were settled. The salary of the former ranged from £30 per annum to £100 and of the latter £400. The office of the Commissioners cannot have been very busy since the staff consisted of a secretary, an assistant secretary, a solicitor and a clerk, and they supervised, at that time, only the Land Tax and the Window Tax. The smallness of this office illustrates the minor role direct

---

[9] See Pitt's speeches for this and similar expressions during 1793.
[10] Dowell (*op. cit.*), vol. III, p. 193 *et seq.*

taxation still played in the revenue of the country; yet for all that it was the beginning of central direction.[11]

The Window Tax was not a success initially and the yield fell off mainly because taxpayers hit upon the simple plan of stopping up windows in preparation for the assessor's visit and re-opening them on his departure. The recasting of the tax by Pelham in 1747 kept the usual administrative scheme of Commissioners, assessors and collectors, but the charge was increased and the Surveyor became a Treasury appointment. Not only had he now the usual duties of oversight, including 'full power to pass through any house or houses, in order to go into any court, yard, or backside thereunto belonging' but he could examine the assessments before they were signed and allowed by the Commissioners and he had to be notified if any stopped up windows were re-opened on payment of a penalty of twenty shillings. Provision was made for the hearing of appeals by the Commissioners. A typical example of an early complaint reads as follows:

In 1719 Robert Wood sent a note to Quarter Sessions (written in a large hand upon a rough scrap of paper) saying 'I desire that you his Magestes Justices of the Peace that you would take information of me Robert Wood of Ashton parish under line that i have but 9 windows'.[12] This was no doubt a simple case, but in 1757, by which time the right to express dissatisfaction and demand a case to be stated to the King's Bench had been introduced, the Commissioners found that an ingenious taxpayer, who had fixed a short glass connection between two windows had, in fact, converted them into one window. The Surveyor expressed dissatisfaction and the judges' decision is short and pointed: 'We are of opinion that this is a manifest evasion of the Act, therefore, the Determination of the Commissioners is Wrong'. This admirable succinctness continued for nearly a hundred years in Window Tax cases; in 1849 the same delightfully simple, straightforward and expeditious formula was still being used.

In general, the Commissioners adopted a responsible attitude towards their duties; they were, in any case, responsible persons, traditionally local landowners and their Chairman was frequently the Mayor. The law was interpreted with considerable severity; the Surveyors included in their assessments 'almost any hole in the wall', including a coal hole, a cellar grating with iron bars and even four perforated zinc plates for ventilating a pantry.[13]

[11] Much of the material used here is from E. V. Adams's article (*op. cit.*).

[12] Robert Wood's letter is from Winifred M. Bowman's *England in Ashton-under-Lyne*, p. 540.

[13] Dowell (*op. cit.*), vol. III, pp. 201–2.

The success of the 1747 Act is illustrated by the fact that the administration of more and more taxes was placed with the Surveyor and the same mechanism utilized. These new taxes, which were later known as the Assessed Taxes, were in essence expenditure taxes. It was a long held taxing principle that the rich should pay more than the poor and since there was no administration yet for taxing income, the alternative was to tax the outward and visible signs of wealth. The number of windows in a house or mansion was one such sign. This was followed by a tax on carriages which was transferred to the Surveyor's jurisdiction in 1785. The duty on male servants, however, of 1777, which levied a guinea duty on all male servants, excluding those engaged in manufacture or agriculture, was assessed and collected from the beginning under the Window Tax Acts. The same procedure was followed for the Inhabited House Duty in 1778 which was levied on the occupier of inhabited houses by reference to the annual value. This was to be the full and just yearly rent which the house was really and bona fide worth to be let. The Surveyor had the power to review the assessments and to make surcharges and the assessors were allowed threepence for each house assessed 'in consideration of the extraordinary case and pains requisite in making and adjusting the first assessment'.[14]

Although the Surveyor was being employed more and more on the administration of the larger revenue producing taxes, there were a number of fiscal experiments with which the Surveyor was not immediately concerned before the outbreak of war in 1793 and which illustrate the wide scope of the attempts to tax expenditure. All these taxes failed to produce the yield expected and some had a decidely harmful effect on the industries affected. There was a tax on the possession of silver plate in 1765 which was repealed by North after having proved 'very vexatious and troublesome in the levying and collecting the same and of small advantage to the public'. It is indeed only notable for John Wesley's reply to the Accountant General's circular 'to all persons whom they have reason to suspect to have plate and also to those who have not paid regularly the duty on the same':

'Sir,

    I have two spoons in London and two spoons at Bristol. This is all the plate which I have at present; and I shall not buy any more while so many round me want bread.

I am, Sir,

Your most humble servant,

JOHN WESLEY'.[15]

[14] Dowell (*op. cit.*), vol. II, p. 242.   [15] Dowell (*op. cit.*), vol. III, p. 242.

The tax on female servants of 1785 lasted a mere six years and was widely supposed to be due to Pitt's aversion to the female sex. Pitt then went, as it was said, from the servant's hall to the taxpayer's stable and laid a tax on 'pleasure horses' in 1784 and, in the same year, a levy on racehorses composed of a basic tax on all starters themselves, plus an additional tax on winners. Other sports, such as shooting, suffered equally from a tax on sporting licences and game-keepers which was also imposed in 1784.

It was possible in the halcyon days before the war with France to take these taxes not too seriously; indeed the House treated some of the more fanciful ones with marked levity.[16] But when war was declared in 1793 the need for increased revenue became acute and Pitt indulged in a frenzy almost of fiscal experiment and improvisation. To the taxes on expenditure introduced in the decade before the war were added other taxes the peculiarity of some of which even Pitt himself grudgingly acknowledged. The first of these was the tax, introduced in 1795, on hair powder, the masculine custom being then for the natural hair to be tied in a pigtail and powdered, in place of the wig; the powdering of female hair had long been fashionable. The royal family was loyally exempted from the tax and junior members of the armed forces; in addition, special provision was made for the unfortunate fathers of large female families whereby payment for two unmarried daughters covered the rest. The caricaturists' fun at the expense of the tax hastened the decline of a fashion already on the wane and soon shorter styles and macassar oil began to replace clubbed hair and the powder bowl.

In the following year, 1796, a tax on dogs was introduced which divided them into three different categories, sporting dogs, pet dogs and packs of hounds with differing rates for each, although it was possible to compound for the pack. Puppies under six months old were exempt; this exemption was later extended to sheepdogs.

As the pressure of war expenditure increased, Pitt turned to a tax on clocks and watches, the rate being different for gold and silver watches. The tax proved so disastrous for the clock and watchmaking industries that, despite the need for every conceivable source of revenue, it was repealed in 1798 and replaced by the tax on armorial bearings in the same year. The rates of duty were related to the liability of the person charged to the taxes on carriages, houses and windows. As in the case of the window tax, the Courts were very strict in their interpretation of what constituted a bearing and their definition came to include almost anything in the nature of a crest.

But these desperate fiscal expedients are only one side of the story

[16] See the discussions in Parliament during 1785 on the tax on female servants, which are entertainingly summarized by Dowell (*op. cit.*), vol. III, p. 253.

of Pitt's run of eighteen consecutive budgets. Fortunately a system of local administration and jurisdiction had now established itself in the field of taxation consisting of the local Commissioners with their right to appoint assessors and collectors; linked with these officials were the semi-professional Surveyors appointed by the Treasury with the right to inspect, examine and supervise assessments before they were finally allowed and, where necessary, to certify surcharges. In addition, both parties, Commissioners and Surveyors alike had the right of appeal direct to the Courts. This mechanism was to prove its worth to Pitt and his successors and, in essence, survived to the present day.

Pitt also brought under the control of the Commissioners for the Affairs of Taxes the expenditure taxes which had come to be known as the Assessed Taxes. The Inhabited House Duty, the tax on carriages, on men servants, which he had inherited, were transferred, as previously mentioned, to the Tax office (see p. 19). The taxes which he had imposed himself upon saddle and carriage horses and racehorses were similarly transferred and there was a certain amount of revision; for instance the Inhabited House and Window Tax were combined in 1798. Three years later the hair powder tax and the tax on armorial bearings were also put under central direction. It is easy to say now that Pitt was slow to recognize the fact that a tax on income would have to be imposed if the country was not to slide into bankruptcy and that the centralization of the assessed taxes was only putting off the evil day. But, in fact, it is very doubtful whether Pitt would have carried the country with him if he had tried to introduce a tax on income before he did; he was forced to use the taxes and the administration to hand as long as possible.

When the war broke out in 1793, Pitt had made up his mind to uphold, by force, if necessary, the 'public law of Europe', despite the fact that it meant being both the ally and the paymaster of reaction; but within five years, the ragged armies of the Republic, with their boyish, impromptu generals, had defeated and dominated the Continent; England remained the sole survivor; but faced with rebellion in Ireland, naval mutiny at the Nore and a victorious Bonaparte, her case seemed desperate. It is against this background that Pitt's fiscal experiments, expedients and forlorn remedies must be viewed and judged.

During this period, the work of the Surveyors was increasing daily and so had the number of their supervising Inspectors, who had been instituted in 1778 to examine the performance of their duties. The system had proved very successful and the Commissioners reported to the Treasury with some satisfaction that 'these officers have been found to increase the revenue very considerably'. An experiment of regionalization was tried, that is of having a larger area supervised by a General Surveyor, but this failed and there were no further appointments to this office after 1797.

The Surveyors had been appointed by the Treasury since the beginning of the century which meant that their initial recommendation would be family connections, or political background. But when the need for a new appointment was notified to the Treasury by the Tax office, that department was requested by the Treasury to report on the suitability of the various applicants so that in general reasonably competent officers would be chosen.

The procedure was for the prospective candidate to be placed under the charge of an established Surveyor and if, after such a probationary period as seemed necessary, the candidate passed muster, the Commissioners would report accordingly to the Treasury and recommend that he be offered an appointment. The Commissioners for the Affairs of Taxes, too, owed their appointments to patronage. In 1795 a half pay Colonel attempted, unsuccessfully, to obtain a Commissionership of Irish Taxes; it was perhaps just as well that he failed since twenty years later he was to defeat Napoleon at Waterloo.[17] A notable leader in the *Edinburgh Review* of 1810[18] summed up the process of Treasury intervention in appointments to Government departments for which Pitt and George Rose, a typical example of the new career politician, were mainly responsible.

'A most important change has, within the same period, been effected upon the whole system of patronage in all departments. It has been organised and brought under the immediate control of the Treasury. That great and overwhelming department's hand has been thrust in every branch of the State: in all the Boards, from the highest to the lowest, patronage formerly vested in the numbers of those Boards is now wholly in the Minister's possession. In every part of the country the Treasury gives away clerkships which used, formerly, to be in the gift of particular Departments.'

In 1797, for example, Rose, then Secretary at the Treasury, wrote: 'Mr. Pitt designed the vacant Surveyorship of the House Tax in Westminster for his bailiff at Holwood'.[19] There was no question of abolishing patronage and influence; but by making them the monopoly of one department, there was clearly less room for abuse, especially when the Treasury was interested in the fitness and efficiency of candidates for appointment.

By 1797 then, a strong administrative organization had been brought into being at the centre consisting of the Treasury, the

[17] Philip Guedalla's *The Duke*, p. 51.   [18] *Edinburgh Review*, April, 1810.
[19] A. Hope-Jones, *Income Tax in the Napoleonic Wars*, p. 62.

Commissioners and their local officials the Surveyors. It now remained to produce an equitable taxing act which would, at once, increase the revenue of the country in its hour of peril and which this centralized control could run efficiently. But before the challenge of an Income Tax had to be faced, Pitt tried one last throw, since he felt such a tax would be 'repugnant to the customs and manners of the nation'. By an Act of 1797 he imposed the so-called Triple Assessment,[20] to be effective for the following year 1798. He demanded 'a general tax on persons possessed of property commensurate as far as possible with their means' and the increases affected all the assessed taxes.

Pitt used the 1797 return of an individual's taxable establishment as the basis for the 1798 assessment, to prevent possible evasion by making false current returns. The taxpayers were divided into two categories. Those keeping a taxable establishment of carriages, men servants or saddle and carriage horses, that is, the presumably richer taxpayers, paid a rate of between three and five times the previous year by reference to that year's assessment; the quintuple rate applied to anyone who had been charged more than £50 in the previous year. The second category consisted of those who had no such establishment as the fortunate members of the first category, but who had paid window tax, inhabited house duty, or other expenditure taxes. They paid at rates ranging from only an additional one quarter to the full quintuple rate at £50 and upwards. There was an elaborate system of calculating the annual value of land and houses with an equally elaborate series of deductions.

The interesting feature of this tax was the provision for exemption, abatement and reduction; these reliefs, however, could only be obtained by making a return in a prescribed form. If such a return was made and relief proved to be due, repayment would be made. The tax was normally payable in six instalments during the year. The main relief was the limiting of tax payable to 10% of total income, a feature of some significance when the first tax on income came to be considered.

The Triple Assessment was not a success, in that the yield was only half that expected. The reasons were twofold. By the simple expedient of incorrectly returning total income, many people paid even less than before and there had been no provision for any proper check on their returns. It was fortunate that with it was associated a scheme proposed by the Speaker, Addington, that voluntary contributions in excess of the Triple Assessment might be made to the Bank of England, since this raised £2,000,000 which was not much less than the

---

[20] Triple Assessment, A. Hope-Jones (*op. cit.*), p. 14 and Dowell (*op. cit.*), vol. III, pp. 175–8. The Assessed Taxes machinery included provision for returns.

main tax itself had produced.[21] But nevertheless, it was an important half-way house to a tax on income. It still taxed expenditure admittedly; but it was not current but previous years' expenditure. In addition, it is not a very long step from limiting high expenditure taxes to ten per cent of total income to taxing simply ten per cent of total income. But even at this late hour, Pitt was still not converted: 'If the amount of every man's property could be ascertained, it would be a most desirable thing to make the people contribute to the public exigence in proportion to their wealth. But there existed no means of ascertaining the property of individuals, except such as were of a nature not to be resorted to.'[22]

The final decision, however, could not be put off much longer. In spite of his own original beliefs and the opinion of the economists, including Adam Smith, in spite of the unknown factor of public opinion, in spite of the comparative failure of previous income taxes, Pitt realized he could no longer finance the sinews of war from a tax which produced only half its expected yield and which had to be buttressed by patriotic charity. As he remarked bitterly: 'There have been men base enough to avail themselves of the general modifications which were intended to relieve those who might have been called up to contribute beyond their means, to avoid that fair assessment which corresponded with their circumstances – I am happy to find the notion has been vindicated by the noble and generous aid of voluntary contribution.'[23] By the Autumn of 1798 he was already working on the 'Heads of a Plan for a Contribution'[24] based on yield statistics prepared by his Treasury officials. On December 3, 1798, he introduced his Income Tax; the Triple Assessment was repealed and the Property and Income Tax was to be effective from January, 1799.

These last few years of the century were also a turning point in the history of the Surveyors. Their functions had become more and more indispensable in the administration of direct taxation as had been tacitly acknowledged by the continuous additions to their care over the past fifty years. A Surveyor who entered the Tax Office in, say, 1777 had seen his simple duty of counting windows extend to responsibility for servant tax, house tax, carriage tax – indeed, all those levies which made up the assessed taxes; he had taken part in the complicated experiment of the Triple Assessment; he had seen his establishment expand and additional supervisory officers created. And now there was this new income tax to be added to all his other miscellaneous duties; small wonder that the Treasury should author-

[21] *Addington, Author of the Modern Income Tax*, by A. Farnsworth, p. 12.
[22] See Pitt's Speeches (1806), vol. III, p. 231.
[23] Pitt's speech on proposing the Income Tax, 3/XII/1798.
[24] 'Heads of a Plan for a Contribution' – A. Hope-Jones (*op. cit.*), p. 15.

ize an addition to his salary of £20 per annum 'to each of the said Surveyors who you shall think entitled to the same from their diligence, care and assiduity.'

The fiscal scene, therefore, immediately before 1799 showed that Parliamentary control of taxation had been effectively established for well over a century. Taxation had, to a large extent, kept pace with economic development in contrast, say, with France, where finance was still in the feudal stage and was on a permanent not an *ad hoc* basis; although as far as direct taxation was concerned the accent was still on expenditure taxes.

But these expenditure taxes had developed, as has been indicated, a comparatively sophisticated mechanism, which was not only taken over, lock, stock and barrel by the new income tax, but to a large extent dictated its shape and efficiency. One of the most important features of this mechanism was its strong local flavour and throughout the succeeding history of income tax and its administration is reflected, too, the history of improvements in communications; the growth of the Surveyor's 'interference' and of central administration are part of the Railway Age. This communications aspect is vividly illustrated in an instruction to Collectors contained in the 1855 'Instructions to Surveyors on that part of their duty which relates to the Taxes'. If sending money exceeding £5 to the Receiving Officer by Bank of England notes 'the Collector must take care to send the notes in halves by different posts'.

From this summary, therefore, it is clear that the imposition by Pitt of income tax in 1799 was not by any means a complete break with the theory and practice of the past, but rather a gradual development in both aspects, the final change-over from an expenditure to an income tax being forced on him by the inexorable pressure of war. But the change, as is usual with historical change, was not dramatic; there had always been direct taxes available as precedents from which the new income tax could and did borrow both mechanism and techniques. Nor did the new tax immediately assume a premier position in the production of revenue; customs and excise still contributed far the greater share of the national revenue. 'The essential difference between the direct taxes of this period and the income tax of the nineteenth century is not one of intention but of execution.'[25]

[25] Kennedy (*op. cit.*), p. 46.

CHAPTER II

The Tax that beat Napoleon[1]

THE first fifteen years of the nineteenth century are as dramatic as any in English history. For the first time for a century, or more, England was playing her full part on the European stage. The first phase of this period ended with the uneasy Treaty of Amiens in 1803, after a series of unsuccessful coalitions against Napoleon. Then came the threat of invasion, the 'Army of England' massed at Boulogne, the rash of Martello towers fringing the south coast. Trafalgar ended this threat and the war settled down to a pattern in which Napoleon was as successful on land as England by sea. The final phase of the war began in 1808 with the Peninsular Campaign, followed by the finally successful coalition which triumphed at Waterloo.

But all this had to be paid for, and by the end of the period national expenditure had reached unprecedented heights. In 1814 the Budget estimate for the Army was £40,000,000, for the Navy £20,000,000 and £10,000,000 for foreign subsidies, quite apart from interest on the enormous national debt and the day to day cost of running the goverment. The paymaster had defeated the taskmaster, but the price was high. Only about one-sixth of war revenue was raised by income tax, but it had shown itself a most valuable addition to the national receipts and, as the efficiency of its administration

[1] The standard work on this period is A. Hope-Jones's *Income Tax in the Napoleonic Wars*, which is based on his research on the P.R.O. papers referred to in chapter III, p. 46. It gives a good general picture of the operation of the Income and Property Tax during the period but, since it was a pioneering work, it contains some errors of detail and some important errors of principle. For instance the Surveyors and Inspectors are confused (see p. 45) and so are divisions and districts (see p. 49). More important is his failure to recognize the importance of Addington in the origins of modern Income Tax, for which he was roundly taken to task by A. Farnsworth in his *Addington, Author of the Modern Income Tax*. This book is mainly concerned with the Act of 1803 and is less about Addington the man than Income Tax law. Nevertheless, Dr Farnsworth does prove his point abundantly by a fully documented comparison of the 1803 Act with corresponding sections of the Act of 1918. The two books are to an extent complementary and one should not be read without the other. The only historian to have given Addington his just due is A. F. Freemantle in his *England in the Nineteenth Century*, vol. I, p. 365.

increased, so too did its yield; during the Hundred Days the British Secretary at War wrote to the Deputy Auditor asking for a list of all the Receivers General of Income Tax, the Land Tax and Assessed Taxes.[2] The exile of Napoleon to Elba had led to a certain relaxation in payments of tax; this could not be permitted now he had escaped. But all these developments were far in the future when Pitt rose on December 3, 1798 to introduce the Income Tax Bill.

Whatever the merits or demerits of Pitt's Income Tax Act of 1799, which, in fact, required two Amending Acts[3] three months later, there is no denying his technical grasp of his subject; his proposing speech was a masterpiece of clarity, elegance and precision. He began by giving a summary of the previous measures which had been adopted to meet the heavy rate of current expenditure. That, however, had not proved adequate, not only on account of the 'evasion, the fraud and the meanness which have struggled to defeat the operation of the assessed taxes', but also because 'there must necessarily be much income, much wealth, great means which were not included'. The Assessed Taxes 'furnished the most comprehensive, the most general and the most efficient scale of contribution', but they were manifestly open to 'artifices of dishonesty'. The problem of avoidance constantly recurs in the speech for it was 'to prevent all evasion and fraud' that Pitt came to the heart of his proposal 'that the presumption founded upon the Assessed Taxes should be laid aside and that a general tax shall be imposed on all the leading branches of income'.[4]

This was the truly revolutionary proposal, the logical extension of the relief provision embodied in the Triple Assessment that the tax payable should not exceed 10% of total income. Pitt still professed to believe in the principle of expenditure taxes as exemplified by the assessed taxes; but they had ceased to be efficient; they were wide open to avoidance; the proposal of a direct tax on income was the only solution. It was not, admittedly, 'perfectly free from the objection of inequality', but it was as equitable as possible, and it had become necessary in order to preserve 'the national honour and the national safety'. That was its basic justification: it was emergency legislation for a time of national emergency.

Pitt proceeded to point out the importance of entrusting the administration of the new tax which must leave 'considerable discretionary power', to Commissioners who 'ought to be persons of a respectable situation in life: as far as possible removed from any suspicion of partiality or any kind of undue influence: men of integrity and independence'. Parliament was somewhat sensitive on this

[2] Letter regarding Receivers General, P.R.O. 182/1360, 29/V/1815.
[3] The two Amending Acts were passed 21/III and 10/V/1799.
[4] Pitt's Speeches: Hansard 3/XII/1798.

point. There had been the famous 'Coventry scandal' in 1798 when the list of Land Tax Commissioners was found to include journey-men, weavers, scavengers, dealers in dead horseflesh and cats' meat, dealers in dung, paupers receiving parish relief, two 'fidlers' and two idiots.[5] For the Commissioners were appointed through the Land Tax Commissioners who were required to forward to the Grand Jury for the county a list containing their own names and ten other duly qualified persons. This qualification was now deliberately made high, namely £300 per annum from real estate, or £10,000 personal estate, or 'both commingled'.[6] This £10,000 was shortly afterwards reduced to £3,000. For the City of London the Commissioners were chosen partly by the Lord Mayor and Alderman and partly by the Bank of England, the great trading companies such as the East India Company, and Assurance Companies. In addition to these Commissioners 'for carrying into execution the general purposes of this Act' – hence the term General Commissioners – Pitt had foreseen that 'in the great cities and in great commercial places special provisions may be necessary' and he had to concede to the mercantile interest Commercial Commissioners to satisfy the demand for secrecy; they made assessments and marked a 'number or letter' against each charge to tax; the taxpayer then received details of the charge still identified only by this number or letter which he could then pay direct to the Bank of England. It might be noted, in passing, that until 1942 it was still possible to be assessed in a very similar manner.

A second, and equally important concession to possible public hostility was the requirement in the first instance of a general return of income only as follows:[7]

'I................do declare that I am willing to pay the sum of ....for my contribution from 5th April, 1799 to 5th April, 1800 in pursuance of an Act passed in the Thirtynineth year of the reign of His present Majesty intituled................ and I do declare that the said sum of................is not less than one tenth part of my income, estimated according to the Directions and Rules prescribed by the said Acts, to the best of my Knowledge and Belief. Dated this day of.................
(Signed).................'

It was only if the Commissioners were not satisfied with this very general declaration that they were entitled to issue a precept in a prescribed form which called for details of income under nineteen different heads of which the first fourteen related to lands, and details

---

[5] Parliamentary reports 4/18/19/IV/98.   [6] 39 Geo. 3 22 ss. 3–4.
[7] Farnsworth (*op. cit.*), p. 17.

of deductions.[8] All the duties of examination of returns and assessments were undertaken by the General Commissioners; the Surveyor could, however, inspect a full return, make surcharges where necessary and appeal against assessments, as could the taxpayer, to the Commissioners of Appeal of whom there were three for each county. Their business was simply to hear appeals where either party was dissatisfied with the assessment of the General Commissioners. There was no right of appeal against the assessments of the Commercial Commissioners.

Such, then, was the administrative framework of the first income tax. The bureaucratic side was represented by the Commissioners for the Affairs of the Taxes, the Auditor's office, which dealt with collection, and the Surveyors in the field; the local day to say running was in the hands of the General and Commercial Commissioners, their clerk and assessors and the Commissioners of Appeal. It was a complex piece of machinery which tried to combine executive efficiency with safeguards against its abuse; its defects are obvious, but it does represent a remarkably clear understanding of the problem which, in various forms, besets any government which genuinely seeks both authority and democracy.

The tax itself was charged at 2s in the pound on all income in excess of £200. Between £60 and £200 there was a graduated rate starting at 2d in the pound, income below £60 being exempt. There was an allowance for children and deductions were permitted in arriving at assessable income for interest on debts, amounts payable to children, or other relations, assessed taxes, annuities and life assurance. Repairs too, could be set against the value of real property.

The Bill aroused very considerable opposition in the Commons. Tierney, one of the chief spokesmen of the opposition in economic affairs, complained of the inequity in 'making income the standard of wealth', contrasting the 'income of a widow who lived only on a pension with that of a person whose capital brings him in the same income by way of interest'. Hobhouse, always a reasonable speaker on economic affairs, emphasised the 'glaring inequality' of taxing 'a man who had £1,000 a year arising from capital and the man who gained the same annual sum by a profession or by business'. He also suggested it 'would strike with peculiar force at industry and the fruits of industry' since the merchant would have less of his profit available to convert into capital. Sir John Sinclair, a Scottish landowner and industrialist, spoke twice on the Bill. In his first speech he feared 'It would encourage a spirit of emigration'; in his second speech he advocated a joint tax on income and capital, although he

[8] Dowell (*op. cit.*), vol. III, pp. 106–8.

admitted that it would be difficult to ascertain the latter, especially as a landed income (and here he was, no doubt, thinking of his Caithness estates), 'is subject to a variety of burdens'.[9] He also made great play with the inequity of taxing income from trades or professions and income from capital alike when the former was subject to many more hazards.

The opposition was not, by any means, confined to the Commons. Despite the menace of the 'Corsican ogre' the tax was desperately unpopular, involving as it did the necessity of Commissioners and Surveyors 'searching and prying' into men's estates. John Horne Tooke, cleric, philologist and wit, perhaps expressed this feeling as literately and as caustically as any contemporary newspaper leader in the following exchange of letters:

From the Income Tax Commissioners

May 3rd 1799

Sir,

  The Commissioners having under consideration your declaration of income have directed me to request you that they have reason to apprehend your income exceeds sixty pounds a year. They, therefore, desire that you will reconsider the said declaration and favour me with your answer on or before the 7th inst.

I am, your obedient servant,

W. B. NUTTLEY, Clerk

Mr Tooke replied:

Sir,

  I have much more reason than the Commissioners can have to be dissatisfied with the smallness of my income. I have never yet in my life deserved or had occasion to reconsider any declaration which I have signed with my name. But the Act of Parliament has removed all the decencies which used to prevail among gentlemen and has given the Commissioners, (shrouded under the signature of their clerk) a right by law to tell me they have reason to believe that I am a liar. They also have a right to demand from me, upon oath, the particular circumstances of my private situation. In obedience to the law, I am ready to attend upon this degrading occasion so novel to an Englishman and give them every explanation they may be pleased to require.

I am, Sir, Your humble servant,

JOHN HORNE TOOKE[10]

---

[9] The extracts from the debate on the Income Tax Bill cover the period from 3/XII/1798 to 29/XII/1798. (Parliamentary Register.)

[10] D. A. Wills, *Theory and Practice of Taxation.*

Not all rebukes, however, were as dignified as this. When the news spread to the Navy it provoked the following typically nautical reaction:

'January 12th 1799: This is a horrible war – the rapacity and greed of the Government go beyond all limits – Parliament met on 20 November last year to consider the present financial position – not content with squeezing us dry in February, 1798 (a reference to the Triple Assessment), it is now actually proposed to place A TAX ON INCOMES! No income under £60 per annum is to pay any duty at all, those from £100–£105 a fortieth part and above £200 a tenth! It is a vile, Jacobin, jumped up Jack-in-office piece of impertinence – is a true Briton to have no privacy? Are the fruits of his labour and toil to be picked over, farthing by farthing, by the pimply minions of Bureaucracy?'[11]

Nevertheless 'Tables of Rates of Duty' were issued to the Service Departments by the Commissioners for the Affairs of Taxes, so that the assessment of tax from the armed forces could be accurately done.

But Pitt rode the storm of criticism in the House and in the country with a nice command of firmness and debating ability. He was forced to make some concessions as, for instance, the Commercial Commissioners, but his speeches during the passage of the Bill show a masterly defence of his proposals from the fundamental basis of a tax on income to the details of the reliefs proposed. An attack on the 'tyrannical powers' of the Surveyor drew this spirited reply:

'The duties of the Surveyor are clearly defined and must be perfectly understood. He is only empowered to bring forward, after the necessary enquiries, materials for the information of the Commissioners and they are bound to act according to their oath for the advantage of the public. With respect to the influence which, it is said, the Surveyors possess at parochial and other meetings, I draw a conclusion directly opposite in their favour: for if they are supposed to possess any weight or influence with men of such high and established reputation as the Commissioners is not this strong proof that their own characters are fair and honest?'[12]

Some of the points he made, however, were more striking for ingenuity than logic: 'The consequences of this tax will be that whoever contributes one tenth of his income under this Bill, will have one tenth less to spend, to save or to accumulate. At the end of the

---

[11] *Man Midwife:* 'The further experiences of John Knyveton, M.D., late Surgeon in the British Fleet during the years 1763–1809.'
[12] Parliamentary Register, Dec. 14/1798.

war those who shall have contributed will be no poorer: they will only be the less increased in riches than they might have been.'[13]

Pitt had still two more Budgets to introduce before his eighteen-year run was completed, but these did not make any significant changes in the Act of 1799. In 1800 there was an alteration in the basis of charge on the occupation of land which gave relief to income below £300 and a certain tightening up of the collection procedure, including an increase in the staff of Surveyors 'of 99 at £90 each'. This proposal drew from Tierney, a strong opponent of income tax, whose remarks on the original Bill have already been quoted, some severe strictures:

'By a paper just laid on the table he found there was to be an addition of 99 inspectors for the purpose of this tax. He wished to avoid harsh expressions when mentioning those persons: they were goodlooking men, in good clothes, selected from the tax office for their activity and vigilance. But what are their habits and what have been their employments? They are persons whose duty it is to go about and see the number of servants, horses, dogs etc. that each man has and to make a true return: in this it is their interest, as well as their duty, to be keen and active. These are the persons that are now to come abroad to survey and inspect men's properties and to get at the truth by getting at the secret of each man's affairs. How is this to be done? I know of no other way than by cajoling, corrupting and bribing the clerks and domestics of the respective houses they wish to examine: actions for which a man ought to be hooted out of society!'[14]

In his last Budget of 1801 he continued the principles and practices embodied in the original Act. It is true he had, as early as June, 1799, been considering 'material alterations'[15] due to the disappointing yield and had, in the following year introduced an amending Bill which was withdrawn after its second reading. It provided, amongst other things, for the checking of statements, where thought necessary, by the Surveyor. But the objections raised in the debates were so acrimonious, involving even accusations of unconstitutionality, that Pitt judged it wiser on this last occasion to bow to the storm. He protested that he still stood by the reforms he had tried to introduce, although at the then current stage of organization in the Affairs of the Taxes – there were, for instance, only about 300 Inspectors and Surveyors, including the reinforcements Tierney had complained of –

[13] Parliamentary Register, 14/XII/1798.
[14] Parliamentary Register, 5/VI/1800.
[15] Farnsworth (*op. cit.*), pp. 26–7.

many would have proved unworkable. Within a week or so of his last Budget, Pitt had resigned over the Catholic Emancipation issue and was succeeded by Addington; even discounting the satiric couplet of Canning,[16] it must have seemed to contemporaries as something of an anticlimax.

Was Pitt's income tax a success or not? At one time Pitt was accepted uncritically as the sole author of the 1799–1816 income tax, if not of the present-day system. Subsequently there was a reverse trend which may have gone a little too far. From the standpoint of yield it was certainly a great disappointment. Pitt's estimate of £10,000,000 for the first year was far too optimistic since the final yield, after the deductions for child allowance, was under £6,000,000. The 1800 estimate of £7,000,000, a somewhat more cautious figure, was not realized either since the yield was again below £6,000,000. The 1801 estimate was, it was hoped, a realistic one of £6,000,000 only, but the yield dropped yet again to £5,300,000.[17] This was the more discouraging, since the tax was originally intended 'to repay the excess of the public debt beyond a given amount'.

The specific reasons for this comparative failure were inherent in the provisions of the tax itself. It was hardly possible to check all the general returns; and there was not the administrative machinery available to examine particular forms of return if they had been called for in all doubtful cases. Secondly the system of allowable deductions, especially for annual interest on debts, was open to widespread abuse due to the lack of any recognized procedure for verification. Thirdly, the institution of the Commercial Commissioners had not proved successful, possibly because they lacked the local knowledge of the General Commissioners, possibly because they had a vested interest in the very assessments they made, and possibly also because they had no power to examine the books of account kept by those whose profits they were empowered to assess. The yield from the commercial assessments in 1800 was barely £1,000,000 out of close on £6,000,000; the estimate had been £4,000,000 later reduced to £2,000,000 in the previous year. Today the Schedule D assessments form nearly half of the total income tax charged – a measure of the under-assessments of those first days.

The general reasons were equally important. It was a new tax; it was suspect as a potential instrument of tyranny, and although its existence had to be recognized it had by no means been accepted. It was, after all, intended merely to be a temporary tax, for the duration of the war. Secondly, it had only just achieved a separate existence. In a probably inspired book, published in 1799 entitled

---

[16] 'Pitt is to Addington   As London is to Paddington.'
[17] Farnsworth (*op. cit.*), pp. 18–26.

Observations upon the Act for Taxing Income,[18] the close connection between the Triple Assessment and the first Income Tax Act was clearly illustrated:

'In the last Act, income was the ultimate means of reducing an assessment founded on the amount of former assessments; in the present it is made the primary means of ascertaining the assessment: both lead to the same end of assessing every part of the community to the amount of one tenth of the Income possessed by them, but pursue different modes to attain that end. It is obvious that the necessity of ascertaining Income as the foundation of charge in the first instance is calculated to forward more effectually every description of Income in the country, than the former mode, which left, unaffected, a very large portion of the Income of many, whose habits of expense were disproportionate to their means. In this consists the only essential difference between the two Acts: for out of this distinction only the various provisions in the present Act, that differ from the last, have arisen.'

A third general reason was the pitifully small and overworked professional staff charged with its administration: it was only one more tax among the many under their care and management.

And yet the transition from a tax primarily on expenditure to a tax on income, however embryonic the latter might be, was peculiarly the work of Pitt. It was he who, in those few winter months of Christmas and New Year in 1799 and 1800, against tremendous opposition, managed to persuade both the Commons and public opinion, to accept his proposals. He shattered the Englishman's instinctive and traditional resistance to direct taxation; the fiscal scene could never be the same again.

Addington's first problem was political rather than fiscal; in fact the peace negotiations with France dragged on so long that the Budget had to be postponed. The treaty was finally signed at Amiens in March 1802, and Addington introduced his first Budget a month later. It opened with the abolition of income tax; this was forced on the new Prime Minister by its unpopularity and the promise that it was a war tax exclusively.

'The Income Tax[19] was a measure much too important for the House to let go during the continuance of war. He was, however, bound to declare that it was his thorough and entire conviction that it was to the wisdom which originated that tax, and the firmness

---

[18] This was published anonymously in 1799.

[19] The Budget speech of Addington introducing repeal was on 5/IV/1802. See also Farnsworth (*op. cit.*), pp. 34–5.

which induced the House to persist in it, that the country was indebted for the comforts we now had: for it was by that system that we were enabled to surmount the difficulties with which, during the last three years, we had to struggle and it was from that conviction also that he now recommended that this burden should not be left to rest on the shoulders of the public in time of peace because it should be reserved for the important occasion which he trusted would not soon recur.'

The actual date of cessation was April 5, 1802.

By June he had directed the Treasury[20] to instruct the Revenue Departments to prepare plans for a general consolidation and revision of all the duties under their care; it was clear that he would look to income tax again, but with suitable modifications to make it both more efficient and more productive, if the war should be renewed. This began to seem more than likely as the year went on, and by the beginning of 1803 the dispute over the cession of Malta came to a head, and war was declared in May.

In the following month Addington brought in his first war Budget. He required a further £12,500,000, of which £4,500,000 was to come from 'Duties on Land and Property'. This was, in effect, the revival of income tax which had been forecast for the 'important occasion'; there were originally two Bills, one an Income Tax Bill and the other a Property Tax Bill, but they were eventually consolidated into one Bill.[21]

But this was no mere revival of Pitt's legislation. The general return was done away with and was replaced by particular returns of income from particular sources. The tax was for the first time divided up into the well-known five schedules. Schedule A charged tax on the amount of land and buildings; Schedule B covered farming profits; Schedule C taxed fundholders in respect of annuities payable out of any public revenues; persons not British subjects and not resident in Great Britain were granted exemption; Schedule D was divided into the six cases which are still familiar today and brought into charge various forms of profits and interest. It was, in effect, the final schedule as it contained the 'sweep-up' provisions of Case VI; and Schedule E embraced the charge on income from offices and employments of profit and annuities and pensions. The second innovation was the introduction of a scheme for the deduction of tax at source which was to be applied to interest, dividends, rent, income from the Funds and the emoluments of Crown servants. The Commercial Commissioners

---

[20] Farnsworth (*op. cit.*), pp. 37–8.
[21] The Budget speech of Addington was on 13/VI/1803. See also Farnsworth, pp. 40 *et seq.*

were abolished, and a curious system of Referees substituted for settling disputes as to the profit of trades; as a contemporary 'Exposition of the Act'[22] explained, 'as without doubt respectable people will be appointed, the Revenue will be secure under such management. It is, whatever may be the event, a striking evidence of the liberality of Parliament and of their anxious desire to avoid every possibility of unnecessary rigour. It must, however, be considered as an experiment only, grounded on the good faith subsisting between Parliament and the people.' The power of the General Commissioners was enhanced by the abolition of the superior Commissioners of Appeal of the 1799 Act (see page 29) and by their appointment by the Land Tax Commissioners without the intervention of the Grand Jury. To assist them, and partly in replacement of the Commercial Commissioners, the Act provided for Additional Commissioners[23] appointed from the commercial interest by the General Commissioners, but with half their property qualification; their duty was to receive Schedule D returns and to make assessments thereon, subject to the right of appeal by Surveyor or taxpayer to the General Commissioners; they could also request the help of the General Commissioners in making their assessments.

The principle of exemption and abatement was retained, but on earned income only; incomes under £60 were not liable, and between £60 and £150 the rate varied from 3d in the pound to the full 1s in the pound, which was half the rate of Pitt's tax. Child allowances[24] were also retained, although it is known that Addington regarded these allowances as 'intricate and troublesome' and had their repeal in mind.

There was considerable opposition to the Bill;[25] one M.P. said his constituents 'considered it a measure so unjust in its principle and partial in its operation that no modification of it could remove their objection', and this sentiment found numerous echoes. It was also of course 'an outrage upon the popular opinion'. Addington could deal with this sort of criticism, but far more dangerous was the attack of Pitt. There were many provisions of the Bill of which he 'strongly disapproved', but his principal objections were to allowing exemption

---

[22] The full title of this work which was a sort of 'guide book' prepared by an expert at the Tax Office is 'An Exposition of the Act for a Contribution on Property, Professions, Trades and Offices, in which the Principles and Provisions of the Act are fully considered, with a view to facilitate its Execution both with respect to Persons Chargeable, as Persons liable to the tax by way of deduction and the officers chosen to carry it into Effect' (1803). Besides its explanatory function, the author also adopts a highly moral tone on occasions.

[23] Additional Commissioners: see S. 18, I.T.A. 1803.

[24] Child Allowance: see Farnsworth (*op. cit.*), p. 97.

[25] The Budget debates cover the period June 13 to August 1, 1803.

and abatement only for earned income and the deduction of tax at the source from income derived from the funds and assessable under Schedule C. The first he described as inequitable and the second as 'inconsistent with national good faith'. In the event, Addington conceded both points for the sake of gaining general acceptance for his Bill.[26] Pitt proved equally accommodating in the end. 'Though in detail, there might be considerable difficulties, he trusted there would be none as to fundamental principles.'

Addington, as a Chancellor of the Exchequer, has been hardly used by historians. There is no doubt about the fact that by adopting the five schedule system and the mechanism of deduction of tax at source, he achieved almost as big a breakthrough as Pitt in his changeover from a tax on expenditure to a tax on income. For these two innovations were fundamental; they have lasted until the present day and he must be given due credit for them. And yet the introduction of two taxation principles of startling originality and durability by Addington seem curiously out of character with a career which, although worthy and painstaking, was not otherwise brilliant. This apparent contradiction can perhaps be resolved.

In 1802, as previously mentioned, Addington had requested the Revenue authorities, through the Treasury, to prepare schemes for revising the taxes under their charge. It may be that the schedule system was discussed then since it was based, to an extent, on the headings in the particular return of income which was called for under the 1799 Act when the general return was not considered adequate. As for the principle of deduction of tax, that appeared as early as 1657 when an Act of that year, providing for a Monthly Assessment of £60,000 permitted certain tenants to deduct tax from their rents. 'Landlords' were 'required to allow such deductions and payments upon the receipt of the residue of their rents and . . . every tenant paying the said assessment shall be acquitted and discharged', etc. The same procedure was laid down in the original Land Tax Act of 1692, '. . . It shall be lawful . . . for the Landlords . . . of such . . . Lands . . . and Premises as are charged with the pound rate . . . to deduct and to retain and keep in his or their Hands four shillings in the Pound for every fee form rent or other annual Rent or Payment charged upon or arising out of the premises . . . and all and every Persons who are . . . entitled to such Rents and annual Payments are hereby required to allow such Deductions.' Now Addington clearly possessed a profound knowledge of taxation history; this is clear from his speech on Pitt's Income Tax Bill of 1798 which gives a most graphic and concise summary of the course of direct taxation. The principle of deduction of tax at source would, therefore, be familiar

[26] Parliamentary Register, 22/XII/1798, pp. 409–10.

to him and it is doing him scant justice to ignore his part in the two signal reforms which took place in his Chancellorship of the Exchequer and to suggest that they were simply the work of a highly industrious Parliamentarian speaking to departmental briefs.

Addington was essentially a practical man. Whether or not the schedular system originated with him, it was clearly a procedure which would go far to meet the public objection to 'making a full disclosure of their fortunes' and, although the principle of deduction of tax at source was not new, Addington saw how it could be adapted to prevailing circumstances and how, especially, it would prevent that 'fraud and evasion' which had so characterized the first income tax. The justification of the wisdom of these reforms was shown by the yield. The estimate for 1803 was £4,450,000; the final yield exceeded that by some £250,000 which was only 20% short of the yield of Pitt's tax, which was levied at double the rate. The yield for 1804 was close on £4,700,000 against an estimate of £4,800,000, but by the time Addington's estimates had been justified he had resigned and Pitt, a dying man, brought in his last Budget in 1805.[27] The rate was raised to 1s 3d in the pound; the Special Commissioners were instituted with duties under Schedule A and Schedule C;[28] otherwise Pitt had accepted completely the Addington amendments.

It is generally agreed that the 1806 Income Tax Act settled the final shape of income tax in the Napoleonic Wars. It was introduced by Lord Henry Petty, son of the Marquis of Lansdowne and a product of the same brilliant financial school as Pitt.[29] He raised the rate to 2s in the pound, saying this mode of increase was preferable to one more gradual which 'would have led to the supposition that this was a fund to be drawn upon to an indefinite extent but, being raised at once to its natural limit, there will be less suspicion of future augumentation'. The withdrawals Addington had suggested of exemption and abatement for small, unearned incomes, repairs allowance for property, and relief for children were now implemented, as was his proposal, originally dropped at the instance of Pitt, that tax should be deducted from income from the Funds by the Bank of England. There was an increase in the number of Surveyors and in the power of the Special Commissioners, giving them the right to act in the event of the failure of the General Commissioners to perform their duties.

The debates were mainly concerned with minor points, and the usual requests for concessions to meet hard cases and 'the extreme

---

[27] Farnsworth (*op. cit.*), p. 87 *et seq*.
[28] S. 30, I.T.A. 1805 and ss. 73–85.
[29] Lord Henry Petty's Budget was introduced 28/III/1806 and the debate was wound up on 10/VI/1806.

injustice and hardship which the bill would inflict' were made. Petty was 'reluctant to relax any of the provisions', but on 'mature consideration' he proposed an exemption to those who earned no more than £50 a year 'when gentlemen recollected how the money was acquired, when they considered that it was frequently by the sacrifice of health and ultimately of life in dangerous and injurious employments, they would readily allow that these persons whom he mentioned were entitled to some superior advantages'. He refused, however, to differentiate, as requested, between incomes that were 'but temporary and unstable and those that were permanent and stable'; and he rejected an appeal for the restoration of child allowance on the ground that it was really a tax on those who had none. Petty might have been a humanitarian, but he was certainly not an egalitarian. 'The honourable member had recommended to him to adopt a mode of raising the taxes of the rich and exempting the poor. Of all the dangerous doctrines that could possibly be held out in a legislative assembly, there was not one that could possibly be more mischievous in its tendency than that of equalising all ranks of society by reducing the higher orders to a level with those of a different class and depriving them of every comfort which they had a right to expect from their exalted situation.'

The period 1806–16 saw no significant changes in the law or the administration of income tax. The powers and duties of the various bodies of Commissioners remained unchanged; their administrative areas, derived from the old Land Tax, stayed the same. Even the rate was stabilized at its 1806 level of 2s in the pound. There were two interesting executive innovations. In 1808 travelling Inspectors General were appointed to visit various areas and comment on the way the local Surveyor had been conducting his district, reporting back to the Central Commissioners at the Tax Office.[30] The duties of the Surveyor himself were more closely defined too in that year and later in 1810.[31] He was required to attend meetings of the General Commissions and to supply full details to all taxpayers on whom he had levied surcharges. These could be very considerable: Joseph Radford,[32] the Surveyor for Manchester and Salford, for instance, received about £470 as his 10% commission on surcharges in 1813, as compared with his salary of £110.

Income tax was now settling down and securing a general, if

[30] The Act appointing the Inspectors General was 48 G.3 C141. See Hope-Jones (*op. cit.*), p. 30.

[31] Hope-Jones (*op. cit.*), pp. 31–2.

[32] His name appears in the Manchester Directory for 1813 as Surveyor of Taxes, his office being at 19, Hanging Ditch and his home at 1, Hulme Place, Salford. He later moved to London; see Hope-Jones (*op. cit.*), pp. 53–4.

somewhat, reluctant acceptance. Between 1806 and 1815, for instance, even the most casual references to income tax in Hansard are very few. One of the rare occasions was in 1811 when an M.P. complained of the oppressive nature of the tax on the 'lowly paid classes'.[33] The Chancellor replied that 'alterations (in exemptions) would produce a material diminution in revenue and there would be no way of supplying it but by laying taxes on the necessaries of life, which would press as strongly upon the poorer classes as the tax from which it was proposed to relieve them'. There was no question – an echo of Lord Henry Petty, five years before – of higher taxes on the rich: 'that would be a complete subversion of all the principles of justice by which the property of all men should be equally protected by the law'.

In February 1815, however, there was a very full statement by the Chancellor, Vansittart, on income tax in the Committee of Ways and Means.[34] Napoleon had been exiled on Elba for almost a year and the question was whether to renew the tax or raise money by some other means. He emphasized the benefits the country had derived from it; and he denied its supposed inquisitorial nature; the Commissioners had always acted according to the 'fair dictates of their judgment' and many of them were J.P.s 'to whom the country was indebted for the preservation of tranquillity'. He contrasted the equitable way the tax operated[35] with the oppressive mechanism of the subsidy in Queen Anne's reign and concluded by saying that it would be better to lay it aside entirely than to alter it. 'Still, however, it ought always to be considered as a resource which Parliament might resort to when public necessity demanded it.'

That time was not far away. On March 1, 1815 Napoleon escaped from Elba. Another state of affairs had now arrived said the Chancellor, and all his plans were now changed. The Government was prepared to wage war against France as long as Napoleon remained on the imperial throne, but this was not by any means the unanimous opinion of the country. On May 1st, for instance, a petition was presented by the Lord Mayor, Aldermen and Livery of London, against a war with France 'as founded neither in justice nor necessity' and 'against that most galling, oppressive and hateful inquisition – the tax on income'. It concluded by praying the House 'to stop a weak, rash and infatuated Administration in their mad and frightful career'. But all the complaints about income tax were forgotten when

[33] Hansard 24/VI/1811.
[34] The Committee of Ways and Means sat 20/II/1815 and there was a further lengthy debate 19/IV/1815. See Hansard accordingly.
[35] The referee principle and the number of people who used it is referred to in Sayer's *Observations and Suggestions* (see pp. 53–4, pp. 163–4).

The Tax that beat Napoleon

Napoleon rallied his veterans to him again from the prison camps of Russia and East Germany only to meet and lose in person to the man he had been fighting by proxy ever since the opening of the Peninsular Campaign seven years ago. The political results of Waterloo are plain to see; one of the economic results was the disappearance of the immediate necessity and justification for a tax on income.

CHAPTER III

The End and the Beginning

In the last analysis income tax was a war tax; it had been born of the war and it had sustained the war; its current yield to the war chest was in the order of £16,000,000.[1] But when the war was over, it was understandable that the Government should be subject to the strongest pressure to redeem an implied promise, that a war tax should not continue in time of peace, and repeal the Income Tax Act. The opposition in the Commons to its retention was led by Henry Brougham,[2] a lawyer with a restless talent and an all-pervading energy. The Government was not, however, prepared to repeal automatically, and Hansard tells of a desperately interesting struggle over this issue in the last six weeks or so of the winter of 1816.

It began with the Chancellor observing in his 'Financial Exposition' on February 12, 1816 that he proposed to continue the property tax[3] while reducing its rate. 'By reducing the property tax to 5% (i.e. half rate), an immediate diminution of £7,000,000 of taxes would be effected of which sum above £4,000,000 would fall to the agricultural share of the country.' In addition, further to alleviate the prevailing agricultural distress, the malt duty was also to be repealed giving the farming interest relief of £5,000,000 in total. Brougham would have none of this; previous attacks on income tax had confined themselves to details; the principle of the tax itself had been accepted as a necessary war-time evil. But this was peace; and patriotism no longer provided a check to full-blooded assaults.

'He could not impress too deeply on the public mind the unequal

---

[1] For the yield of the war income tax generally see Hope-Jones (*op. cit.*), ch. VI.

[2] Henry Brougham: a good popular biography is that of Francis Hawes which brings out his 'fitful, defective and strange greatness'.

[3] It should be noted that when the Chancellor talks of property tax, he actually means income tax; and even down to the present day, there has been a certain confusion about the terms property tax and income tax. The title 'Income Tax Acts' was not introduced until quite late in the Victorian era. The use of the term 'property tax' where later generations use 'income tax' is a reflection of the importance of income from land in the early nineteenth century.

manner in which this tax operated, nor could he sufficiently reprobate the inquisitorial mode of its collection. It injured in a higher degree than it produced revenue and he was willing to admit that it was a most productive tax. The very circumstance of its being so productive formed one of his strongest grounds of objection to it. (Hear! Hear! from the ministerial benches.) It did so, because such a productive tax was likely to render ministers more saving and economical than those in power, profuse and extravagant. He hoped that this tax would never be agreed to by Parliament. He hoped that the country would rise as one man against it.'

George Rose followed with a reasoned defence of the tax. It had saved the national credit and sooner or later, if it were repealed, other taxes would have to be raised to secure equivalent revenue. 'The tax bore hard on certain classes of people; but any other tax that would produce £12,000,000 annually would bear on them harder still.'

The anticipation that within a few weeks the table would be covered with petitions against the tax was fully realized; one of these was from the Lord Mayor, Aldermen and Commons of the City of London which seems, by its language, to have been drafted by the same hand as that of May 1, 1815. The continuation of the property tax would be a violation of assurances and the solemn faith of Parliament. The petitioners trusted 'it would not be necessary, neither would it be possible within the limits of a petition to enumerate all the grievances arising from it'. References to 'inquisitorial vexations', 'partiality and injustice', 'degrading expositions', and 'multiplied oppressions' abound. Admittedly relief was needed by agriculture; but industry was equally oppressed. In sum, the tax was 'hostile to every sense of freedom, revolting to the feelings of Englishmen and repugnant to the principles of the British constitution'. This was the pattern for many similar petitions of which Brougham took full advantage.

He also exploited the possibly deliberate misunderstanding of an order which the House had made for a return of all the persons assessed to the income tax in London, the amount of the assessment and the appeals against it with the relevant decisions. The innocent reply from the Tax Office was that the Commissioners 'knew of no Income Tax but one that had expired in 1802'; did the House mean the property tax? Brougham was indignant: 'Did the House require the schooling of the Board of Taxes?' The Chancellor explained that the order should have been sent to the Treasury; and he was sure no disrespect was intended and gave the text of an amended order which had the proper reference to statute and not the simple phrase 'to the Income Tax'. Brougham tried to insist on the reinsertion of the words, but the Chancellor closed the discussion by saying he had no objection to the words proposed but 'it would be best to refer to the acts by which the contribution was granted'.

There was a fresh spate of petitions in March, and on the 4th the Chancellor made a further statement that the Government had at no time promised to discontinue the tax at the end of the war,[4] although he agreed that the House ought to be given the opportunity of considering whether such an impost should be levied in time of peace. On the following day, in the face of more petitions, one of which contained the interesting statement that out of fifty French passports granted to Englishmen, forty-five were 'emigrants flying from the weight of taxation at home', he summarized his proposals with regard to income tax which had been briefly stated in the 'Exposition' of the previous February and cleared up, to his own satisfaction at least, some misrepresentations 'as to the proportion of the burthen that fell upon individuals in trade'.

Brougham returned to the attack again holding up a new batch of petitions, in particular one from Honiton, in which complaint was made about 'compelling the petitioners to lay open their concerns to a team of inspectors and spies'. He then went on to relate how an acquaintance of his had bought some cheese which, to his horror, was wrapped in an income tax return; the cheesemonger had 'lately bought a great lot of waste paper which had been exposed to sale by the Commissioners'. The Chancellor had heard this story before; the honourable and learned member had been misinformed; but he was prepared to meet the complaint of 'inquisitorial proceedings' by reinstating the referee principle of 1803. This was only a sop and Vansittart must have known it as it seems that only twenty people availed themselves of the procedure when it was originally introduced.

On March 18th, the Chancellor rose again for the last time 'to submit his proposition for the continuance of the property tax'. The petitions, although very numerous, did not contain the signatures of a majority of the population, 'nor could it be expected that many people would carry public spirit so far as to petition in favour of a heavy tax'. The petitioners had not understood the subject; there was

[4] The debates on repeal commenced 12/II/1816 with a speech by the Chancellor. A series of petitions to Parliament followed, beginning the next day. Brougham then renewed his attack on 28/II/1816 and on 5/III the Chancellor made a further statement. Brougham continued to press home his advantage and made a further set speech 7/III/1816, in which the waste paper story occurs. This story crops up again (Hansard 5/V/1851) in a speech of Sir Henry Willoughby and the Chancellor in his reply referred to the Brougham canard. On 11/III there were further petitions followed by a debate on 12/III. On 18/III came Vansittart's last ditch defence and the defeat of the motion for continuation. See Hansard accordingly.

no implicit promise that the tax would be repealed when peace came; and the tax which he was proposing was, amongst other things, so light in its incidence that it could hardly be said to resemble the old war income tax. There still were some snags. 'As to Schedule D, he confessed he had never been able to discover any complete remedy for the complaints of persons included in it', but he was willing to include a clause whereby 'an individual in trade might be charged according to his estimated profit of the last year so that he would not be called upon to make a fresh return' – unless his profits had diminished.

But it was too late for any concessions; the temper of the House and the country was for total abolition. The debate concluded with a speech by Wilberforce which could hardly be heard for the shouts of 'Hear, Hear!' But by the 'thundering peal' of applause which accompanied the close of his speech, it was understood that he had once more expressed his determination to vote against the Bill. The House then divided; two hundred and one were the votes for the continuation of the Property Tax; against it, two hundred and thirty-eight, a majority of thirty-seven. So ended, for the time being, Pitt's bold experiment reinforced by Addington's brilliant amendments. So ended too, the complaints about the unwarranted interference with individual liberty and the nagging fear that this might be followed, not only by the tax as a permanent feature – 'Is it possible to imagine that if this tax is once imposed, we shall ever be able to get rid of it?' – but that this extension of bureaucratic power into everyday life might be the herald of an all embracing tyranny. But despite the very real hostility which ran as a continuous thread through the whole first phase of income tax, there were three most important by-products.

In the first place the machinery set up and developed contained many of the features of modern administrative and executive practice, even to a certain independence of the legislature. It was not yet the modern Civil Service by any means; but the lesson was plain that the sort of problem which the introduction of income tax had posed needed the skill and attention of the expert, of such men as Winter,[5] the Secretary to the Tax Office, and Gray,[5] the Deputy Auditor

[5] Matthew Winter and Richard Gray; the former was Secretary to the Board until 1822 and the latter Deputy Auditor General until 1825. A good deal of their correspondence is contained in the papers at the Public Record Office at reference E182/1360. There are some undated papers at reference E182/1361 but these are in too poor a state now to be inspected. This correspondence has been well used by A. Hope-Jones. It is a pity that the correspondence of their successors has not been preserved in such detail; of course, since the war was over there was not the same need for such close co-operation, especially after the abolition of the Property Tax. See also Silberling's article in the *Quarterly Journal of Economics* (38), 'Financial and Monetary Policy of Great Britain during the Napoleonic Wars'.

General, who worked so well together in their long tenure of office during the life of the war income tax.

Secondly, it had been manifested that a graduated direct tax could be made to work. Admittedly it had its flaws: there was evasion especially in the assessment of profits under Schedule D; the system of surcharges was sometimes abused by the Surveyor since he received commission on them; there were too many defaulting collectors; and it was imposed at a higher rate than at any time until the twentieth century. But some of the more discerning could see that a graduated income tax, properly administered, is an equitable method of taxation and an equally equitable substitute would be hard to find.

Thirdly, despite the objection to interference in the private affairs of the citizen and to the inquisitorial nature of both officials and returns, this interference had, in fact, been borne for fifteen years. Admittedly the reason was partly the stress of war and partly the fact that assessments were, in the main, made by amateur Commissioners, but that is not so significant as the fact that this interference, including the deduction of tax at source, had been the basis of the successful yield of the war income tax from 1803 onwards. Direct taxation could never again lapse into the old casual quota-based system of the centuries before Pitt and Addington.

There is a curious postscript to the drama of the last days of income tax. Mere repeal was not enough. 'The documents held by the Commissioners for the Affairs of the Taxes were, it was ordered, to be cut into small pieces and conveyed to a paper manufactory,' where they were to be pulped under the eyes of a Commissioner, so that no trace of the hated tax would remain. But duplicates of the Land Tax returns and the assessed taxes had always been sent to the King's Remembrancer and as a matter of ordinary routine, this procedure was extended to the income tax records. It seems that that diligent officer did not think it worth while to remind anyone that he had in his office the complete records for seventeen years; and, in fact, at some unknown date they were bundled into sacks and sent to the Public Record office. There is a legend that Brougham himself helped to stoke a bonfire of the hated records in Old Palace Yard, Westminster; Gray, the Deputy Auditor, whose office windows overlooked Old Palace Yard, must have smiled a very sardonic smile at the thought of the duplicates safe in the keeping of the Exchequer Court.[6]

But scarcely had the smoke from Brougham's bonfire died away than it was necessary to make a considerable reappraisal of the

[6] Hope-Jones (*op. cit.*), Introduction – 'The King's Remembrancer Documents'.

general taxation position. Customs and excise were still the mainstay of the national income, and even with the cost of government mounting, the National Debt at £861,000,000, and the problems arising from the return to the Gold Standard in 1819,[7] Huskisson,[8] at the Board of Trade, found it possible to make an impressive reduction in tariffs throughout the 1820s. He even managed an amendment to the Corn Laws in 1828 by bringing in a graded set of duties, after his sliding scale had been rejected in 1827. Direct taxation, on the other hand, lacked any such organizing intelligence and became increasingly a jungle of levies, some makeshift, some efficient, some with a yield hardly commensurate with the vexation the collection aroused, and all subject to evasion.[9]

There were, first of all, the taxes on specific professions and trades. These included taxes on the legal profession for practising certificates costing £12 in London and Edinburgh, £8 elsewhere, on the Banks for their licence to issue notes, on auctioneers and appraisers, on pawnbrokers and finally on hawkers, who had not only to pay for a licence to cover themselves, but one for their beast of burden as well. There were increases in the legal and hawking licences in 1815.

Then came the taxes categorized as 'taxes on persons providing the means of locomotion'. Among these were the taxes on persons keeping various types of coaches, post horses and horses let for hire; journeys by post-chaise were both popular and efficient; as Dr Johnson had observed of that mode of travel: 'Sir, life has not many things better than this.' The tax on coaches was reasonably profitable, yielding over £350,000 in 1824, but, with the tax on horses, it was revised by Althorp in his elaborate Budget of 1832, when he also introduced a tax on railways, based on $\frac{1}{2}$d per mile for every four passengers. This became most remunerative and contrasted with Pitt's abortive attempt to tax canals and Althorp's attempt to tax passengers travelling by steamboat, which was quietly dropped.

Neither of these two classes of taxation was very productive, but probate duty and legacy duty proved excellent stand-bys, raising between them about £2,000,000 by the late 1830s. Tax on insurances was equally successful raising close on £1,000,000 for example in 1832. Stamp duties also provided a steadily increasing revenue, but the tax on property sold by auction became overgrown with exemptions and, despite its yield of £250,000, was listed for repeal at the first available opportunity.

[7] N. Gash: *Mr Secretary Peel*, p. 241 *et seq.*

[8] See, *inter alia*, C. R. Fay: *Huskisson and his Age*.

[9] The summary of the various taxes remaining, apart from those under the control of the Tax Office, may be studied in more detail in Dowell (*op. cit.*), vol. III, pp. 20–64. The yield figures are those used by him.

There remained the Assessed Taxes,[10] which contained almost as many complications as all the foregoing classes combined. They were levied under sixty or more different Acts, and the law had been modified by some 2,000 appeal cases which, as previously stated, contained simply the bare decision without any reason. These taxes had originally been concerned principally with window tax and inhabited house duty, but to the charge of the Tax Commissioners had been added the taxes on coaches, menservants, saddle and carriage horses, racehorses, game certificates, hair powder, dogs and armorial bearings which, in total, were in 1816 yielding some £2,500,000. There were revisions and increased exemptions during the period. For instance, agricultural horses were declared not liable to the tax on horses and 'working' servants such as gardeners and gamekeepers were exempted from the tax on servants. In addition, in 1823 'Prosperity' Robinson, who had succeeded Vansittart as Chancellor of the Exchequer, reduced all these taxes by one half. An example of the anomalies which abounded in the range of taxation was the curious distinction between the tax on horses entered for a race which was operated by the Commissioners for Stamps and the tax on racehorses which was under the control of the Tax Commissioners.

Window Tax and Inhabited House Tax, however, were the props of the assessed taxes and the main concern of the Surveyor now the Property Tax had been repealed. The yield of the former, in 1815 was £2,000,000 and of the latter close on £900,000. Trade premises and warehouses were made exempt from both taxes in 1817, and in 1823 the rate of both was reduced by one half in the general reductions which applied to the whole of assessed taxes. In 1824 there was a further extension of exemption to offices so that by the 1830s the yield of both taxes was approximately halved. One of the first fiscal acts of the Reformed Parliament in 1832 was to apply further reductions in Inhabited House Tax to premises partly occupied for trade purposes, such as shops and public houses. By 1834 Althorp had a considerable Budget surplus which he used to repeal the Inhabited House Tax, although it had been suggested that the repeal of the window tax would have been the more popular move. A contemporary notice of assessment (see page 50) gives some idea of the details called for in this multiplicity of taxes; and it can be seen how, again, expenditure rather than income had become the test of liability.

This notice, it will be observed, was dated before the reductions of 1823 which explains the severity of the duty charged; the rates then

---

[10] The Assessed Taxes may also be studied in Dowell, vol. III, pp. 169–310 but their history is traced from beginning to end in the case of each tax which means a certain amount of repetition.

remained unchanged until Baring introduced an all-round increase in the assessed taxes of ten per cent in 1840.

CONTEMPORARY NOTICE OF ASSESSMENT

'No. 10 Assessed Taxes, 1st part for the Year ending 5th April,1818.
To...................of the Parish of....................
Your first Assessment in my Duplicate for the present Year delivered to me on The 20th day of July – under the Acts relating to the Duties of Assessed Taxes amounts to the Sum of £74.3.6. – the Particulars of which are stated on the Back hereof and the Assessment may be seen at my House as under-mentioned. If you have any Cause to appeal against the same, you must give Notice in Writing within 28 Days after the said 20th day of July – to the Surveyor or Inspector for this District or to one of the Assessors of this Parish. The Day of Appeal is fixed for the 16th Day of August 1817.

Signed....................Collector
Residing at.........................

N.B. These Duties are payable by Instalments Quarterly viz. the 20th of June, 20th of September, 20th of December and 20th March, or within 10 Days after: and the full Amount for the first half Year, if not former paid as aforesaid, will be collected or levied on your Goods and Chattels on the 10th of October next and the full amount for the Second half Year, if not paid as aforesaid will be collected or levied In like Manner on the 5th April next, or within Twenty-one Days after the respective periods; in Default of Distress or Payment you will be subject to Proceeds for the Recovery thereof from the Court of Exchequer with Costs: and if you remove from this Parish without discharging the Taxes due, or leaving sufficient goods whereon Distraint may be made, you will be liable to a Penalty of Twenty pounds.'

Standard economic theory was still dominated by the classical figure of Adam Smith and *The Wealth of Nations*.[11] He designated four canons of taxation: equity, equality of contribution, certainty of imposition, convenience of payment and economy in collection. He rated highly a proportionate tax on houses since 'There is not, perhaps, any one article of expense or consumption by which the liberality or narrowness of a man's whole expense may be judged of than by his house rent'. He might not perhaps have opposed any of Addington's five schedules, apart from Schedule D which could be criticized according to his teachings more from its administrative interference than its intrinsic injustice; but in general he opposed

[11] The quotations from Adam Smith are from the Cannan edition.

49

	No.	Amount of Duty £	s	d
Windows	32	21	6	6
Inhabited House Duty	Rent £30	3	7	6
Servants Sch. C No. 1				
Under Gard. & Occal. Groom Trade &c.	1	2	8	0
Bailiffs &c.	1		10	0
Travellers or Riders				
Clerks &c.				
Shopmen &c.	1	2	0	0
To take care of Race Horses				
Waiters at Taverns &c.				
Occasional Waiters in Taverns 6 Months				
Ditto less than 6 Months				
Ditto in private Houses				
Occasional Servants				
To let to Hire				
Stage Coachmen and Guards				
Private Use				
Additional Bodies same Wheels				
To let to hire				
Post Chaise				
Stage Coaches				
Two Wheel Carriages	1	6	10	0
Drawn by two or more Horses or Mules				
Additional Bodies same Wheels				
Taxed Carts				
Coachmakers &c.				
Carriages made for sale &c. 4 Wheels				
2 Wheels				
Taxed Carts				
Own Use	3	15	13	6
To hire				
Race Horses				
Draught not in Husbandry 11.1s.	20	21	0	0
Mules carrying Coal 3s.				
Small Farmers under 201.1s.				
Used in husbandry 17s. 6d.				
Under 8s. hands 8s.				
On Farms under 50 1.3s.				
On Farms under 701 per Annum 3s.				
701 and under 1001 5s.				
1001 and under 1301 7s. 6d.				
1501 and under 2001 10s. 6d.				
Greyhounds at 11. each				
Other Dogs	2	1	8	0
Packs of Hounds				
Horse Dealers				
Hair Powder				
Armorial Bearings				
		£74	3	6

'capitation taxes' as 'arbitrary and uncertain'. 'The state of a man's fortune varies from day to day and without an inquisition more intolerable than any tax and renewed at least once every year, can only be guessed at.' His assessment therefore 'must, in most cases, depend on the good or bad humour of his assessors'. The objection of the average M.P. to an income tax was the very simple one, that it was a war tax and there was no place for it in the fiscal system of peace. The ordinary taxpayers, having by their petitions forced Parliament to drop income tax, now turned on the assessed taxes which were manifestly unfair in their incidence; their objection was practically to any taxation whatever.

Fiscal practice corresponded exactly with fiscal theory. Since an income tax was opposed by the greatest of economists, the majority in Parliament, and the main body of taxpayers, it was clear that it could never be resurrected without a complete and national rethinking of the whole problem of finance. That being so, the only current recourse was to the two old stand-bys of classical financial policy – the raising of loans and the taxing of necessaries. There was a long and potent tradition of indirect taxation and, after all, even although the system was cumbersome, anomalous, and encompassed a multitude of articles, it did work. Moreover, in a boom period, it was possible to reduce the duty on account of the increase in consumption. This was a financial policy of expediency at once 'imprudent and unattractive'.[12]

If fiscal theory and practice did not provide a favourable climate for a tax on income, still less did the political atmosphere of the period.[13] The government of England had rested traditionally on the landed aristocracy which controlled the country through Parliament and the local magistracy; this was true even of specialized legislation such as the Income Tax Acts, which were basically administered by the General Commissioners who themselves were, as Vansittart had pointed out, very often also Justices of the Peace (see page 40). After 1815 many factors contributed to upset the delicate balance of this mechanism. The end of the war meant an all round slackening of central control. Agricultural depression created a chronic source of discontent in general and an impatience with any attempt to retain income tax in particular, as the repeal debates of 1816 showed. Finally, there were the ever-increasing problems posed by an explosion in population, a working class often on the brink of riot,[14] and

[12] Halévy: *The Triumph of Reform*, p. 93. The financial policy of the period is discussed at pp. 88–97.

[13] N. Gash: *Mr Secretary Peel* and *Politics in the Age of Peel*, especially pp. 6–14 in the former book.

[14] R. J. White: *Waterloo to Peterloo*.

a dynamic but often inhuman industrial development. Little real government existed: Halévy, the great French historian, mindful, no doubt, of his own country's tightly organized administration, called the England of 1815 a 'disorderly society'.

It was small wonder then that the function of the government, which meant in practice the Cabinet, was quite simply to govern; and it was often a hard enough task to carry on the day to day administration of the country. There was no question of a party system; Parliament had not yet learned to call ministers to account; allegiance was owed to a leader, not a set of principles. Still less was there room for doctrinaire innovations; when changes came, they came, like the Reform Bill, because the pressure of public opinion made it necessary for action to be taken if the machinery of state were to survive.

The financial history of the period illustrates how the accepted theory and practice in both economics and politics was being overtaken by the march of events. This is not so surprising when it is realized that the office of Chancellor of the Exchequer was regarded as a post of subordinate importance. Vansittart, for instance, was not a politician of first rank. For a time, all went well. Direct taxes were paying their way and the yield of indirect taxes was up, even although rates had been reduced, in the boom conditions of the 1820s. 'Prosperity' Robinson, who had succeeded Vansittart, well earned his sobriquet. The financial crisis of 1825 shook this facile stability, and the general policy was then drastic economy, since there was no surplus and no possibility of introducing new taxes. It is known that in the last days of the Wellington–Peel ministry of 1828–30 Peel was corresponding with the Treasury on the question of income tax,[15] and had even received a qualified assurance that, if it were introduced, the Whigs would not oppose it. But all was forgotten in the turmoil over reform, and in 1831 Lord Althorp found himself as Chancellor with no special qualifications for the office. His Budget proposed reductions amounting to £3,000,000 and new taxes of £2,750,000, but by the time his suggestions had been debated, it was much less of a Free Trade Budget than had been intended. When the Reform Bill had been passed, Althorp ran into trouble again and was faced with a demand for the simultaneous repeal of both the malt and the assessed taxes, together with associations formed for the purpose of refusing to pay taxes. 1834 was the high water mark of Whig finance with further remissions to cover a surplus of over £1,500,000. Peel's short ministry of 1834 to 1835 could accomplish little in the way of retrenchment, and the last four years of Whig finance were a series of deficits as taxes were repealed without any replacement. Baring, a member of the famous banking family, assumed the Chancellorship

[15] Gash (*op. cit.*), pp. 613–18.

too late, and by 1841 Peel was saying of him, 'Can there be a more lamentable picture than that of a Chancellor of the Exchequer seated on an empty chest – by the pool of bottomless deficiency – fishing for a budget'.[16] The *laissez-faire* theories of Adam Smith and the popular 'ignorant impatience of taxation'[17] had produced a policy of expediency which had pushed the country almost to the verge of bankruptcy.

But ever since the abolition of income tax in 1816 there had existed a definite body of informed public and private opinion in favour of its retention; not all the petitions after the war were pro-repeal; some prominent Manchester businessmen, for instance, led a petition for its retention. David Ricardo,[18] the foremost economist of the nineteenth century, who had entered Parliament as the member for Portarlington in 1819, was very decidedly in favour of direct taxation, and had already proposed a scheme for taxing not only income but capital also as part of an overall plan for redeeming the national debt. This was generally considered to be too extreme, even by the advocates of a tax on income itself, but it was widely discussed, especially by the progressive 'Manchester School' of economic thinkers and reformers on whom Ricardo had initially a marked influence.

Economic speculation, however, was by no means the exclusive preserve of the expert. An example of a current pamphlet is 'A letter addressed to the late Earl of Liverpool in the year 1822 showing that Unjust Taxation is the cause of the evils complained of with a Just System then suggested, to which is now added Preliminary Observations'.[19] This, as may be deduced from the title, is a somewhat confused piece of pleading, but it does recognize that many of the country's economic problems were caused 'in great measure by taking off the property tax, although unjust, instead of the internal taxes of the country, which are so much more so'. The remedy was the taxing of 'superfluous income' according to a scale graded from one per cent on an income of £50 to fifty per cent on an income of £2,500. The author may be permitted the last word on the subject: 'it might perhaps be called a plan of theoretical perfection, which can never be realised in practice.'

A far more reasoned and professional production was *Observations and Suggestions with a view to the Substitution of an Income or*

---

[16] Dowell (*op. cit.*), vol. III, p. 118.

[17] The phrase is Castlereagh's and was at the time much resented. It often appears in contemporary cartoons. One is in the Board's waiting room.

[18] Referred to by Mr Warburton in the debate of 26/III/1833 on the motion for appointing a Select Committee for taxation reform. For his influence on the Manchester School see W. D. Grampp, *The Manchester School of Economics*.

[19] Published anonymously in 1833. There is a copy in the library of the Board of Inland Revenue.

Property Tax for the Present Taxes.[20] This is a book of nearly four hundred pages with a seventy-page index. It is divided into three parts, the first dealing with the advantages of a tax on income over the prevailing system; the second with suggested amendments to the Property Tax repealed in 1816; and the third, of somewhat academic importance, with a plan for using its yield to reduce the National Debt. Income tax itself 'had never undergone that fair, dispassionate and complete treatment that it needs'. This the author proceeds to give, recommending in his preface that those interested should not read it all, but only such parts as 'they may see occasion or be inclined to attend to' as 'the perusal of it throughout would be a tedious task'.

The taxes on expenditure were inefficient as far as the State was concerned since the amount of an individual's contribution depended on the amount he was willing to spend, whereas income tax had to be paid on earnings which the earner would hardly wish to restrict. Ricardo is quoted with approval for his advocacy of a 'well regulated tax on profits'. Income tax could be graduated and give relief to the family man. The assessed taxes were regarded as 'obnoxious', and it would be possible to abolish them without any loss of income and with a gain in ease of administration since less people would be liable to direct taxation; in fact, the cost of collection could be cut by over half to 6d in the pound. To summarize, 'the principle of an Income Tax is founded on Justice'.

Some modifications of the previous system were desirable, but Adam Smith's argument for taxing rents of lands and houses only should, logically, have been extended to income in general. There were 'short returns' under Schedule D, admittedly, which arose 'in some degree from ignorance or misconception of the allowed and of the prohibited deductions' and which had given rise to complaints on 'inquisitorial and vexatious' methods when queries were raised on them. But certainly deduction of tax at source should be retained:

'The late plan of stopping the Tax from Income at its place of payment not only prevented the possibility of escaping it, but it obviated much of the necessity of resorting to any troublesome and

[20] There is a copy of this book in the Board's library, published in 1831. The title page appears to be missing. The copy in the British Museum is slightly revised and was published again anonymously in 1833. It is, however, indexed under the author's name, but it is not known how this was discovered. It must have been an open secret to contemporaries since Sayer is mentioned as the author in Warburton's speech (Hansard 26/III/1833). His name occurs in the Public Record Office correspondence already referred to (E182/1360) but he never became Secretary. Possibly his 'indifferent health' referred to in his Preface had something to do with it.

unpleasant proceedings for ascertaining the amount of income and was, doubtless, on the whole more satisfactory to all parties.'

The book was originally published anonymously and for private circulation. The author makes the interesting assumption that 'the long desired and expected Financial Reform would be brought forward in the proposition of an Income or Property Tax'. This may well have been an inspired remark since the book came out in February 1831, so that it, or a draft, could well have been read by both Peel and Goulburn, the Chancellor, before the Cabinet came to discuss the question of an income tax in the following month.[21] For its author would be well known to them; he was Benjamin Sayer, assistant to Edward Bates the Secretary to the Board from 1822, and his name appears frequently, indeed more frequently than his superior's, in the Tax Office correspondence with the Auditor's Office. A revised and expanded edition of the book was published in 1833, but it was another nine years before its author's hopes were realized.

The publicists of an income tax had their views fully reflected in Parliament during the 1830s. In March 1830, Poulett Thompson, the Whig member for Dover, proposed a motion for a general committee for taxation revision, and although it was defeated, there was considerable sympathy in the government for it, especially in the Herries–Goulburn–Peel camp. The battle was resumed after the Reform Bill when, in March 1833, a Select Committee was again proposed[22] 'to revise the existing taxation'. The opening speech came out boldly with the proposition that an income tax could be justified in peacetime: 'from the decreasing capital of the country and the diminishing wages of the working classes it was impossible that the present system of taxation should stand': and the income tax should be graduated. The seconder quoted, with approval, both Ricardo and Sayer and said 'he would recommend his (Sayer's) book to the perusal of hon. Members'. Althorp's reply mentioned the inequity of income tax in that fixed income, such as from property, or wages paid the full amount, but there was evasion in the case of trading and professional incomes. As for a graduated property tax, what was it but saying that a man who had £20,000 a year in comparison with one possessing £1,000 a year possessed too much property? 'If the principle were to be carried out to that extent, it would come, eventually, to the equalization of all property. Nothing could be more dangerous than to hold out such a prospect.' In the following month Sir John Key[23] moved the repeal of both the House and Window Taxes and the

[21] Gash (*op. cit.*), p. 616.
[22] Hansard 26/III/1833. The proposal was defeated by 66 votes.
[23] Hansard 30/IV/1833.

opposition was led by Peel; if these taxes were abolished, some substitute was necessary, 'and in the present circumstances of the country
either a Property or an Income Tax would be a great calamity'. But
there was one significant remark later in the speech: 'He would not
say that circumstances might not arise in war, or even in peace to
justify such a tax.' In the event both motions were defeated.

But Robinson,[24] the mover of the 1833 motion, was undaunted
and raised the question of the reform of the financial system in both
1835 and 1836. The objections to a property tax 'resolved themselves
into nothing more or less than a reluctance on the part of the wealthy
classes of the community to put their hands into their own pockets'.
The Chancellor reverted to the old argument of no property tax in
peacetime for the ingenious reason that there would be no property
tax to fall back on to increase revenue in time of war: 'No: let
indirect taxation be the source of your revenue in peace and leave
direct taxation in the shape of a property tax for the advent of war.'

There was then a good deal of economic speculation in the 1830s
favourable to an income tax; and there was clearly less antagonism
than there had been among politicians of both sides to an income
tax, certainly when presented under the aegis of 'commutation of
taxes'. After all, as a speaker had recently reminded the House, its
repeal had been carried by a majority of thirty-seven only. But if an
income tax were to be restored at any time, the Tax Office required
an organization flexible and capable of immediate expansion. Fortunately that was, in fact, the case.

When the Property Tax was abolished in 1816 there was naturally
a certain run-down of staff. Retirement plans were drawn up by the
efficient Winter, the Secretary to the Board, which were approved by
the Treasury in 1817.[25] The ordinary Surveyor in the field still had
enough to occupy himself, despite the repeal, as his 1818 Instruction
Book shows.[26] This is divided into two parts: 'Instructions to Surveyors of Taxes on that part of their Duty which relates to the
Assessed Taxes' and 'Various points under the several Schedules to
which the Particular Attention of the Surveyor is directed'. His duties,

[24] Of the two subsequent motions of Mr Robinson, the more interesting is that
reported in Hansard 24/III/1836 from which all the quotations have been taken.

[25] P.R.O. papers E182/1360 of 9/VII/1817 and 31/VII/1817.

[26] The Instruction Books quoted from are in the Board's library and are listed
as follows:

Instructions to Surveyors of Taxes 1818.
Instructions to Surveyors of Taxes 1838.
Instructions to Surveyors and List of Forms 1841.

The second of these is wrongly titled; the title page and the first two pages are
missing, but from the contents it is clear that the Instructions are those to
Receiving Inspectors. The books are still officially in the 'Confidential' category.

with regard to Assessed Taxes, not only required strict attention to the returns of income, but equally strict compliance with the complicated and almost ritualistic assessment procedure. The second part related to Window Tax, Inhabited House Duty and all the other miscellaneous imposts down to game certificates. The Surveyor was warned that 'Country Houses and Mansions appear greatly under-rated. The assessment should be based on what a House was worth to be let; that is what others in their circumstances would give for the occupation of such Houses, taking into consideration all the advantages such as grandeur, locality, quality of land, etc.'. And when it came to dogs:

'Many representations have been made of the evasions under this schedule, not only in number of dogs kept, but in the rate of duty; a strict attention must, therefore, not only be given to the number returned, but where only one is returned, the Surveyor's enquiry must be limited to the description, as that and not the use of the dog renders it liable to the higher duty if Hound, Pointer, Setting Dog, Spaniel, Terrier or Lurcher.'

The staff of Inspectors, however, those officials who supervised the work of the Surveyors, was reduced to seventeen. Their names are listed in a Treasury minute of June 20, 1817,[27] and there was also a change in the basis of their salary. The Board was authorized and required 'to cause salaries of Four Hundred Pounds to be paid to each of the Inspectors undermentioned, who are proposed to be retained, in lieu of all emoluments whatever from the per centage or Penalties arising from increased charges'. The Surveyor, however, still retained his surcharges and the Board issued a further circular on the subject in 1824. In 1837, however, there was a proposed new plan for remunerating Surveyors[28] 'vizt. that instead of paying them by a fixed salary of £90 a year, together with an allowance of 20 per cent on the amount of their surcharges, the whole number of Surveyors should be divided into four classes and that a salary should be assigned to each class according to the amount of the assessments of the Districts'. This plan was, at this stage, somewhat premature.

An Instruction Book for the Inspector, that is, the officer who supervised the Surveyors of 1838, gives a vivid and detailed account of his duties. This book is signed by Charles Pressly, the Secretary to the Board.[29] Much of it is concerned with the Inspector's duties as

[27] P.R.O. papers E182/1360.

[28] This is contained in some as yet unedited papers which include drafts of the Board's reports to the Treasury.

[29] Charles Pressly succeeded Bates (see p. 55) and remained as Secretary until 1859 when he became a C.I.R. See also ch. IV, p. 67.

Receiving Inspector, that is with the actual administration of tax collection, the examination of accounts, for instance, or the comparison of the duty charged with the amounts in the previous year. But he was also 'to state his opinion of the general conduct and competency of each Surveyor, also whether they are punctual in their attention to their correspondence and in making out the accounts required of them'. There was a special form of report provided, with a special column for observations on their 'assiduity, judgment and discretion'.

The Surveyor's Instruction Book of 1841, on the eve of the re-imposition of income tax, shows very little change from the print of 1818. The directions regarding Inhabited House Duty had, of course (see p. 48), disappeared, but the main content is still the detailed procedure required for making assessments in accordance with the strict letter of the law; for instance with regard to supplementary assessments, the duty of making these 'most essentially belongs to the Commissioners . . . and the Board desire that the Surveyors will strictly confine themselves to the care of forming the certificates of increased charges and not take upon themselves the execution of business which it has been specifically directed by the Legislation shall be the act of the Commissioners'. This book also was signed by Charles Pressly, but whereas he addressed the Inspectors in the familiar second person, the Surveyors are instructed in the formal third person.

The repeal of the Property Act had, in the end, achieved nothing and settled nothing. Looking back over the quarter century, since 1816, it was clear that financial crisis had only been averted in the 1830s by boom conditions which had artificially inflated the yield of direct taxation, so that even when the rate was reduced, the gap in the revenue was, at first, covered by increased consumption and by paring the cost of government to the limit. But now the fiscal honeymoon was over; now the government had to face the problem of recurring deficits with a patchwork system of direct taxation and a collection of indirect taxes possessing a mass of complex and varying rates. On the credit side in the sphere of direct taxation, the Board of Stamps and Taxes could deploy a well-drilled and well-instructed team of Surveyors and Inspectors with an expertise in assessment and collection, and backed by an experienced Head Office, all of which was essential to any taxation reform. For events were moving rapidly on the political front, although from two very different angles. The Chartists had already begun their agitation for that programme of constitutional reform which seemed so revolutionary to an electorate hardly used to the 1832 Reform Bill. But of more immediate and commanding importance, because publicized by a powerful propaganda machine and directed by two first class and complementary intelligences, was the Anti-Corn Law League. The genius of Peel at this period lay in his ability to reconcile these various conflicting elements with a general reform and stabilization of the fiscal policy of the country.

CHAPTER IV

The Giant from Repose[1]

WHEN the last two uneasy years of Whig rule, following the Bedchamber crisis, had finally dragged themselves to a close, Peel and his new Conservative party, as predicted, won a comfortable majority in the General Election of 1841. The electors were tired of the Whigs; the enthusiasm which had generated the great Reform Bill had long since been dissipated in annual imbalances, commercial depression and social unrest. 'When Sir Robert Peel undertook the government in 1841, it was a period of confusion and darkness . . . the new Minister found an empty Exchequer, a growing deficit.'[2] On the credit side he had 'an apparently invincible working majority'; on the debit side he had to face a ready-made solution in the repeal of Customs dues – which might commend itself to his party – and its natural corollary, a revision of the Corn Laws, which had the eager backing of a powerful and not always scrupulous pressure group whose policy was anathema to the interests and traditions of his supporters.[3]

'A constitutional statesman,' wrote Bagehot, 'is in general a man of common opinions and uncommon abilities.' This description perfectly fits Peel in his attitude towards income tax. He had considered the possibility of reimposition in 1830 (see p. 52), although he had spoken against it in 1833 (see p. 56). He was, however, well aware of the growing body of opinion in favour of a tax on income. By 1842 he was convinced the time had come. The secret was well kept, and speculation had busied itself with all manner of rumours from the complete abolition of protection to its intensification over a new range of subjects.

In spite of the fact then, that he was a late convert and never intended the tax to be permanent, his Budget of 1842[4] must still rank as one of the most famous in the nineteenth century.

---

[1] Adapted from a phrase of Gladstone's in his 1853 Budget speech, 'Sir Robert Peel in 1842 called forth from repose this giant . . .'
[2] A. A. A. Ramsay's *Sir Robert Peel*.
[3] S. Maccoby, *English Radicalism 1832–1852*, p. 225.
[4] Hansard 11/III/1842.

'I propose that, for a time to be limited, the income of the country shall be called upon to contribute a certain sum for the purpose of remedying this growing evil (the deficit). I propose that the income of this country should bear a charge not exceeding 7d in the £ for the purpose of supplying not only the deficiency in the revenue, but of enabling me, with confidence and satisfaction, to propose great commercial reforms; and by diminishing the prices of articles of consumption and the cost of living will, in the pecuniary point of view, compensate you for your present sacrifices; whilst you will be, at the same time, relieved from the contemplation of a great public evil.'

Peel went on to say that on the rate he proposed of 7d in the £ he estimated the yield at something over £3¾ millions. 'He trusted that Parliament would not be unwilling, in case of necessity, to continue the duration of this tax for a period of five years', but he suggested that the experiment should be limited to a period of three years 'in order to give Parliament an opportunity of continuing it at the end of that time, if necessary'. Ireland was exempted[5] largely for administrative reasons since, having no assessed taxes, there was no machinery for collection. Coupled with this was the beginning of a great Free Trade plan which affected 750 articles of the Customs tariff of about 1,200 articles so that 'the duties upon raw materials would only, in a few instances, exceed 5% and those on partially manufactured articles would never exceed 12% and on completed manufactures the maximum duty would not exceed 20%'.

So important did Peel consider the occasion, the launching of a new fiscal policy, that he had taken the unusual step of introducing the Budget himself, and he himself replied to many of the opposition's questions until its passage the following June. There was plenty of criticism ranging from the simple statement that 'an Income Tax was the most unpopular tax that was ever introduced in England'[6] to that veteran opponent of Income Tax, Lord Brougham's nine resolutions put forward on March 14th, which he followed with a long speech three days later. But even as early as 1842 there were objections to the principle of levying the same rate on the 'permanent occupation of property', and on those 'who obtained their annual income by their own exertions', and pleas for the introduction of an abatement mechanism so that incomes just above the exemption limit should only pay tax on the difference between the amount of their income

---

[5] See Dowell (*op. cit.*), vol. II, p. 306; vol. III, p. 120 gives details of the repeal in 1823 of the Assessed Taxes.

[6] Wakley (Hansard 2/III/1842).

and the limit, not on the full amount.[7] There were some cogent arguments on the problem of evasion.

'In the debates of 1816 it was stated that the great manufacturing interests of Manchester were assessed at only £300,000 per annum while at the same time Glasgow, the manufacturers of which were not one half as extensive as Manchester, were assessed at £600,000; making it clear that if Glasgow had been fairly rated, Manchester had not paid one quarter of what was fairly due.'[8]

There was danger too from imposing an income tax in peacetime since its effect might be to drive capital out of the country. One of the most effective speeches was by Roebuck,[9] the leader of the main Radical objections to income tax. He also criticized its inequity in taking income from property and from labour on the same basis, and he suggested a tax at half rate on earned income.

But Peel and his Chancellor, Goulburn, fortified by their commanding majority, successfully resisted every criticism including, at the committee stage during May, an amendment to alter the procedure of assessing on the three years' average, and one to allow the setting off of losses sustained in one schedule against profits in another. In the end, therefore, the Budget was passed in the same form as it had been proposed. In fact it can justly be called a 'reprint' of the Act of 1806[10] with two important modifications. Instead of the old exemption for incomes up to £50 with a graduated scale for 'industrial incomes' between £50 and £150, there was now complete exemption for incomes below £150; and secondly there was a considerable enlargement of the powers of the Special Commissioners[11] who had been instituted in Pitt's Act of 1805 (see p. 38). This arose directly out of the old bogey of secrecy which had led to the introduction of Commercial Commissioners and the referee system in the war income tax. Now a person chargeable under Schedule D could make his returns to and be assessed by these Special Commissioners. This was, as Peel said, an attempt to reconcile 'the impartial and just imposition of the tax and the prevention of evasion and fraud; he sought to apply a remedy to those special evils which were alleged to arise from an inquisitorial examination of the concerns of the trader or professional man'.[12]

[7] The pleas for differentiation and abatement were made by Baring (Hansard 18/III/42) and Sir Robert Inglish (Hansard 8/IV/1842) respectively.

[8] C. Buller (Hansard 23/III/1842).

[9] Roebuck's speech: Hansard 29/IV/1842.

[10] The Acts of 1806 and 1842: see E. R. A. Seligman, *The Income Tax*, p.132, and Dowell (*op. cit.*), vol. III, p. 119.

[11] Ss. 120–133 I.T.A. 1842.   [12] Hansard 18/IV/1842.

When the tax came to be reviewed in 1845, there were further criticisms. Lord John Russell complained that 'the man of most integrity and most honour, and who gave his returns fairly, was subjected to the greatest imposition of the tax'.[13] Another M.P. raised the question of a life insurance allowance;[14] many made the standard complaints about the harshness and inquisitorial nature of the tax.[15] More important, from the viewpoint of principle, were the renewed arguments for differentiation between income from property and income from trades or professions; Buller[16] and Sheil,[17] for example, returning to those arguments which they had put before the House three years ago. The latter, as befitted an Irish Whig-Radical, made an emotional appeal against imposing 'the same tax upon the income which is the product of a man's thought, and may be called the sweat of his mind, and upon income which is as stable as the state', and ended his speech with: 'This tax is not only inquisitorial but most criminal: it holds out inducements to fraud – leads us into that which we pray we may not be led and teaches men to handle with a desecrating familiarity the word of God.'

But Peel was undeterred. He had opened again, as in 1842, making the Budget speech himself, by stating that he anticipated a surplus of £3 millions in 1844–5, one of £2·6 millions in 1845–6, but a deficiency in 1846–7 if the tax were not reimposed. If it were, another three years of the tax would see the fiscal foundations of the country securely based.[18] As it was, while still offering no Corn Law changes, he continued his Free Trade programme. There had been minor remissions of excise duty in 1843 and 1844;[19] now the second round of revisions was made involving the removal of 450 items from the tariff list, the abolition of the duty on the export of coal, the taxes on glass and property sold at auction.[20] He proposed no changes in his income tax.[21] 'I do maintain that any attempt at modification would be attended with the ustmost risk', and had no trouble with any of the divisions. But the 'landed interest' was beginning, increasingly, to suspect a policy from which it derived no benefits. This suspicion deepened into certainty[22] when Goulburn introduced the Budget of 1846 which proposed the repeal of the duties on corn. Peel could claim, as he did, that no other man could carry the necessary measure but himself, since he had been forced back into office after Lord John Russell's failure to form a government. But it is

---

[13] Hansard 17/II/1845.   [14] W. Ewart, Hansard 5/III/1845.
[15] General criticisms: see e.g. B. Hawes, Hansard 5/III/1845.
[16] Buller, Hansard 10/III/1845.   [17] Hansard 18/III/1845.
[18] Hansard 14/II/1845.   [19] Dowell (*op. cit.*), vol. II, p. 306.
[20] Dowell (*op. cit.*), vol. II, pp. 308–9.   [21] Hansard 14/II/1845.
[22] See Maccoby (*op. cit.*), pp. 257–8.

difficult not to feel that it was a tractical error to rely on his indispensability and fail to try and convert the Conservatives to ideas he had held for some time, or at least to educate them to the necessities and realities of the position.

So the Whigs were back in power again and Lord John Russell, following the example of Peel, himself introduced his government's Budget on February 18, 1848.[23] He proposed to continue the tax for a further five years, the first two years at 1s in the £, reverting to the old rate of 7d in the £ for the three subsequent years. In the event, the government was obliged to abandon the increased rate and the tax was finally renewed at 7d in the £ for three years only. The discussions which followed were mainly notable for a renewed attempt, this time by Bright, to secure some measure of differentiation, and on March 3rd, on the Chancellor's moving the Order of the Day for going into Committee of Ways and Means, a resolution was moved 'that if the Income Tax be continued, it is expedient to amend the Act and not to impose the same charge on incomes coming from professional and precarious sources or on those derived from realized property'. Goulburn, the ex-Chancellor, spoke against the resolution: it was simply saying, 'You shall give up a portion of your property for the benefit of the public' and Sir Charles Wood, the current Chancellor, declared that 'any attempt to make one tax perfectly equal and perfectly just would be an unavailing and useless attempt . . . by attempting to make the tax more equal and more suitable to the existing circumstances of the party taxed, you render it necessary to make a more rigid inquisition into their circumstances and, therefore, the more burdensome and odious the tax will be'.[24] The Prime Minister himself intervened in the debate and the motion was lost, but in spite of this, the matter was again raised by G. G. Turner who went further than any speaker so far, in advocating graduation also;[25] and these two proposals were echoed by Cobden. 'If a distinction were made between permanent and precarious incomes, if a graduation of duty were established you would have no remonstrances . . .' 'Why,' he had also asked, prophetically, 'did you not appoint a Committee on the subject?'[26]

Russell was forced to resign in February 1851, four days after the Budget had been introduced, but he returned to office the following month, since no alternative government could be found, and the Budget was reintroduced in April. Sir Charles Wood made no change in his original proposals. which were to continue income tax but to substitute another house tax for the Window Tax; and he was equally against making any change in the method of charge.

[23] Hansard 18/II/1848. (Also the discussions on differentiation.)
[24] Hansard 3/III/1848.   [25] Hansard 6/III/1848.   [26] Hansard 13/III/1848.

'Having considered the subject most anxiously and I believe read through every word of every debate which has taken place on the Income Tax, from the first imposition by Mr Pitt up to the present time and many publications beside, I have come to the conclusion that the only practicable mode of levying the tax is that which every person who had ever proposed the tax has advocated – namely, by a uniform rate on all descriptions of income, from whatever source derived.'[27]

This Budget, wrote Disraeli was 'universally derided';[28] before the year's end, Palmerston had resigned over his unauthorized approval of Louis Napoleon's *coup d'état*; in February 1852 he had had his '"tit for tat" with Johnny Russell'; so that within a year Disraeli found himself transformed from Chancellor's critic to Chancellor. 'You know as much as Mr Canning did,' said the new Prime Minister, Lord Derby, to his apprehensive lieutenant. 'They give you the figures.'[29]

Before these dramatic events, however, Hume had moved, in 1851,[30] that 'the duration of the tax should be limited to one year with a view of instituting an enquiry by a Select Committee', and this had been accepted by Lord John Russell. Hume lost no time; by June 2, 1851 he had his list of nominations ready. One of the Committee members was Disraeli, which meant that his Budget of 1853 is in many ways a reflection of both current fiscal theory of which much can be culled from the evidence given before the Committee and current fiscal practice as approved by members of Parliament – especially the Tory members.

Disraeli had little time to prepare a Budget for April,[31] and since the Hume Committee had not yet reported there was no real objection raised to the continuation of the tax for a further year. But despite the interim nature of his proposals the House was fuller than it had been since Palmerston's '*Civis Romanus sum*' speech in the Don Pacifico debate, and it was not disappointed. Even the Queen expressed her approval.[32] Two points from the speech might be noted. On income tax he said: 'One of the main causes of its odium is that there is no difference as to the rate of assessment upon incomes of a temporary and of a permanent character.' And on taxation in general he declared: 'The feelings of the people must be considered, as well as the principles of science.'[33]

[27] Hansard 17/II/1851.
[28] See Monypenny & Buckle: *Life of Disraeli*, vol. I, p. 1101.
[29] Monypenny & Buckle (*op. cit.*), vol. I, p. 1160.   [30] Hansard 5/V/1851.
[31] Disraeli's April Budget – Monypenny & Buckle (*op. cit.*), vol. I, pp. 1177–81.
[32] Monypenny & Buckle (*op. cit*), vol. I, pp. 1180–1.
[33] Hansard 30/IV/1852.

But it was an even more dramatic occasion with a House 'crowded to suffocation' when Disraeli rose to present his considered Budget,[34] after a few short months breaking-in as Chancellor. Facing him was a bloc of almost all the financial experts of the day – Wood, Goulburn and Baring, all ex-Chancellors, Gladstone 'already a power in economic debate', Cobden, Bright and Lord John Russell himself.

Disraeli had the task of trying to reconcile the fiscal interests of town and country and in addition, to give expression to the ideas which had been discussed in the Hume Committee. With regard to indirect taxation, the policy of remission was continued; half the malt and hop duties were cancelled together with a reduction in the tea duty. There was one decrease in income tax; the farmer was to be assessed on one third, not one half, of his rental. To balance these reductions, the tax was extended to 'precarious incomes' over £100 and 'permanent incomes' over £50. A further measure of differentiation was a reduction of the rate on 'precarious incomes' to three-quarters of the rate on 'permanent incomes', a measure aimed at securing the support of the commercial interest. The rate was held at 7d in the £, but the tax was extended to Ireland. Finally the house tax was to be applied to houses of £10 per annum rateable value.

The general reception of the Budget was deceptively favourable in the country at large, but opposition in the House began almost at once with Gladstone's criticism of differentiation. When the debate began it was clear that the Budget 'presented too many assailable points to have much chance of being adopted'; nor did the Government speakers possess the calibre of the Opposition. The real objection was to the House Tax reduction rather than differention. Disraeli made his final defence on December 16th. The division took place at nearly 4 a.m. and the Government was defeated by 286 to 305.

Looking back on Disraeli's Budget, the primary reason for failure was its attempt to reconcile two irreconcilable interests. In some ways it was before its time, especially in its distinction between earned and unearned income. Its main technical fault, which the Opposition could have stressed, but did not, was the inequity of taxing Schedule A on the gross figure, whereas Schedule D was not only on the net, but was also at the three-quarter rate, which increased the original disparity between the two schedules. Its main political fault shows in the proposal to tax Schedule E income of £100, while leaving exempt a farmer with a rental of £299. This was compensating the landed interest with a vengeance. Disraeli's letter to Lord Derby, November 30, 1852, had been prophetic: 'I fear we are in a great scrape and I hardly see how the Budget can live in so stormy a sea.'[35]

[34] Monypenny & Buckle (*op. cit.*), vol. I, p. 1242, Hansard 3/XII/1852.
[35] Monypenny & Buckle (*op. cit.*), vol. I, p. 1241.

Generalizations are dangerous; in dealing with nineteenth-century history, however, some are unavoidable because of the mass of detail. But in attempting to summarize the parliamentary attitude to income tax from 1842 to 1853, it is quite clear, in the first place, that no responsible member would now claim to finance the cost of government wholly by indirect taxation, especially during the process of remission. The attitude to differentiation is not so easy to define. There had always been a differentiation school, but the mechanism for applying the principle varied. Mill,[36] for example, thought that savings, when invested to provide for a taxpayer's future, should be exempted, but parliamentary ideas followed the technique of trying to calculate the capital value of 'precarious income' and taxing that, which raised many practical difficulties. It should be noted that graduation had also been mentioned (see p. 64), but in general this principle was opposed. One other feature of the debates and questions on income tax during the forties is that there was clearly developing a new element on both sides of the Commons – the parliamentary income tax expert.

Experts, both inside and outside Parliament, had the chance of expressing their opinions on income tax during the sessions of the Committee chaired by Joseph Hume, that inveterate committee-man, which had been appointed in 1851. Its brief was 'to enquire into the present mode of assessing and collecting the Income and Property tax and whether any other mode of levying the same, so as to render the Tax more equitable, can be adopted'.[37] Amongst its members were Cobden, Disraeli, Sir Charles Wood, Ricardo, Thomas Baring and Roebuck. The Committee examined numerous witnesses whose evidence is recorded in two volumes: the first, dated May 17, 1852, is devoted mainly to official witnesses; the second, dated June 22, 1852, gives the conclusions of various actuaries and economists. It found, however, that 'there was not sufficient time for discussing and preparing a report that could do justice to this complicated subject'.[38] Hume himself did prepare a draft report,[39] but it did not secure general acceptance amongst a majority of the members of Committee which finally contented itself with reporting to the House simply the evidence taken.

The first witness was Charles Pressly.[40] He had entered public service in 1818, acted as Secretary to the Board of Stamps and Taxes

[36] Mill developed his ideas on Income Tax fully in the evidence he gave to the Hume Committee, pp. 284–324 of the Report.
[37] vol. I (iii).   [38] General Report – vol. II (V).
[39] Hume's draft – vol. II (XIX–XXXII).
[40] The detailed quotations are from Qq. 61 and 62, vol. I. For the comment on the exemption limit, see vol. II (XXII).

for many years (see p. 57) and had been appointed a Commissioner in 1849. He gave a general summary of the working of the Act which he freely admitted had the 'same general powers and provisions' as the Act of 1803, the 'great change' from Pitt's Act being the deduction of tax at source. He was concerned about the amount of evasion which he thought arose mainly from the high exemption limit of £150, on which 'the Commissioners of Inland Revenue were not consulted' when the 1842 Act was being drafted.

There followed the Solicitor of Inland Revenue who was mainly asked about evasion and the three Special Commissioners[41] (see p. 62) to give an account of their duties, the office being still comparatively new. This, in effect, disposed of the central administrative staff and the Committee then turned its attention to local affairs. They had called both George Offor, the Chairman of the General Commissioners in the Tower Hamlets division of London, and his clerk, Richard Till.[42] Between them they presented a vivid picture of the running of a busy London division contributing about 'one thirtieth of the whole tax, taking all the sources'. The Commissioners met in March annually 'to put the Act into operation for the ensuing year' and appointed their assessors, who were instructed 'by a book printed at the expense of the Commissioners of Inland Revenue as a guide'. These assessors issued returns, handed to them by the Surveyor, and the Schedule A assessments were compiled from these when completed. The Schedule D assessments were made by the Additional Commissioners 'to the best of their ability', and any appeal against these was heard by the General Commissioners; there were 'about 4,000 (appeals) in the year'. It was just as well they had an 'adjoining hall that will hold 300 appellants with accommodation for them to sit'. The Surveyor was of 'very great assistance' indeed. Without him the Commissioners would often be 'at a very serious loss: besides which he is the officer to protect the Crown'. The two main difficulties were assessments under Schedule D and the unfairness of not allowing repairs under Schedule A. Apart from these two points, 'I do not think the machinery could be more simple, more perfect, or more efficient'. The tax should be made permanent: 'we should then carry it on with a good deal better success.'

The Committee then heard from an Inspector who had thirteen Surveyors under him, a retired Surveyor and six Surveyors still in office.[43] The most significant contribution came from the Surveyors

[41] The Special Commissioners had been appointed under the 1842 Act.
[42] The detailed quotations are from Qq. 2455, 2487, 2489, 2491, 2462, 2730–35 2633 and 2634, vol. I.
[43] The detailed quotations are from Qq. 159–161, 749, 834, 882, 340–69, 2930, 2987, 369–90, vol. I.

for the City of London, for Manchester and for Birmingham, although it is interesting to note that the Inspector had been in the Department since 1813 and so provided continuity between the war and the peace Income Tax. The Surveyors were punctilious about their attendance at Appeal meetings. 'I have never been absent from an Appeal meeting since the year 1842', and all agreed there was a good deal of evasion. Edward Walsh, the London Surveyor, handed in a list of representative cases where the assessment had been made in a figure greatly in excess of the return; in one extreme case £500 was returned and £14,000 assessed. This evasion, however, might have, to an extent, been balanced by some of the City merchants. 'If the amount is between £8,000 and £9,000, they make their return an even £10,000 and so on.' His total charge of Schedule D tax was close on £250,000; but John Nicholson of Manchester could only muster between £70,000 and £80,000. The town was then, of course, partly rural and 'you cannot call for accounts from a farmer'. The traders' returns, he thought, were substantially accurate; they often 'volunteered to show me their accounts if I wished it'. Both he and John Lee of Birmingham agreed that one of the best precautions against under-assessment was the comparison of one trader's profits with another of the same type. John Lee said his Commissioners were very well aware of the gross profit percentage brassfounders, for instance, should make; and if a case differed from the normal, they would want to know why.

It was now the turn of the experts. The Committee was attracted by the arguments for making a distinction between permanent and temporary incomes and the latter part of their enquiry was devoted to hearing on this subject various actuaries and economists. Some of the arguments and calculations of the former seem as full of sophistry as those of the medieval schoolmen since, in many instances, they were trying to discover the capital value of a variable income source such as profits assessable under Schedule D. It was small wonder that Pressly remarked, 'It is very difficult, on reading the evidence, to see the precise system these gentlemen would recommend: they appear to me to differ very much in the principle.'[44] In fact, little more was heard of 'differentiation by capitalization' after 1852.

The economists[45] could no more agree than the actuaries. Warburton, the M.P., thought there should be the 'same rate upon each annual income'. Babbage, who had done a good deal of pamphleteering on taxation, also considered it should be imposed at an 'even rate'. John Stuart Mill, whose evidence occupies some forty pages,

[44] Q. 5055, vol. I.
[45] The detailed quotations are from Qq. 5145, vol. I, p. 324, vol. II (Babbage), pp. 284–324 (Mill), Q. 5511, vol. II (Thynne).

considered the chief defect of income tax was its lack of distinction between permanent and temporary incomes; the exemption limit should be lowered although incomes should only be taxed on the excess above that limit; but he was totally opposed to graduation. The root and branch opposition to exemption, as a principle, came from F. Thynne, who thought 'none should be exempt since all are equally protected by government'. Another extreme view was that of the Liverpool Association which was 'anxious to place their opinion on record'; the body held that direct taxation should be substituted for all indirect levies.

A main interest of the Committee is, however, not the theories embalmed in its evidence, but the remarkably clear account given of income tax administration four generations ago. There was the central administration of the Board, its Solicitor and the supervising Inspectors who had, during the period, ceased also to be receiving Inspectors:[46] that part of their functions being taken over by the Excise Department. There were ten of these Inspectors for the whole country. It is quite clear that as well as dealing with the broad principles of policy, these officers were very much concerned with the day to day details of administration. The evidence of the Chairman of Commissioners described the local mechanics of assessment by the assessors in the case of Schedule A and the Additional Commissioners for Schedule D and brings to life the crowded appeal meetings with the Surveyor's invaluable, if possibly sardonic, presence to help matters along; and the occasional appeal to Somerset House for elucidation of some obscure point. And finally, there were the Surveyors themselves, the local officers in the field.[47] They were divided into six classes, beginning at £160 and rising to £400; they numbered only 140, for when the Act of 1842 was passed the government did not feel it necessary to increase the establishment, but gave them assistance by appointing eighty expectant or supernumerary Surveyors. They were no longer given a percentage on increased charges, either for income tax, despite S. 162 of the 1842 Act, or for the assessed taxes, although by some curious anomaly the percentage still operated in the case of a surcharge for game licences. Their method of arriving at assessable profits was very much rule of thumb, in spite of the fact that the Inspector General himself had published a commentary on the 1842 Act.[48] With regard to an allowance for depreciation,[49] for instance, the Special Commissioners told the Committee that such

[46] Qq. 1320–21: 165, vol. I.
[47] Q. 2469, p. 22, vol. I; Qq. 165, 303, 333, vol. I.
[48] A copy of the Inspector General's 'Commentary on the 1842 Act' is in the Board's library.
[49] Depreciation: Hume Report, vol. I, pp. 67–80.

an allowance was generally made; as the Surveyor for the City of London said: 'We generally take in the great manufacturing districts, the scale allowed by the manufacturers themselves sitting as Commissioners.'[50] The Birmingham Surveyor, however, was not as accommodating; he was willing to allow a deduction for repairs, but not for wear and tear; he had seven cases on this very point which were noted for hearing before the Special Commissioners.[51]

As far as the theory of income tax is concerned, the Hume Committee's witnesses were, on the whole, conservative. It should be borne in mind that the yield of income tax held steady at £5½ to £5¾ millions between 1842 and 1851 which at about 10 per cent put it well behind customs which provided 38 per cent and excise 25 per cent of national income; so that, although it was an important revenue producing item, it was not, at the time, vital; and it was still regarded as a temporary tax. Current taxation theory in 1840 tended to practicability as being the test of a good tax rather than equality;[52] differentiation was treated as impractical. As for graduation, it had always been suspect as a mechanism for the distribution of wealth and as such, wholly unacceptable. By 1851 it would be fair to say that only the Radicals would have agreed that income tax should be permanent and should possess the elements of both differentiation and graduation. Orthodox economists were coming round to the idea of differentiation only. But Parliament, which counted for most, was, on the whole, anxious to retain the tax, if at all, as it stood. Here the experts could meet them; for on the whole, they too showed a strong preference for Income Tax as against any other form of duty.

But the development of both theory and administration practice would have been stultified without wholehearted and intelligent provincial co-operation. To take the case of Manchester,[53] for instance, whose efficient surveyor of the Napoleonic war period, Joseph Radford (see p. 39), was eventually succeeded by an equally efficient John Nicholson (see p. 69). As soon as the Act of 1842 became law, there was a meeting of the Land Tax Commissioners in the Town Hall on July 4, 1842, to choose seven General Commissioners, together with seven reserves to fill future vacancies; judging by the shaky writing of one of the Commissioners, the first of those reserves might be needed before long. 'The first seven gentlemen immediately proceeded to put the Property and Income Tax Act into execution

[50] London practice, vol. I, Q. 1285.

[51] Birmingham practice, vol. I, Qq. 369–90.

[52] Current taxation theory in 1840 – see J. R. McCulloch, *Treatise on the Principles . . . of Taxation*.

[53] The Manchester General Commissioners: The information on pp. 71–74 is taken from the Minute book of the Clerk and is reproduced here by permission of the present clerk, Mr G. K. Daniels.

and made the following appointments and took the oath required.' They signed precepts for their Assessors and appointed their clerk, John Owen. He wrote to Charles Pressly, the Board's secretary, on the same day telling him the appointments had been made. He also enquired what allowance he could claim for the official use of his office and whether his appointment was annual, or for all those years for which the tax was presumed to last.

On July 22nd the assessors were sworn in, but there were the usual administrative troubles. Owen had to write to Pressly: 'I trust you will excuse the liberty of my pointing out that the supply of forms of return hitherto furnished to Mr. Hall, the Surveyor has been quite inadequate for the division, and in several of the Townships, the Assessors are at a stand for want of them.' This was not the only problem. Before long, he was writing to Pressly again on such miscellaneous points as residence, mines, railways, bank interest, his Commissioners' jury service, and whether 'a medical man will be allowed to deduct any and what part of the expenses of a Carriage and Horses employed by him in going to visit his patients'. On the last query, Owen should have read the *Guide to the Property and Income Tax Act* which, as already mentioned, was written by the Inspector General, since it stated there that where 'an apothecary keeps a horse, which he uses to visit his patients, and also on other occasions not connected with his business, no deduction can be made for the expense of his keep, although he alleges he should not keep a horse if it was not for his business'. In this connection, ten years later, the Birmingham Surveyor was allowing the expense of a horse, but not the carriage so, possibly, practice had changed. By May of the following year Owen had sent so many queries to Somerset House that he was writing to say the delay in replies was causing 'much inconvenience'. Not that the replies, when they came, were always satisfactory. 'A clear and distinct opinion, with the ground as principle on which it is founded, should be given by the Board.' Otherwise, the relevant parties 'protest loudly'.

Meanwhile the Additional Commissioners had been appointed and, with regard to the Special Commissioners, Owen had written to suggest that the General Commissioners ought to be consulted on the 'propriety of the nominations'. They were, indeed, busy enough with their other duties. They had met in August, 1843 to examine the collectors on their arrears which the collectors submitted to them, together with their comments, hopeful or otherwise, on the defaulters: 'will pay up', 'will settle' or 'will probably pay'. One collector, with a long list of defaulters, asked to resign, but was told sternly 'to proceed diligently and bring the accounts to a close'. Soon afterwards, they were having their appeal meetings. If an appellant did not attend he was suitably admonished by the Clerk: 'Your case was expressly mentioned to them and as you did not appear, the amount must be levied. There is no alternative, but payment.' If the required figures were not made available, the appellant would be told: 'Until you furnish such account, you cannot be further heard.' Taxpayers were often recommended to read *The Guide to the Property and Income Tax Act*; although on the question of horses the clerk might have taken his own advice.

The Clerk to the Commissioners took the initiative in raising enquiries arising from returns:

'The Commissioners of Income Tax have desired me to enquire from you the reason why your Return is so much less this year than in previous years. They do not wish to make surcharges if they can be avoided and perhaps you will be good enough to give an explanation. Should you wish for an interview you will, on any day, find me, or Mr. Seymour, the Surveyor at this office.'

His office also made the requests for accounts and discussed details of what deductions should be made in such varied cases as solicitors and coal merchants.

Occasionally there were matters of more than local application. In 1843, Owen wrote about 'Interest on Money deposits in Bankers' hands'. This interest was claimed as a deduction from the bankers' profits, but 'the bankers refuse to pay the Income Tax on the interest in question: they also refuse to give us a list of depositors'. The Board, however, refused to support any drastic action and the Commissioners had to content themselves with issuing returns wherever the receipt of such Bank Interest was 'known or suspected'.

This account of the early days of the newly introduced Income Tax in a busy, mainly industrial division gives a very different impression from the normally accepted version of the inquisitorial Surveyor, the independent Commissioners, and the somewhat aloof Somerset House. In fact, the Surveyor still owed his position to influence; there was, as yet, no examination for entry into the Civil Service and certainly no training on appointment; his expertise could derive only from experience. His principal function was to hold a watching brief and to assist the Commissioners when called upon. His duties under the Act were mainly permissive – what the Surveyor 'may' do; he had, at this stage, very little power of initiation, apart from causing notices to be delivered when, in any particular case, the assessors failed to do so. It is quite clear that the administrative success of the Act rested on the efficiency of the General Commissioners and their clerk; it was they who put all the searching questions. It is equally clear that their liaison with Somerset House was close and direct.

For instance, in 1849 the Clerk to the Manchester Commissioners wrote to the Board's Secretary: 'If the Board will give them instructions how to act, the Commissioners will feel obliged.' Manchester was not exceptional in this, since the Chairman of London's Tower Hamlet Commissioners had said in evidence:[54] 'We refer the appeal to Somerset House for their assistance in properly construing the Act: they send their opinion to us and it is always conclusive with us'; or again: 'I have a case here in which the Commissioners at Somerset House gave us their opinion.' The Clerk to Commissioners had to get the permission of the Board's Secretary to burn the documents relating to the 1845–7 assessments, and was involved even in requisitions for stationery:

'Mr. Sanderson, Surveyor for Manchester and Mr. Hall, Surveyor for Salford have informed me that the application for "envelopes" for use under Schedules D and C must be made through the Clerk to the Commissioners. I have, therefore, to inform you that the calculation for the two Districts will be as under, viz:

Manchester	6 reams
Salford	1 ream

I shall be obliged by the above quantities being furnished as soon as possible.'

And so the first ten years of a peacetime income tax ended with the defeat of Disraeli over a Budget attacked as being too Tory, with the gradual hardening of expert opinion in favour of differentiation, but not yet of graduation, and with an administration so centralized that its Head Office, in the person of the Secretary to the Board could maintain an immediate and detailed two way contact with the local bodies of Commissioners. They, in general, were happy to accept official rulings on the Act, since the Surveyor was more a local officer than a direct representative of Somerset House. It is hard to see how it could have been otherwise. If the Commissioners had made an early assertion of their independence, there could have been so many varying interpretations of the Act that a reasonably uniform administration would have been virtually impossible and it could well have perished in a welter of contradictions. Fortunately, the General Commissioners and their Clerks were willing to lean on Somerset House for the time being. There may have been injustices; but at 7d in the £, although inequity might rankle somewhat, it was not expensive.

[54] See the Hume Report, vol. I, Qq. 2469/70.

CHAPTER V

Gladstonian Finance

JUST as the decade in fiscal history from 1842 to 1852 is dominated by the name of Peel, so the years from 1853 to 1866 are similarly dominated by the name of Gladstone. In some ways the two men were alike. Both gained double Firsts at Oxford in Greats and Mathematics; both found it difficult to decide on a political party in the early stages of their carrers; both possibly settled for the wrong one; and they both believed in strictly disciplined government expenditure. Speaking of his master, Peel, Gladstone once observed, smacking his lips, 'He was a rigid economist! Oh, he was a most rigid economist!'[1] Even their periods are comparable in the extension of the Free Trade programme, the increasing interest in financial theories and the publication of another somewhat inconclusive Report. And in the political ebb and flow of the times which witnessed six changes of government in eight years,[2] the inept handling of the Crimean War, the Indian Mutiny, the American Civil War, and the death of the apparently indestructible Palmerston, income tax was slowly consolidating its position as a fiscal reserve; its fiscal indispensability was not yet appreciated, much less admitted.

Gladstone's 'five-hour speech on the introduction of the Budget of 1853 stands out as one of the most memorable Budget statements ever made'.[3] In some ways Peel had had an easier task for, although as Gladstone himself said in the 1853 debate, 'We have no conception now of the strength of feeling which Peel had to overcome', he was imposing income tax for a specific and well recognized purpose which recommended itself to the free trade conceptions of the period, whereas Gladstone was faced with the necessity of defining his attitude towards it.

He was brought sharply up against this problem in the first Budget.[4] He realized that the whole success of his measures centred round its 'deep and vital importance', an importance which was not

[1] P. Magnus: *Gladstone*, p. 112.
[2] These took place between 1852 and 1859.
[3] Lord Ponsonby: 'Great Victorians', *W. E. Gladstone*, p. 211.
[4] Hansard 18/IV/1853.

to be measured solely by its yield of £5·5 millions. It might be possible to reconstruct it, but this raised social questions of the 'most serious import'; it tempted statesmen to extravagance and taxpayers to evasion. He was against charging different rates for 'realized and precarious incomes'; he argued that differentiation already existed in that some deductions were allowed under Schedule D, but none under Schedule A, quite apart from the evasion which existed under the former Schedule. He was also against the plan proposed by the actuaries in the Hume Committee for 'everyone knows that it is a mathematical speculation on paper', of no practical value. 'The income tax in its operation ought to be mitigated by every natural means compatible with its integrity, and above all it should be associated in the last term of its existence as it was in its first, with those remissions of indirect taxation which have so greatly redounded to the profit of the country.' In effect, therefore, Gladstone considered himself first as heir to Peel's policy of using income tax as the compensating mechanism for the loss of import duties and equally of his conviction that it 'was not well adapted for a permanent portion of the financial system'.

His first practical measure, therefore, was the prolongation of income tax for a specific term of seven years and at specific rates, that is at 7d for two years, 6d for the next two years and 3d for the final three years, extinction thus coming in 1860. Relief was restored for payments in respect of life assurance policies or deferred annuities up to one-sixth of total income.[5] The limit of exemption was reduced from £150 to £100, but on the incomes between these two figures the rate of tax was to be 5d only for the duration. These measures were combined with the extension of the legacy duty to real property, and the fourth round of revisions of the customs tariff, complimentary to those of 1842, 1845 and 1846. The Act was also to apply to Ireland.

Apart from Disraeli's meteoric period as Chancellor, this was the first Budget speech of eloquence and authority since Peel and went a long way towards restoring the influence and prestige of the Chancellor's office which had been languishing in the hands of nonentities. The Budget speech again became an event eagerly awaited by the ordinary man to whom, for the first time, the dry bones of finance came alive. But the traditional picture of Gladstone's matchless eloquence and orphic voice dominating the House was only true while he was speaking. 'The merit of his performance'[6] did not deter Hume from proposing, for the last time, the actuaries' plan of his Report,[7] or Irish M.P.s from objecting to the extension of the tax to

---

[5] Life assurance relief had been provided in Pitt's income tax, but was not included in Peel's reintroduction of the tax in 1842.
[6] Greville 3rd Series: p. 59.　　[7] Hansard 25/IV/1853.

Ireland. One of them, Sir Fitzroy Kelly, fired the first shot in the battle for differentiation which was to occupy the attention of Parliament and Committees for many years to come. The Chancellor had his defenders, Lowe arguing that even graduation would not produce a just tax;[8] it would simply be the 'apple of discord'. Disraeli congratulated his rival on producing a Budget which copied so many features of his own of 1852 and said, with some prescience, that income tax was going to be established 'most probably for ever'.[9] Gladstone refused to admit the justice of this forecast which was admittedly, at that time, very much a matter of opinion. But it was a grave error of judgment to provide for the extinction of a tax without ensuring that fresh remissions of taxation, fresh additions to expenditure and, above all, the defence of the realm would not enforce its continued existence.

'The Crimean War revealed to us many imperfections in our military system: but the strain on our finances brought to light nothing but their soundness and vigour.'[10] Income tax came into its own again as an elastic element in the Budget. Gladstone refused to borrow, believing 'the expenses of war are a moral check'.[11] He increased its rate by one half to 10½d ingeniously placing the whole of the increase in the first half year so that it would all be received in the year. By May, however, it was clear that a further increase would be necessary and the rate was doubled, now rising to 1s 2d. In a long and involved financial statement, Gladstone took occasion to refer to differentiation in particular, and the whole question of reform, but 'we cannot think of opening the general question of a graduated income tax'.[12] Palmerston had now succeeded Aberdeen as Prime Minister, but on the appointment of a committee of enquiry into the conduct of the war, the Peelites, including Gladstone, resigned out of loyalty over the implied censure of Newcastle, one of their dwindling group;[13] Sir George Lewis became the reluctant successor to Gladstone and he had the task of presenting the War Budget of 1855, which raised the rate to 1s 4d.[14]

It was Sir George Lewis also who introduced the next two succeeding Budgets. By 1856 the Crimean War was over, but the 'war ninepence',[15] as the additional duty was termed, was continued until the end of the year. It could, in fact, legally have been enforced until 1858, but in 1857 the rate was reduced to 7d;[16] it was intended to

[8] Hansard 2/V/1853.   [9] See Monypenny & Buckle (*op. cit.*), 1322/3.
[10] See Sir Stafford Northcote: *Twenty years of Financial Policy*.
[11] Hansard 6/III/1854.   [12] Hansard 8/V/1854.
[13] See inter alia Connell, B., *Regina v. Palmerston*.
[14] Sydney Buxton: *Finance & Politics*, vol. I, p. 153 and note.
[15] See Buxton (*op. cit.*), vol. I, p. 157.   [16] Hansard 13/II/1857.

remain at that level until its expiry in 1860. Sir George was not the most inspiring of Chancellors; on hearing the news of the reduction to 7d 'a considerable number of members hurried from the House'; they had heard all they wished to hear. Like Gladstone, he had had to face the advocates of differentiation. Typical of their consistent hammering is a speech in the 1856 debate: 'He thought it most unjust to levy the same rate of taxation upon industrial and professional incomes and upon real property',[17] or, from the 1857 debate: 'He considered it most unjust to levy the same rate of taxation upon incomes derived from fixed and funded property and upon those derived from such precarious sources as trades and professions.'[18] The Chancellor could only make the standard reply that it was necessary either to keep the present system with all the injustices, or to start all over again;[19] he added that the phrase 'precarious income' was something of a misnomer since incomes derived from such prosperous concerns as banks have a 'character of stability'. But his worst moment was a combined attack from both the Peelites and the Conservatives in the persons of Gladstone and Disraeli which greatly alarmed the Queen.[20] Sir George stoicly defended himself[21] and, on the move to cut down the estimates, successfully argued that taxation 'should be regulated by expenditure', not expenditure by taxation, a lesson which his two assailants were soon to learn the hard way.

It was Disraeli's turn first, for early in 1858 Palmerston fell and Derby formed his second minority Government with Disraeli again as his Chancellor. More fortunate than with his 1852 Budget, he secured general acceptance with his proposal to reduce the rate to 5d.[22] 'The nation had made a solemn compact with the Chancellor and had only consented to allow the income tax, unjust, unequal and inquisitorial, as it was to continue for a limited time on the distinct understanding that it should ultimately be repealed.' This arrangement was considered more binding than debt repayment. In retrospection it may have been the wrong decision, but as Disraeli realized, it was at least consonant with the temper of the time.

The period after the fall of the Tory Government over the 'fancy franchises' of the first Reform Bill was as politically stable as the previous seven years had been unstable, for not only did the same Government stay in power, but until 1865 the same Prime Minister, Chancellor of the Exchequer, and Foreign Secretary remained in office. This meant, as far as Gladstone was concerned, the oppor-

---

[17] Muntz, Hansard 8/IV/1856.   [18] Major Reed, Hansard 20/II/1857.
[19] Hansard 8/IV/1856.   [20] *Regina v. Palmerston (op. cit.)*, pp. 208–12.
[21] Hansard 13/II/1857.
[22] Monypenny & Buckle (*op. cit.*), vol. I, 1531 and Buxton (*op. cit.*), vol. I, p. 166.

tunity of planning ahead, of being able to regard his Budgets as a series rather than as isolated annual events. His first Budget[23] was inevitably provisional in nature, but in it income tax was, for the first time, treated as an elastic element. It was imposed at a rate of 9d for incomes over £150 and 6½d for incomes under £150 simply to fill up the deficiency of approximately £4 million and Gladstone re-used his 1854 technique of imposing the whole of the increase in the first half year, despite Sir Stafford Northcote's criticism of the practical difficulties involved in the deduction of tax from annuities, for instance; and Hubbard's disappointment that 'the only means the Right Hon. Gentleman, the Chancellor of the Exchequer could find to extricate himself from the financial difficulties of the day was by an aggravated use of that obnoxious and most mischievous impost – an unreformed income tax'.

But Gladstone's eyes were firmly fixed on the year 1860, when the ghost of the promise of repeal in that year which had bedevilled Budgets since 1853 was finally to be laid. The occasion did not lack drama for Gladstone had been suffering from a throat infection and Palmerston had to apologize for the postponement of the Budget. Eventually the Chancellor opened it on February 10, 1860, and excepting that he 'spoke for four hours instead of the expected five and occasionally had recourse to sips of some mucilaginous mixture, there was no trace of weakness, physically or mentally'.[24] He had no choice but to renew income tax, and its rate was fixed at 10d for incomes above £120, and 7d on incomes between that sum and £100. This was combined with the fifth round of tariff reductions, leaving only 143 articles and subdivisions of articles liable.

The Opposition was not sparing in criticizing the failure of the high hopes of 1853. Disraeli compared his rival to the contemporary conjurer who had for forty-eight hours actually convinced people he could creep into a pint bottle; 'The Right Hon. gentleman has enjoyed the position of a bottle conjurer for seven years. That is a long time and the person who had been the hero of a popular delusion for seven years, enters into one of the first categories of human achievement.'[25] The reasons for this failure were clear. The abolition of income tax within the seven-year period had depended principally on the stability of government expenditure; but that had, in fact, consistently increased from £56 millions to its present £70 millions. Revenue had shown the expected elasticity, but not in sufficient measure to cope with the £14 millions rise in outgoings.

Gladstone also had to deal again with the opposition of the ex-

---

[23] Hansard 21/VII/1859. Hubbard's speech also.
[24] *Illustrated London News*, February, 1860.
[25] Hansard 10/II/1860.

perts. On March 30, 1860 Hubbard[26] said he trusted 'that the Chancellor of the Exchequer would concur on some subsequent day in the appointment of a Committee of Enquiry who might recommend some revision of the tax, so as to make it less objectionable'. Gladstone, in a brilliantly reasoned reply, admitted the 'great inequalities in the income tax', but did not see his way to the appointment of a Committee which 'would be an unworthy attempt to escape from our proper responsibility' unless there was a very strong desire for such a Committee 'on the part of the country and a large portion of the House'. He then referred to the Hume Committee of 1851 and warned members that 'the most dangerous of propositions that could be made in a country like this would be an attempt, upon abstract principles, to devise a graduated tax on incomes, aiming at an adjustment of different rates of assessment according to the means of the taxpayer'. Disraeli sprang to the defence of the Hume Committee: 'it was formed of the best men in the House'. He omitted, with becoming modesty, to recall that he himself had been a member, but he did mention the many advocates of differentiation who had given evidence. There was a further motion on June 14, 1860 'calling attention to the present mode of assessing the property and income tax with a view to the more equitable assessment thereof'. Gladstone professed to consider the mover had exercised a 'wise discretion' in not calling for a Parliamentary Enquiry: a differentiation policy 'would cause a greater amount of injustice than it would cure', and he went on to mention two 'highly intelligent' pro-reform members who had sat on the Hume Committee and who, after hearing the evidence, decided that 'the reconstruction of income tax was impossible'.

The following year, however, Hubbard, in a massive speech, again moved the appointment of a Select Committee.[27] He was tired of the 'stereotyped reply' that income tax was only temporary, to subsidize fiscal reform, or to provide for a 'most unhappy war'. It now brought in one-sixth of the total revenue, so how could it be 'placed before the House in the light of a compensation tax'? There were three types of income; spontaneous or interest on capital; precarious, which was the product of capital 'utilised by the application of skill and labour'; and the product of unskilled labour with which 'they now had no concern'. He proposed an elaborate series of abatements for precarious incomes and argued for a repairs allowance in arriving at the value of lands and houses. He thought the loss on Schedule A would be made up by more honest returns under Schedule D because under the present unfair system, the evasion under that schedule was due

[26] Hubbard's speech, Gladstone's reply and Disraeli's comments: Hansard 30/III/1860.
[27] Hubbard's 1861 Speech and Gladstone's reply: Hansard 19/II/1861.

to the endeavour of the Schedule D taxpayer 'to do justice to himself in his own way'. Gladstone's reply was remarkably playful. 'It would be a most pleasant process to go about deducting all day'; but some-one had to pay. 'The abatement of one man', he continued, 'is the taxation of another', and he was convinced the scheme in general would aggravate the sense of injustice and 'flood Schedule A as well as Schedule D with immorality'. He concluded somewhat ruefully that 'necessity drove us to the income tax in 1842 and necessity has attached us to the use of it. (No! No!). When I used the word 'attached', I meant not as a bridegroom is attached to his bride, but as a captive is attached to the car of his conqueror'; the motion he advised should be negatived as it must result 'either in evil or dis-appointment'. It was, however, carried by the slender majority of four.

The six Budgets from 1861 to 1866 seem something of an anti-climax when compared with the great occasions of 1853 or 1860. The first two, however, those of 1861 and 1862, hardly deserve the epithet 'commonplace'.[28] Income tax was only, it is true, reduced by an unspectacular penny, but the incorporation of the whole year's financial proposals in one Bill so as to force through the Lords the rejected repeal of the 'taxes on knowledge' was a constitutional *coup d'état* of immense significance. There was no income tax change in 1862 which saw a mark-time Budget. But now public opinion was beginning to consider whether taxation could not be reduced by the simple process of curbing government expenditure, which Gladstone was always deploring, although he was, together with the Cabinet, collectively responsible for it, 'a spendthrift weeping over pence – a penurial prodigal proposing enormous expenditure'.

In May the irrepressible Hubbard[29] was again on his feet in the House proposing his abatement scheme rather than, as he explained, moving a series of amendments on the Income Tax Bill. He was not satisfied with the latest Report, for reasons which will be discussed later, for that Report had not proposed any alterations in the tax. 'In his opinion it was absolutely necessary that some attempt should be made to adjust the burden now thrown so unequally upon skill and intelligence as compared with property.' Gladstone was at his most devastating in his reply.

'The proposal of my Hon. friend would have the practical effect of taking away one fourth of the revenue at present derived from the Income Tax which now amounts to £10,000,000. I must take the

---

[28] The Budgets of 1861 and 1862: Buxton (*op. cit.*), vol. I, p. 289, Hansard 15/IV/1861 and 3/IV/1862.
[29] Hubbard's speech and Gladstone's reply: Hansard 13/V/1862.

liberty of saying that I proceed in this discussion upon the vulgar calculations that proceed from the Board of Inland Revenue and that I do not proceed upon imaginary calculations of the magical results which are to follow from the improved morality of a considerable portion of the people.'

The scheme would operate unfairly, especially in the case of small fixed incomes as against large, so called precarious incomes. 'I can easily imagine that many a benevolent, clever and honest man, whose business it has not been to consider practically the subject of taxation, might say "let the rich pay: let those who can bear the burdens of society, bear them".' And why had legislation taken another course? 'Because there has been wisdom enough in legislative bodies to detect mere plausibility and to perceive that the true interest of society lies in securing to every man the fruit of his accumulations. . . .' He ended with an impassioned plea that 'when plans like that of my friend are introduced – arbitrary, capricious and inapplicable in principle, and without any practical recommendation, merely upsetting the principles of taxation as they now exist, and getting rid of one set of anomalies and evils which at all events are more tolerable by being more known as traditional in order to bring in novel inequalities and novel abuses and with them, that source of all evils, discord between class and class – the House will have virtue and manliness enough to reject it.' The House had – by a majority of thirty-seven.

But by the spring of 1863 it was possible, both to economize in government spending and not only to reduce income tax by a further 2d, but to give further relief by increasing the abatement limit to £200, involving a deducation of £60 from all incomes between £100 and £200; the reduced rate was abolished.[30] It seemed as if the plan for its extinction was on again. Gladstone had to fight off yet another attack by Hubbard, and told him tartly that the 'inequalities and anomalies of income tax, as they now exist, have this advantage, that they are in some degree understood'.[31] But he was less successful in his attempt to bring charities within the ambit of taxation and, in spite of a most incisively argued speech, sentiment in the shape of taxing the widow's mite and the beds of sickness, triumphed over reason. It was Roebuck,[32] the veteran Radical, who raised the question of differentiation on the Budget debate; 'the breadwinner', he pleaded graphically, 'may simply become the breadeater'. Gladstone was unmoved. 'By removing one or two anomalies', he argued with a familiar technique, 'we should be introducing three or four anomalies

[30] Gladstone's 1863 Budget: Hansard 16/IV/1863.   [31] Hansard 24/III/1863.
[32] Roebuck, Gladstone and the differentiation debate: Hansard 23/IV/1863.

which would leave us in a worse position after our trouble than we were before.'

'At this point in our history the revenue developed in a marvellous manner',[33] and it was possible to combine with the current economics further remissions including yet another penny off income tax, bringing it down to 6d and again within sight of total remission if such was the country's wish; for Gladstone considered it undesirable that it should 'creep unawares into perpetuity'.[34] This sentiment was repeated by Sir Stafford Northcote in a debate initiated yet again by Hubbard,[35] in which the former pointed out that there was no question at present of the Chancellor asking the House to make income tax permanent.

The same pattern of economy, remissions and a buoyant economy was continued in 1865 when income tax was reduced to 4d, a penny less than it had ever stood before; indirect taxation received an almost equivalent relief. The final Budget of the period, which left income tax unchanged, but contained some remission of customs duties, came after the death of Palmerston, Lord John Russell succeeding him as Prime Minister. It was as if the departure of that seemingly ever present figure had closed an epoch in history; for in 1866[36] Gladstone had to take into account a financial crisis at home[37] and the rise of Prussia abroad. Nevertheless he had the satisfaction of having reduced public expenditure to £66·4 million; probably in all those seven consecutive years at the Exchequer nothing had gratified him more.

One of Gladstone's most consistent critics, it will be clear, was John G. Hubbard, an independent M.P. and a Governor of the Bank of England. From the sixties onwards he had spoken often and at length, on income tax reform and finally had forced through a motion, as has been mentioned (see p. 81), for the appointment of a Select Committee under the same terms as that of ten years earlier. Hubbard himself, as the protagonist of reform, was appointed Chairman. The members, however, were selected by the government Whips and have, to a certain extent, justifiably been labelled as 'Gladstone's nominees'.[38] Gladstone himself took part in twelve out of the nineteen sessions held.

---

[33] Dowell (*op. cit.*), vol. II, p. 347.

[34] Hansard 7/IV/1864.

[35] Northcote and Hubbard: Hansard 14/VI/1864.

[36] The 1866 Budget: Hansard 3/V/1866.

[37] The most spectacular example was the collapse of the banking house of Overend and Gurney on 'Black Friday'. See, for example, J. A. R. Marriott: *England Since Waterloo*, p. 284.

[38] 'Gladstone's nominees' – see Clapham: *Economic History of England*, vol. II, p. 403.

The first witnesses were Charles Pressly,[39] now Chairman of the Board – he had given evidence ten years ago when he was a Commissioner – and Joseph Timm,[39] the Solicitor to the Board. They gave a general account of the income tax administration, stressing the importance of the General Commissioners whose conduct was very satisfactory, and the better qualifications of the officers of the department which was due to the fact that they were better paid. The Government, they thought, should also appoint both the assessors and collectors. If the principle of differentiation were adopted, the loss to the Revenue would be nearly £2 million and there would be no corresponding decrease in evasion. Pressly refused to be drawn on whether or not the principle of differentiation would, in his opinion, be a desirable reform; it was a 'political question' or a 'question of principle' which 'I would rather not enter into'; as he said later: 'It is not my province to advise on the principle of the income tax – only to carry it out.'

After this dignified rebuke, the Chairman turned with relief to William Newmarch,[40] the Secretary to the Globe Assurance Office, who was 'quite ready' to adopt the Chairman's preliminary memorandum. He received a very searching cross-examination from Gladstone, especially on the question of life annuities which showed up a good number of inconsistencies in his beliefs, and he had to admit that there were a number of cases where differentiation might work unfairly (Gladstone was a pastmaster at suggesting examples of this kind); and where there might be administrative difficulties; but these were 'ingenious cases suggested by a refining mind' not 'of practical weight, with regard to the property of a great community like ours'.

Hubbard himself[41] then gave evidence and was, in fact, examined longer than any witness. His scheme for differentiation was, he thought, perhaps not a perfect scheme, but it was practicable. He would not admit that there would be a 20% fall in the yield of tax under Schedule D since, as he went on to argue later, it would diminish fraud, and the administration might feel more confidence in the law if it were fairer and 'pursue their duty more diligently'. He agreed, as the previous witness has done, that there were inconsistencies, such as the granting of the suggested relief to sleeping partners in receipt of enormous incomes, 'happy people that they are'. And he got into serious trouble when he tried to define income for taxation purposes

[39] The quotations from Pressly's and Timm's evidence (pp. 1–17) are taken from Qq. 109–110, 111, 208, 267, 121, 148, 273.
[40] Newmarch's evidence (pp. 17–61), Qq. 333, 996, 975.
[41] Hubbard's evidence (pp. 61–94); Qq. 1113, 1148, 1486, 1752, 1201, 1566–7, 1351.

as 'the net revenue which is available for the purpose of expenditure', for that led finally to the thesis that savings ought not to be taxed, although Hubbard was not prepared altogether to subscribe to it as that was 'dangerous ice'.

Hubbard was followed by two Clerks to Commissioners.[42] Both thought that a certain abatement on trading and professional incomes was justified, and that public opinion was opposed to the present practice. Till, the City of London Clerk, also held that a man's savings should not be taxed and that a 'reduction of a moderate amount' might even increase the Schecule D yield, since taxpayers would not them claim deductions to which they might not be entitled. He was somewhat roughly handled over this since he had previously said he was astonished at the general honesty of returns and finally remarked, which was not surprising after his cross examination, that he 'was not in a condition to go into any further inequalities'.

Two more officials were heard[43] – the Surveyor for the City of London and the Collector for Marylebone. The former was of the opinion that the commercial returns of the City of London were fairly made on the whole; it followed that if a deduction were made in Schedule D 'on a given principle' the advantage gained from more honest returns 'would be very insignificant in comparison with the loss of revenue'. The Collector was very much of the same opinion; he thought in the majority of returns 'a considerable margin' was reserved and that even if some concession were made, he was 'hardly disposed to think that the public would voluntarily make accurate and just returns in all cases under any circumstances'.

The professional men examined were concerned with two main points, the equity of introducing some form of deduction for Schedule A and, of course, the justice of differentiation itself. On the first issue there was no doubt in the minds of the architect[44] and the two surveyors[45] examined that property owners felt aggrieved in having no allowance for repairs and other outgoings. This point had also been raised by the Collector and there seemed to be general agreement that a 15% deduction would be reasonable. The three doctors[46] and the solicitor[47] were even more emphatic about the need for some

---

[42] The evidence of the Clerks to Commissioners (R. Till and J. C. Burgoyne pp. 110–128), Qq. 1828, 2102, 2064, 2035, 1860.

[43] The evidence of the Surveyor (Edward Walsh, pp. 128–38) and the Collector (J. W. Knight, pp. 236–42), Qq. 2148, 2239, 3878, 3879.

[44] The architect's evidence (C. Lee, pp. 138–41).

[45] The Surveyors' evidence (F. Vigers: pp. 142–3, H. A. Hunt, pp. 233–6; see also Q. 2288 and John Clutton, pp. 190–1).

[46] The three doctors' evidence (J. Lavies, W. Fergusson and G. Webster, pp. 195–206), Qq. 3228, 3423.

[47] The Solicitor's evidence (W. S. Cookson, pp. 206–11), Qq. 3462, 3473, 3474.

form of differentiation. The former thought in the first place that 'truer returns would be made', but their main argument was that some concession should be made because of the 'personal exértion' involved in earning their incomes, although they were trapped into a good number of inconsistencies during their evidence. The solicitor, however, was made of sterner stuff; he refused to discuss 'the general principles of the income tax'. He admitted there were anomalies and hard cases; but he stuck firmly to his point that 'people who derive incomes without any labour or effort of their own have their hands and brain to resort to besides, although they do not choose to employ them to produce money: whereas professional men have to depend entirely on their labour: they have no further resources whatever'. He admitted there were no other taxes which drew this distinction but the 'income tax was entirely *sui generis*'.

The experts[48] called were actuaries, statisticians, economists and accountants. Most of them pursued their own pet theories, including Mill who had been a witness before the Hume Committee; he went so far as to claim that savings should not be taxed in order to avoid 'double taxation'. The sturdy commonsense of the accountant saved the day. He was generally of the opinion that tax on income and tax on property should not be equal, but he did not believe any reform in that direction would increase the correctness of returns. 'I am afraid', he commented 'their morality would not be much increased . . . many of them have no consciences at all.'' His own clients made correct returns, but the 'lower order of traders' did not.

As might be expected from as much conflict of evidence the Committee 'after full consideration' reported that 'the plan proposed by their Chairman does not afford a basis for a practicable and equitable readjustment of the income tax; and they feel so strongly the danger and ill consequences to be apprehended from an attempt to unsettle the present basis of the tax, without a clear perception of the mode in which it is to be reconstructed, that they are not prepared to offer to Your Honourable House any suggestions for its amendment'.[49] Hubbard claimed the Committee was doomed from the start in a pamphlet printed for private circulation in the form of a letter addressed to John Stuart Mill;[50] and certainly much of the cross-examination was as prejudiced as it was deadly.

On the face of it, the theory of differentiation could be justified on

[48] The experts:
   William Napier, pp. 144–7,   Manager of the Land Improvement Company
   Charles Ansell,   pp. 147–61, Actuary
   William Farr,   pp. 161–90, Statistician
   J. E. Coleman,   pp. 191–5, Accountant: also Qq. 3118, 3159, 3160, 3169.
[49] The Committee's full report is on pp. III and IV.
[50] Hubbard's letter to J. S. Mill: Shehab (*op. cit.*), pp. 145–6.

equitable grounds, but its advocates betrayed themselves into inconsistencies and manifest illogicalities such as the exemption of savings.
The criticism of the opposition was purely destructive; the plan of
the Chairman had many practical defects and the exposure of these
was the principal exercise of many of the Committee members; time
and again Gladstone and Lowe exploited the inequity of giving relief
on large commercial incomes, even those received by sleeping partners, while leaving unrelieved comparatively modest incomes from
land or securities. For both inside and outside the House Gladstone[51]
had consistently opposed differentiation, but not on principle; he
believed simply that the tax should either be left alone or abolished;
it should not be tampered with. He even remarked on one occasion
that there was more to be said in favour of a graduated tax. At the
back of his mind he always cherished the illusion of extinction; he
could never bring himself to accept the tax as permanent. So the
whole weight of his vast authority was thrown against reform and
honestly so, for he felt he was legislating for the 'interests of the
country at large . . . without distinction of class'.

Meanwhile under the pressure of war and the wealth of theoretical
discussion, including a second Committee, if not an agreed Report,
both the central and local administration of income tax were settling
down. The Board's Chairman was Charles Pressly[52] who had been
in the Department since its formation, from junior clerk to Secretary,
and Commissioner before succeeding to his present office, and this
provided valuable continuity at the top. He and his officials had, even
at this early stage in their history, developed a strong sense of
responsibility and a remarkable appreciation of the increasing technical problems. It has been said they were 'in terror of their master's
(Gladstone's) wrath'[53] but the only evidence for this seems to be
Pressly's refusal to discuss, for example, differentiation as a principle
which he fully justified on the ground that his job was to administer
income tax, not to speculate on its theoretical basis.[54]

The reports of the Board itself are the best evidence of the way in
which it was developing. Its first report, four years after its formation,
came in 1857, for the year to March 31, 1856. This commented on all
the duties controlled by the Board which then comprised excise,
stamps, probate, legacy and succession duty, as well as income tax,
'the most important of all duties under our management', and with

[51] See Hansard 14/VI/1860 and 24/III/1863 for Gladstone on differentiation and
graduation respectively.
[52] Hubbard Report, Qq. 1863–4 and 2.
[53] 'In terror of their master's wrath' – see Clapham (*op. cit.*), vol. II, p. 403;
he is quoting Hubbard.
[54] Hubbard Report, Q. 148.   [55] Board's Report 1859, pp. 23–4.

it the Assessed Taxes and House Duty, substituted for Window Duty in 1851. The whole series from 1857 to 1866 gives details of the comparative increases in duty through the expansion in commercial profits despite the overall fall in revenue when rates were reduced; in 1859, for example, there was an increase in Schedule D profits[55] assessed, of £4 millions for which it is notable that the industrial towns, especially Manchester, were largely responsible. But, even so, there are annual complaints that 'the amount of evasion of the duty under Schedule D must be very considerable', and cases are quoted where the returns showed £6,500, but the assessable profit turned out to be £32,000 or, more flagrant, where the return gave £190,000, which should have been £250,000.[56] There were, happily, payments of conscience money, one of no less than 10,000 guineas.[57] The Board also had to deal with 'many painful appeals to our compassion and forebearance', the claims to exemption in 1857 reaching the remarkable total of quarter of a million.[58] These examples of evasion, however, do give point to the argument that if, possibly, differentiation would increase honesty, it would be worth trying.

There was not a great deal of change in the organization at Somerset House. The Board was laying greater emphasis on supervising[59] its Surveyors which 'had been productive of good results'; these inspections were most carefully made and the 'praiseworthy exertions' of the Surveyors favourably commented on. The ever-present Charles Pressly at last retired in 1862 after over forty-four years of public duty on a pension, to mark the value of his services, of his full salary of £2,000 per annum;[60] not that he was being entirely lost to the Revenue for he volunteered to remain as a Special Commissioner. Thomas Keogh, the Secretary to the Board had died three years earlier and here Gladstone, to economize, did not fill the post, but appointed the two assistant Secretaries to act as joint Secretaries at a saving of £1,600 a year.[61] In 1862 the 'Chief Inspection Department' was created with Edward Hyde as the first Chief Inspector; he had under him a staff of 210 Surveyors of six different grades, ranging in salary from the assistant at £150 per annum maximum to the senior Surveyor, of whom there were only twenty-five, with a maximum salary of £450.

The local organization of assessment and collection of Income Tax had assumed a form which was to endure for many years, although the Board was of the opinion that 'the mode in which that business

---

[56] Board's Reports 1860, p. 21 and p. 25; 1862, p. 29.
[57] Board's Report 1865, p. 25.   [58] Board's Report 1858, p. 28.
[59] Board's Report 1860, p. 30; 1865, p. 25.
[60] Board's Report 1863, p. 24, p. 25 and Appendix (ii).
[61] Board's Report 1860, p. 23.

is at present conducted is, in general very imperfectly understood'.[62] A 'concise account' was, therefore, given of the arrangements which are the same as those previously outlined (pp. 43–4);[63] not that they always worked in practice as well as they were supposed to in theory.

The General Commissioners already had come in for some comment in Parliament; it was said there was a want of confidence felt in their impartiality and there was too large a discretionary power in their hands.[64] It is to this period also that the delightful story of Jane Welsh Carlyle's trip to the Kensington Commissioners belongs.[65] The Board was careful to avoid any general criticism; however, it was reported that during the 1861 collection period when the tax for the first three-quarters of the year had to be paid before March 31st, 'some local Commissioners not only did not co-operate, but offered a very decided opposition . . . but these were the rare exceptions'.[66] Their Clerks could be equally at fault; the Clerk to Commissioners for the City of London had 'so many other engagements' that he only held sixteen meetings during the year.[67] The Clerk for Louth, having been told to discharge an assessment improperly made in his district, refused to do so. When the Board made the discharge themselves, the clerk, of course, lost his poundage and 'observed no measure in his hostility and resistance' and it was nearly five years before the district was in full working order again.[68] But, in general, the Board hastened to add, they are 'gentlemen of ability from whom we receive much valuable assistance'. The Board would also like to have seen the collectors as Government officials; the results had been 'very beneficial' when the Board had made the appointment on the occasions where the General Commissioners had been unable to.[69] An attempt to transfer their appointment to the Crown failed, however, despite the number of defalcations.[70] They also noted, with approval, the Scottish practice of using the Surveyor as the assessor.[71]

But the most significant feature of the Board's reports is the increasing importance of the Surveyor, who is beginning to emerge as the prototype of the modern government servant. Although still appointed by patronage, he had to undergo a departmental examination for promotion, 'a system which has the advantage of testing the knowledge and diligence, not only of the young men themselves, but of the Surveyors under whose superintendence they have gone

---

[62] Board's Report 1862, p. 16.
[63] Board's Report 1862, pp. 22–30.   [64] Hansard 23/V/53.
[65] Her 'Letters and Memoirs', 20/XI/55 and 21/XI/55.
[66] Board's Report 1861, p. 19.   [67] Hubbard Report, Q. 2135.
[68] Board's Report 1862, pp. 26–7.
[69] Board's Report 1859, p. 27 and 1864/p. 31.
[70] See for example Hansard 23/III/1860.
[71] Board's Report 1862, p. 28.

through their course of instruction'.[72] Then, as has been mentioned, his work was closely supervised by the Board (see p. 88), for he was becoming far more active than in the first decade of his increased duties; many are the references to his 'zeal and alacrity'.[73] Under Schedules A and B the duties now devolving upon the Surveyor 'are frequently almost equivalent to making the assessment';[74] under Schedule D he is now 'permitted to make any observations which occur to him'[75] and frequently induces the Commissioners 'to make alterations in the assessments'.[76] These became much more frequent when districts were subdivided and Surveyors were able to make personal surveys;[77] London, for instance, was so split in 1866 and a marked increase in profits assessed followed. He is in fact 'the advocate for the Revenue'.[78] But sometimes even he incurred the Board's displeasure, especially in the matter of increased remuneration. In 1859 some of these officers 'made an appeal to the public by the dissemination of a pamphlet containing a most exaggerated view of their case'. The report continues: 'In justice to the Surveyors of Taxes, we ought to state that they are, generally speaking, most efficient officers; not surpassed, as we believe, by any public servants of the same class in intelligence and judgment, in the discharge of very troublesome and invidious functions.' So far, so good; but the sting was in the tail. 'At the same time we are not prepared, at this moment, to recommend any alteration or addition to their present salaries or emoluments.'[79]

The period from 1853 to 1866 was one of the most significant in the history of Income Tax. In the first seven years, its extinction was planned, but war expenditure kept it alive. In the subsequent six years, it became clear that the price to be paid for remissions of indirect taxation,[80] combined with annual government expenditure of £70 millions was an income tax even if its rate was only a few pence. But if it were to be retained, its critics argued, then it should be revised. Gladstone would have none of this; he still hoped extinction was possible; if not, then better to keep its familiar anomalies than create novel abuses. Indeed, although it may not have been premeditated, he did income tax a service by setting his face against elaborate reforms until some clear cut scheme was available.

Certainly, owing to the spectacular personality of the Chancellor and the dearth of any other domestic legislation of note, there was a wealth of discussion on finance during the period. Besides the main

[72] Board's Report 1862, p. 25.
[73] Board's Report 1866, p. 46.
[74] Board's Repport 1862, 24.
[75] Board's Report 1862, p. 24.
[76] Board's Report 1862, p. 25.
[77] Board's Report 1866, p. 26.
[78] Board's Report, 1862, p. 21.
[79] Board's Report 1859, p. 30.
[80] Hansard 15/IV/1861.

issue of differentiation, all manner of schemes were proposed from Bright's idea of electing Commissioners from the general body of taxpayers to the London Surveyor's suggestion that Stipendiary Commissioners should be appointed. And, behind the speculations of economists, the Committee witnesses and the Parliamentary experts stood the growing authority and organization of Somerset House, with its cadre of trained professionals. The story of these thirteen years is the story of the restoration of prestige and power to the Chancellor of the Exchequer's office and the emergence of a new type of specialized government servant.

CHAPTER VI

Taxation in Twilight

IN the period 1866–74 Gladstone was forced to share the political scene with Disraeli; and probably the highest praise which can be accorded to Disraeli is that, in the face of his rival's tireless industry, all-round parliamentary powers, lucid and compelling oratory and high morality he was able, at times successfully, to oppose his own particular combination of courage, insight and mastery of political tactics. It was this combination which forced through a lukewarm House of Commons and an apprehensive Upper Chamber, the Reform Bill of 1867[1] and ended 'the monopoly of liberalism', for all it finally owed a good deal to Gladstone's amendments. It represented a calculated risk that an extended voting list would eventually send a Conservative majority back to Westminster.

But an ungrateful electorate said immediately: 'Thank you, Mr Gladstone', and his administration of 1868–74 has been called 'the greatest reforming Parliament since that born of the original extension (of the franchise) in 1832'.[2] The catalogue of its changes included the measures concerning the Church and agriculture in Ireland, the Army reforms of Cardwell, the overhaul of the Judicature, the Education Act of 1870, the Trade Union Act of 1871, and the opening to competitive examination of the Civil Service except the Foreign Office.

It was, to summarize, a period in which the country was becoming more democratic and more literate. It was a period when, during his final months of office, Gladstone had his last chance of abolishing income tax. And that chance lost, it was gone for good; the once ever expanding economy was soon to be threatened by the decay of agriculture, and first the commercial and then the political challenge of resurgent Europe.

The heated controversies of twenty years or so had produced, by the mid-sixties, a qualified acceptance of income tax. This qualification varied in accordance with the school of thought. The reformers' qualification was the hope of amendment. The traditionalists' quali-

---

[1] Monypenny & Buckle (*op. cit.*), vol. II, pp. 278–87.
[2] R. C. K. Ensor, *England 1870–1914*.

fication was the hope, growing ever fainter, of abolition. The opinion of both these schools found full expression, both in Parliament, Committee and contemporary periodicals and pamphlets. But there were two minority groups, the root and branch objectors to any income tax whatever, and those whose income was below, or not a great deal above the exemption limit.

The opposition to the principle of direct taxation was now fast diminishing. Probably the most articulate expression of this was Sir Morton Peto's *On Taxation*.[3] He was the M.P. for Finsbury and he wrote and dedicated the book to his constituents. It is perhaps not so opposed to Income Tax as Seligman[4] seemed to think. He argued that Peel never contemplated the tax would last and that was why its irregularities were never amended. To these general abuses were now added two specific objections: its adaptation to make up permanent deficiencies which was an encouragement to extravagance, and the amount of evasion under Schedule D. If income tax were to be a permanent source of revenue, it must be remodelled[5] 'to permit of fair assessment' at 'a moderate rate of duty'. 'If this cannot be done, the tax must be abandoned. It is too oppressive, too unequal, too immoral in its character to permit of its continuance.'

The author then pointed out the anomalies which had been exposed by the Hume Committee (see pp. 67–71), and which had never been remedied. It seems, in general, that he approved the scheme of differentiation which Hume had advocated; and it would be unfair to say he was wholly opposed to a tax on income; he simply objected to it in its present form. Indeed, at the conclusion of his book he quotes, with approval, Gladstone's advocation of a mixed system of direct and indirect taxation.[6] This, to mention another extreme group, was very different from the avowed aims of the Liverpool Financial Reform Association,[7] founded in 1848, which was still active in the 'sixties, and which proposed 'the abolition of all Customs and Excise Duties, the substitution of Direct Taxation and the establishment of perfect freedom for trade and industry'.

Julius Partridge,[8] however, published a minute under the auspices of the National Association for the Promotion of Social Science in which he declared categorically that 'as to our direct revenue, a perfectly new system must be adopted. Income tax must be totally abandoned. A wealth tax on all wealth of every description, beginning at

---

[3] *On Taxation*, see pp. 68–99.   [4] (*op. cit.*), p. 162.
[5] *On Taxation*, p. 82.   [6] *On Taxation*, p. 339.
[7] Hubbard Report (*op. cit.*), p. 45.
[8] *Papers on Taxation: Direct and Indirect* – National Association for the Promotion of Social Science, 1861.

a low minimum is the only equitable direct taxation; to complete its utility, a new method of administration must also be adopted'. A further paper by Duncan McLaren[9] suggested a property and house tax instead of an income tax. Judging by these two dissertations, it is unfair to dismiss the abolitionists as introducing 'no new argument against the principle of income taxation'. Of course, there was the usual lunatic fringe which frequently haunts any minority group such as the author who wrote '*Penny Taxation*:[10] Self Collecting; Calculated to produce Twelve Millions Annually; Suggested in Liquidation or Curtailment of the Income Tax', which seems to have been a cross between an entertainment tax and a stamp duty. The author had written to Mr Gladstone 'at considerable length'; the letters had been 'graciously acknowledged' but, nothing further having been heard, the scheme was now being made public. Even he, however, did not suggest entire abolition at the present juncture 'for the sinews of war must be constantly strengthened'.

There was, however, a considerable section of the public which had little direct interest in the arguments for or against differentiation or even for abolition – the weekly wage earners. They had not suffered too heavily under the 1799 income tax since there was total exemption under £60 and a graduated rate starting at 2d in the £ above that figure (see p. 29). But there had been considerable collection difficulties, when liability existed; and, in fact, some of the Royal dockyard workers[11] had discharged their liability under a Government-sponsored, primitive scheme of deduction of tax from wages. At Peel's limit of exemption, £150, when income tax was reintroduced, not only were the ordinary weekly wage earners exempt, but very many of the middle class too.

This high rate of exemption had been criticized by some of the experts. The Liverpool Financial Reform Association which, as already mentioned, advocated direct taxation only, had proposed lowering the limit to £50. Reduction was also the opinion of Charles Babbage[12] who stated: 'Abolish all exemptions – or else reduce the exemption to the lowest possible point and disqualify from voting all electors who claim the exemption.' He admitted, however, that 'it is obviously impolitic[13] to allow any tax to descend below the point at which the cost of collection exceeds the produce. It is also hopeless to attempt to collect it from those whose entire income just enables

[9] *Papers on Taxation* (as Julius Partridge).

[10] This pamphlet was written by William Hewitt and published in Bristol, *circa* 1860.

[11] The deduction scheme is referred to by Sayer (*op. cit.*), p. 164.

[12] *Thoughts on the Principles of Taxation with reference to a Property Tax*, p. 18.

[13] See p. 13.

them to subsist'. Julius Partridge[14] thought that taxing wages 'would create a mob insurrection' quite apart from the problems of collection. The general theory was that fiscal exemption bred political irresponsibility; the Crimean war was a case in point; the belligerence of the lower middle classes might have been sparked off by a hatred of the Czar, but it was also reinforced by the comforting thought that they would not have to pay for it.

As usual, Hansard mirrored the general theory and practice regarding exemption. As Gladstone[15] put it, 'there was a certain point in the progress down the scale of direct taxation beyond which it was not advisable to pass. The sums to be levied, for instance, might be so small that they would not pay the cost of collection, or if they were collected, the vexation attending it would be such that it would not be expedient to attempt it'. He had, however, reduced the exemption limit to £100 in 1853, but this was not 'to trench on the territory of labour'.[16] This phrase was repeated by the Chancellor of the day, Sir George Lewis, in 1857, but some M.P.s thought that 'the operations of the income tax[17] on persons having under £150 a year, was incredibly severe', and that the exemption limit ought to be raised to Peel's £150. This theme recurred at the Committee Stage when a member unkindly remarked that 'the Chancellor of the Exchequer,[18] possessing a very large income himself, could not appreciate the pressure of the tax upon a man with only £100 a year. It deprived such a man of many of the comforts of life and seriously interfered with the education they were most anxious to afford to children.'

This appeal *ad misericordiam* was reinforced by the reading of a letter from the managing partner of the Minton China Company who had been asked to make a return of the wages of all workpeople 'amounting to £80 per annum and upwards'.[19] They had been charged to tax, had to make personal appeals and thereby 'lost from one to two days' wages'. This year he was refusing to make such a return, 'whatever the consequences'. The Chancellor replied that he received about £350,000 from the source of tax on wages, 'a much larger sum than I feel justified in surrendering'. He also went on to relate the story of the widowed Mrs Smith who had been distrained upon by the Collector for her late husband's tax.[20] The Board, in the person of Charles Pressly, on hearing her story, had immediately sent her to the Surveyor with instructions to withdraw the demand without costs 'and a shilling was given to her to pay her omnibus fare'. Mr Smith, incidentally, had been both a hatter and a Post Office sorter; his

[14] *Papers on Taxation* (*op. cit.*), p. 15.
[15] Hansard 23/V/1853.
[16] Gladstone, Hansard 18/IV/1853.
[17] Hansard 13/II/1857 (Williams).
[18] Hansard 10/III/1857 (Williams).
[19] Hansard 10/III/1857 (Child).
[20] Hansard 12/III/1859.

joint wage had brought him over the exemption limit. For wages in general were still not regarded as a suitable subject for taxation; as Hubbard had said when proposing his Committee, he was not concerned with the 'product of unskilled labour'.[21] Skilled, or unskilled, even by 1868 half the total national incomes were below £100. The average wage for a clerk was just below that figure; a manual wage earner would be taking home between £70 and £80 and an agricultural labourer not much above £20.

But still there were a considerable number of skilled workers and senior clerks who would be earning over the exemption limit.[22] Sir George Lewis had put the number at 20,000 in 1857, but it must have been greater than that if the tax yield was £350,000; and the collection difficulties would multiply with the number involved. There was one obvious solution which Edward Walsh,[23] the Surveyor for the City of London, had put forward in his evidence before the Hubbard Committee; in reply to a question whether 'it would be desirable and proper to ask employers generally to return the salaries of their clerks', he replied: 'I think it would be very much better if we could get the employers to pay the tax for their clerks.' He went on to say that there was often great difficulty in collecting the full amount of tax due at any one instalment, and that the 'indulgence of the Board of Inland Revenue has been very great' in accepting payment by 5s monthly instalments. Hubbard specifically asked him whether he had any doubt about 'the policy and propriety of calling upon employers of labour to assist you by giving you lists of their clerks and, in fact, collecting the tax upon their salaries' and he replied: 'I think it would be very desirable if it could be done.'

The Civil Service itself had always operated a scheme for deducting tax from salaries[24] and this had even been extended to the Royal Household salaries by 1854. Why then was it not found possible to have solved the pressing collection difficulties by a type of Pay As You Earn procedure? The simple explanation is that such a scheme was tried in the early 'sixties and is referred to in the Board's report of 1864.[25] In that year was heard the case of the Attorney General *v.* the Lancashire and Yorkshire Railway Company when it was determined that the Board was not justified in requiring the company to deduct tax 'from such of their servants as are engaged at weekly wages'. They had to be assessed from their residences as the law prescribed. The Board quite justifiably commented that it was a hardship to the weekly wage earner to pay his tax in comparatively large amounts instead of by small deductions; but no more was

---

[21] Hansard 19/I/1861.   [22] Hansard 13/II/1857.
[23] Hume Report, Qq. 2218–2219.
[24] Taxes Out Letters 12988/68/6, 29/VI/42; 6/VII/1854.   [25] See p. 28.

heard of that bold experiment for some time to come. The question of the hardship imposed on the small taxpayer by the reforms of 1869, when the one yearly payment system was introduced (see p. 101), was raised in Parliament two years later, but a motion to have two half-yearly instalments was lost by a majority of thirty-nine.[26]

Meanwhile the advocates of differentiation were continuing their battle, both outside and inside the House. The criticisms which Gladstone and his nominees had levelled against the reformers forced them to revise their theories and formulate a more logical defence. The *Westminster Review*,[27] for example, in a lengthy and elaborate article, was prepared to drop the element of personal exertion which the doctors,[28] for example, had stressed in the Hubbard Report and the vexed question of the exemption of savings which Mill[29] had put forward and rest the case for differentiation on the precarious nature of the source of earned income: 'It is solely the precariousness of the duration of industrial incomes, not the fact of their being industriously earned, that entitled them to exemption.' The amount of relief claimed was the old one third of earned income and it could still be countered by the old arguments that a flat one third gave too much relief to some and too little to others; and that in any case it was at the expense of those to whom no relief was given. Further it left unsolved the problem of Schedule A income which was still assessed on the gross, a grievance intensified by the fact that at least some expenses were given before assessing income both under Schedule D and Schedule E; in this connection the reformers seemed to have forgotten that allied to Hubbard's original scheme for differentiation was a measure of relief for Schedule A (see p. 85).

This simplification of the case for differentiation, however, did represent real progress, especially in discarding the exemption of savings theory; in addition, Hubbard's placing of pensions in the category of fixed incomes was dropped and they were now held to attract the suggested one third exemption. For the first time, too, linked with the 'new' differentiation, was more than a hint of progression 'by an income tax that would counter balance the pressure of indirect taxation on the smaller incomes'. For it still remained the fact that despite all the reductions in indirect taxation, 1862–3 could boast only £10·6 millions from income tax, while customs and excise produced £39·2 millions; ten years later, income tax had fallen to £7 millions while customs and excise was close on the £47 millions mark.

But in the somewhat scant fiscal literature of the period, mention

[26] Hansard 18/V/1871.
[27] See *Westminster Review XXI* (N.S. 1862): quoted by Shehab (*op. cit.*), p. 158.
[28] Hume Report, see Q. 3423.   [29] Hume Report, see Qq. 3538 *et seq.*

should be made of a paper given to the Economic Section of the British Association early in 1874 by P. Hallett.[30] His main contentions have been summarized as follows:

'First of all, equality should constitute the first and supreme maxim of any tax distribution policy. Secondly, equality could only be effected among people equally situated and so any attempt to equalize the tax burden of the different classes should be preceded by the preliminary step of equalizing for computation purposes, the value of their incomes. Thirdly, the source from which the income is derived is the fundamental factor in this process of equalization.'

Coming to practical matters, he suggested a 'wear and tear' allowance which he defined as the general cost of maintenance; something like this was already being given under Schedule D. He was also in favour of a depreciation allowance which, as has been mentioned, was allowed by the Commissioners in some divisions, but not in others (p. 71). There was also to be a third deduction for 'risks', for example, fire, wreck, disease, injury, sudden death, etc.

There are two general objections to Hallett's scheme. In the first place it tends to ignore the relevance of size of income to taxability. Hallett himself never seems to have considered the matter. Secondly it was far from clear how the suggested reliefs of wear and tear, depreciation and 'risks' were to be given. Such allowances would imply the submission of trading accounts in the case of Schedule D for examination by the Commissioners and the Surveyor, an exercise for which the current assessing machinery and staff were hardly adapted in the early 'seventies.

The most interesting point, however, brought out by research into the subsequent history of the paper, shows that it stimulated the formation of a committee by the British Association to enquire into 'the practicability of adopting a common measure of value in the Assessment of Direct Taxation'. Hallett was appointed Secretary of this committee, which included, amongst the members, three old advocates of income tax reform, Hubbard, Newmarch and Farr. By endorsing the committee's report, which was pure Hallett, they endorsed in effect the 'new' differentiation and thus provided a direct link with the Committees of 1851–2 and 1861.

Inside the House, the particular issue of differentiation and the general question of finance were both overshadowed by the problem of parliamentary reform, over which the Liberal Government had fallen in 1866. It is small wonder that Disraeli, Chancellor of the

---

[30] P. Hallett: See Shehab (*op. cit.*), p. 165 *et seq*. His researches on Hallett and the subsequent history of his paper are invaluable and have been closely followed here.

Exchequer for the third time and Leader of the House, gave a 'somewhat perfunctory performance' in introducing his Budget of 1867.[31] The current surplus was mortgaged to terminable annuities, and by autumn a credit was needed for the Abyssinian expedition. Income tax was, accordingly, increased from 4d to 5d.[32]

This was Disraeli's last Budget; in February 1868 his chief, Derby, resigned and Disraeli became Prime Minister. 'I think Hunt must be the Chancellor of the Exchequer' he wrote to Derby, 'and I have prepared the Queen for it.'[33] Ward Hunt had been the Secretary to the Treasury and it was he who, in the absence of Disraeli through illness, had suggested the penny increase.[34] He added a further penny, making the rate 6d when he introduced his Budget in 1868.[35] This increase was to cover mounting military and naval expenditure, but the Government was charged by the Opposition with a general lack of economy. Not that it mattered a great deal; the days of the first Disraeli Government were numbered. Parliament was finally dissolved in November[36] and a Liberal administration was then swept into power on a wave of almost unprecedented popularity. For a third time in sixteen years, a Conservative minority Government had unsuccessfully 'appealed unto Caesar'.

The decision to rely on income tax increases alone for additional revenue was justified by the fact that the money was needed for emergency purposes which had been the original reason for imposing the tax in the first place and by the knowledge that the imposition and subsequent remission of indirect taxation would cause economic disturbance. This represents yet another departure in the case of income tax. Not only was it being treated as the elastic element in the Budget, but its rate was being raised without any addition to indirect taxation. 'No wonder that from this time forward, on any and every emergency successive Chancellors of the Exchequer turned', Mr Ward Hunt said, 'as the most obtuse among them could hardly fail to do, to the Income Tax and put it up or down as poverty or plethora dictated.'[37]

The choice of Robert Lowe[38] as Chancellor of the Exchequer by Gladstone, while surprising, was not altogether infelicitous, for although he had no special aptitude for figures, nor the best of eyesight, he had a quick and lively mind and a peculiar brand of sardonic

[31] Hansard 4/IV/1867 and Buxton (*op. cit.*), vol. II, p. 35.
[32] The Income Tax increase took place in November, 1867.
[33] Monypenny & Buckle (*op. cit.*), vol. II, p. 324.
[34] Dowell (*op. cit.*), vol. II, p. 353.
[35] Hansard 23/IV/1868. See also Buxton (*op. cit.*), vol. II, p. 46.
[36] See Buxton (*op. cit.*), vol. II, p. 56.   [37] Buxton (*op. cit.*), vol. II, p. 48.
[38] See, *inter alia*, on Robert Lowe, Monypenny & Buckle (*op. cit.*), vol. II, p. 442.

humour. The reformers had been quiet under the brief Conservative regime, but very early in the Liberal period, a motion was proposed 'That it is expedient to include in the financial arrangements of the Government for the ensuing year the unconditional repeal of the income tax on trade profits and personal property of all kinds and that any deficiency be raised by an increased tax on land and fixed property.'[39] This was differentiation *in excelsis* and Lowe's reply[40] should be quoted at some length for it illustrates perfectly the Gladstonian view of Income Tax.

'The notion of income,' he said, 'is one that is very difficult to seize. It is like "now". In a moment it flies from you while you stop. It is the notion of a man's annual revenue, abstracted altogether from the sources whence it comes and the purposes for which it goes. That is the idea of an income: and the moment you begin to say you ought to pay more on this schedule and less on that, or abolish, as the Hon. Gentleman says a Schedule altogether, you are not amending the income tax but destroying it and making, instead of it, an unfair and bungling property tax. Unless you look at income without reference to the sources whence it comes, or whither it goes, it is impossible to maintain an income tax by any argument . . . The real evil of the income tax, in my judgment, is not that it is levied in a partial manner on land, or realized property, or profits of trade, but that, from the necessity of the case, persons having such income, as that included in Schedule D are judges in their own cause and that in many instances holds out a temptation to those persons to give too favourable an interpretation of their liability. But to say that there is an objection to income tax is only to say that this tax is a tax; for the ingenuity of the human mind never did and never will devise a tax to which there are not objections more than plausible and which would be absolutely convincing and irrisistible if taxation were not a necessity.'

'The motion,' says Hansard, 'was withdrawn.'

Three weeks later, Lowe presented his first Budget.[41] The prospects did not seem at all encouraging and, unlike the prosperous years of Gladstone's Chancellorship, the revenue showed 'not the slightest symptom of elasticity'. Government expenditure on social services had increased, although the efforts of Cardwell at the War Office and Childers at the Admiralty had cut expenditure on the armed forces. Even with the rate remaining at 6d only a small surplus could be anticipated.

Lowe altered this most unpromising situation by changing the collection dates of all the direct taxes. Income tax was normally

[39] Hansard 16/III/1869.   [40] Hansard 16/III/1869.   [41] Hansard 8/IV/1869.

collected three times a year: imposed in April, a half was collected in October and the remaining two quarters in the following January and April, which meant only three-quarters of the tax being harvested in the year in which it was due. Now the income tax imposed at the beginning of the financial year was to fall due in the following January, with three months' grace in appropriate cases; but March 31st was the dead-line. The Assessed Taxes (see p. 48) were collected in October and April, based on a return made in the previous April of the dutiable articles used during the previous twelve months. Under the proposed arrangement, a return had to be made of the articles which were to be used in the coming twelve months from January to December; the tax was due at once in one sum by a licence system. But this summary procedure was accompanied by a revision and simplification of the miscellaneous duties; the hair powder tax finally disappeared – it was no loss at a current yield of £1,000 and the taxes on locomotion were repealed (see p. 47), apart from that on railway passengers where the Government and the companies affected could not agree on terms.[42] Land Tax and Inhabited House Duty had been due in October and April; now they were to be paid in January.

The immediate financial effect of these changes was remarkable. As far as income tax was concerned, five quarters were collectable in 1869; the payers of Assessed Taxes[43] would, by the new system, be paying almost twice in one year, so a concession was granted 'for this occasion only' whereby three-fifths merely of the tax was demanded in the New Year of 1870, the balance being held over until the following April and in the case of Land Tax and Inhabited House Duty, an extra half of the taxes would be received in the current year. Thus, by shortening the period over which the taxpayer might spread his payments and reducing the length of credit allowed by the State, Lowe, as if by magic, created a surplus which reached nearly £3·4 millions. This he used not only for the revision of the direct taxes mentioned above, including 1d off income tax, but also for further remissions of indirect taxation. Admittedly the surplus was in the way of being a windfall; but the remissions were justified by the fact that the originally small balance had been due to war expenditure which it was hoped would not recur. Lowe spent nearly two hours speaking on his revised collection system; his audience had to agree it was worth it in the end.

The Budget of 1870, after the previous year's masterpiece of ingenuity, was inevitably something of an anticlimax. Expenditure had remained steady, the revenue had increased; it was possible to make further reductions in indirect taxation and take a further 1d off income tax. Whether these constant reductions were truly in the

---

[42] Dowell (*op. cit.*), vol. II, p. 356.   [43] Buxton (*op. cit.*), vol. II, p. 87.

national interest in view of the size of the national debt, was a question which historians of taxation have never satisfactorily answered. Some took a highly moral tone:

'But the evil desire for immediate fruition which characterized the times would not permit the Chancellor of the Exchequer to keep a large surplus. "Give! Give!" was the cry of a people who had become accustomed, in a time of advance in the national prosperity by leaps and bounds, to expect a benefaction on Budget Day as regularly as a postman expects a Christmas Box.'[44]

Others have judged the position on its immediate merits. 'I think it is clear (putting aside for the moment the question of whether the remissions themselves were wise and expedient) that financially they were fully justified.'[45] Probably, considering the current state of public opinion, any Chancellor of either party was virtually committed to a policy of remission; Disraeli had dealt with the problem in exactly the same way in 1858 (see p. 78).

1870 was the year of the Franco-Prussian war; and Lowe indirectly was one of its victims. For although by the time the 1871 Budget was introduced,[46] the actual fighting was over, the Army needed another £3 millions. Lowe made two errors:[47] he grossly underestimated the revenue; and he proposed to raise the amount required by a tax on matches, an increase in the legacy and succession duties and by complicated income tax adjustment which would have involved the levying of the tax based on a percentage not pence. These proposals raised objections which seem out of all proportion to their intrinsic merits or demerits, even granting the Chancellor had made the assumption that income tax was permanent and that it was sound economic policy to use it as a makeweight. The real agitation, however, might well have been against the personality of Lowe himself; the Budget speech was decidedly provocative in parts: 'it was annoying to be taxed at all; it was especially aggravating to be taxed by Mr Lowe.' In the event, the House would have none of his 'fancy schemes';[48] and this 'harum-scarum' Budget was quietly dropped for the 'sweet simplicity' of twopence on the income tax.

Lowe was also faced later in the year with a revival of activity from the advocates of differentiation. There was a short debate on the occasion of the income tax resolution of the year, in which the usual arguments were put forward and the usual replies made.[49] But a full dress debate took place later in the month on the motion of Chad-

---

[44] Dowell (*op. cit.*), vol. II, p. 357.   [45] Buxton (*op. cit.*), vol. II, p. 93.
[46] Hansard 20/IV/1871.   [47] Buxton (*op. cit.*), vol. II, pp. 119–120.
[48] Monypenny & Buckle (*op. cit.*), pp. 479–80.
[49] Hansard 4/V/1871.

wick,[50] the auditor and M.P. for Macclesfield, for the appointment of a Select Committee with an all embracing brief, not only to enquire into differentiation, but into the question of an allowance for depreciation and the whole administration of the Income Tax Acts. Reform was essential because the tax had now become permanent was the theme of an extremely lengthy but able speech, during which the House was nearly counted out. He concluded by making thirteen points which he thought such a Committee might well enquire into. Lowe's reply was typical:

'a great many of the subjects which had been raised in the debate deserved the consideration of the Government . . . but (an echo of Gladstone), there was no subject in the whole range of political economy, or the practical administration of the Government, that had undergone a more thorough, or sifting enquiry than the general abstract principle upon which an Income Tax should be founded. He felt perfectly confident that if a Committee were appointed, the result they would come to . . . would not be different from the result that had hitherto attended such investigations . . . if an Income Tax must be maintained, it must be a uniform tax.'

The motion was lost by a majority of 9 only.

The twopence imposed in 1871 came off in the following year[51] and the limit upon which abatement was allowed was raised from £200 to £300; in addition the abatement itself was increased from £60 to £80. Lowe was at pains to point out that 'it had nothing to do with any attempt to graduate the Income Tax . . . but on the ground that there is no class of the community so severely pinched by taxation as the lower class'.

The year 1873 has been called the *annus mirabilis* of fiscal years. It saw the so-called 'Prosperity Budget'[52] in which there were remissions of duty amounting to £3·75 millions, including a further penny off income tax; even so, a surplus of nearly £5 millions remained. Despite this promising state of affairs, the Budget speech was one of stupendous dullness and not even a debate on differentiation following the Financial Statement aroused the Chancellor. It could very well have been of Lowe that Disraeli was thinking when he spoke in Manchester in the previous April of the Treasury Bench reminding him of 'a range of exhausted volcanoes. Not a flame flickers on a single pallid crest.'[53] Before the year was out an administrative scandal over the Post Office, in which of course Lowe was not personally involved, forced a Ministerial shuffle and Gladstone himself took over the Chancellor's seals.

[50] Hansard 19/V/1871.   [51] Hansard 25/III/1872.
[52] Hansard 7/IV/1873.   [53] Monypenny & Buckle (*op. cit.*), vol. II, p. 531.

This was but one of many indications that the Liberal Government was steadily losing ground in the country. It had already resigned once, in March 1873, after defeat over the Irish Universities. Disraeli, however, refused a fourth minority office, and Gladstone's Cabinet was compelled to resume, diminished both in nerve and reputation. Suddenly on January 24, 1874, the address of the Prime Minister to the electorate appeared. 'In the drab intoxication of Treasury figures, Gladstone lost his grip on the grand problem of politics',[54] for Parliament was to be dissolved and his appeal to the country[55] was based on 'the question of finance and the question of economy' in general and the abolition of income tax in particular.

The Liberal Government fell just before the end of the financial year, 1873, but their record in effect covers the period from 1869 to 1873. It was a period of intense legislative activity which threw a considerable burden on the various Departments of the Civil Service concerned, and the changes and reforms produced by the annual Finance Acts are reflected in the yearly accounts of their stewardship by the Commissioners of Inland Revenue.

The two reports for 1866 and 1867 continue the pattern of the first nine, that is they comment on the immediate position in the year under review, give an account of 'our Revenue for the last financial year with an explanation of any notable variations and finally set down details of the duties under our management' which still, it must be emphasized, comprised excise, licence and stamp duty as well as the Assessed and income taxes. For income tax the yield was analysed under each schedule and figures were given of the amounts assessed, the relevant duty arising and the number of persons assessed. Tables were also provided showing the number of repayment and abatement claims. The theme of evasion under Schedule D recurred annually. 'We have, as usual, abundant evidence from the number of fraudulent returns which have been detected that Schedule D contributes far less than its fair proportion to the Revenue' and an example was given of a business returning £10,000 and accepting a assessment of £30,000. Far more ingenious was the man who returned £1,161[56] when his profits were well in excess of that figure, his reason being that 'an odd figure would look better than a round sum'.[57]

In the following year the Commissioners were able to make an estimate of what this evasion might amount to: 'An extensive demolition of houses by the Metropolitan Board of Works gave rise to a great number of claims to compensation. Two hundred of these were examined by our officers and in 40% of the cases inquired into the

[54] J. L. Hammond & M. Foot: *Gladstone and Liberalism*, p. 123.
[55] See his Greenwich speech 28/II/74 and Buxton (*op. cit.*), vol. II, p. 167.
[56] Hansard 23/III/1860.   [57] Board's Report 1867, p. 24.

revenue had been defrauded of its dues.'[58] The aggregate taxable income returned by the parties themselves was £73,642 and the amount ultimately found to be correct was £171,370, being in excess of the returns by about 130 per cent. The Commissioners then proceeded to apply the margin of error to Schedule D as a whole and arrived at the conclusion that the Schedule D revenue was deficient by nearly £1·5 millions. 'We see no reason to distrust this estimate,' they continued; and although not all cases were wilful, they agreed 'what we are chiefly concerned with is the effect on the public income which is the same whatever may be the cause of the deficiency'.

In fact, during 1868, there was an increase in Schedule D tax which was due to the assessments arising from railways, mines, ironworks, gasworks, etc., being transferred to Schedule D from Schedule A.[59] The profits assessed in London itself, however, showed a decrease reflecting the financial crises of the period which resulted in extensive failures in both banking houses and joint stock companies.

The reports for the subsequent years to 1874 continue to give examples of the evasion of tax under Schedule D, but also contain perhaps the first example of an avoidance device, which was, in this instance, a scheme for making dividends payable nominally abroad so that they would thereby be entitled to exemption.[60] They also comment on the changes in collection[61] (see pp. 100–101) which they had 'so long advocated' and the transfer of the Assessed Taxes into a system of licences. This meant it was possible to reduce the number of surveyors and districts.[62] In practice a number of older men were retired[63] and the administration devolved upon 'younger and more energetic' officers. It may be that they did not, as instructed, always show 'every proper civility and attention'[64] to taxpayers, and there was something of an agitation about the change in regime at the Exeter district.

The M.P. for that constituency complained that the city was in 'a state of great excitement owing to the surcharges which had been made in all directions'. Not only had new Commissioners been appointed, but a new Surveyor also 'and the opinion was general that these surcharges were either the act of the Government Surveyor or that the Government had themselves sent down special orders to raise the assessments all round so as to swell the Budget receipts, both of which impressions he did his best to remove'.[65] The upshot of this was that the Board appointed a special Inspector 'to investigate and report upon the matter'. His survey disclosed that of the 1,098 persons

[58] Board's Report 1868, p. 23.   [59] 29 Vict. C.36 S.8.
[60] Board's Report 1872, p. 37.   [61] Board's Report 1869, pp. 1–2.
[62] Board's Report 1870, p. 40.   [63] Board's Report 1871, p. 51.
[64] Taxes Out Letters, 3/II/1852.   [65] Hansard 25/III/1872 (Bowring).

liable under Schedule D only 222 made returns satisfactory to the Commissioners 'so that 876 either made no return or were surcharged for making untrue returns'. On appeal the claims of only forty-five were allowed. 'These results,' the Board wrote to the Mayor of Exeter, 'appear to show conclusively the assessments in Exeter have been generally made with due regard on the one hand to the requirements of the public service and on the other hand to individual interests.' In the 1871 report they comment mildly that, as seems fairly evident, 'The previous Surveyor had been somewhat lax' and the whole incident underlines the conclusions they had drawn in 1868 (see p. 105).[66]

The reports to the end of the period continue to show the Board rather sensitive on the question of surcharges and the instructions governing them are quoted to demonstrate the essential equity of the system.[67] In all, the conclusion is that although some specific complaints were made, there was no general demand 'for enquiry and redress' and despite the continued evasion under Schedule D, the yield of tax was steadily rising.

There was one most important development at the end of the period in 1874 when both the taxpayer and the Crown were given the right to require either the General or Special Commissioners to 'state a case'[68] for the High Court on the ground that their determination was 'erroneous in point of law'. Previously there had been no appeal tribunal beyond the Commissioners themselves. Taxpayers did apply to the Treasury[69] from time to time for relief but the reply was almost invariably: 'The Commissioners have full jurisdiction in the matter' or 'The decision of the District Commissioners is final.' Occasionally, when the case concerned such exotic characters as the dragomans of the British Embassy at Constantinople,[70] they did concede that 'persons of so peculiar a character' were not liable to income tax, but in general there was a routine formula of refusal to interfere. This right of appeal now established in the case of income tax, had always existed for the Assessed Taxes, where already a long series of decided cases had accumulated which assumed the nature of precedents.

The eight years from 1866 to 1874, or from Gladstone in the ascendant to Gladstone in decline, may seem curiously inconclusive. There was the failure to apply income tax to a considerable body of wage earners, partly through administrative difficulties, for example, their nomadic habits, and partly through the genuine desire of Government and employers not to embitter labour relations or cause

---

[66] Board's Report 1871, p. 52.   [67] Board's Report 1872, p. 35.
[68] 'Stating a case', 37 Vict. C.16.
[69] The examples of applications to the Treasury are taken from the Taxes Out Letters dated respectively 29/X/1842, 7/III/1843.
[70] Taxes Out Letters, 9/VI/1843.

workers to emigrate, all of which made income tax a less potent engine of finance, in both peace and war, than it might have been. For in many ways, income tax was simply a well organized system of raising money, and if it was too much trouble to collect, the criterion of liability became not so much equity or forbearance as executive convenience. There was the failure of the differentiationists, in the face of continued opposition from Gladstone and his school, to make any real progress towards realizing their policy in spite of rationalizing their arguments and their conviction that 'income tax was not necessarily like a house of cards which, if touched, would come down altogether'.[71]

On the credit side was the increasing efficiency of the Board and their Surveyors, now freed from the dead weight of the Assessed Taxes and able to concentrate on their more important functions. Allied with this went an increased interest in the technical questions of income tax, exemplified by, say, William Chadwick, the M.P. whose firm was concerned in 'the auditing and making the Income Tax Returns of upwards of forty or so manufacturing and mercantile concerns, including some of the largest establishments in the country'.[72] Such problems as the allowability of depreciation, the possibility of a wear and tear allowance, what deductions are permissible in arriving at the balance of the profits or gains were all being discussed, although it must be admitted that the Board was not always clear in its requirements, as witnessed one of its circulars. 'Circumstances have arisen which have induced the Board to provide for the Surveyors of Taxes a form of letter to be used in making applications to public companies for copies of their "Balance Sheet of profit and loss" and of their reports.'

This was the heyday of *laissez-faire*; and the principles of its doctrine affected even income tax, the idea being that if given the right conditions, the principle of self assessment under Schedule D would be honestly applied. The experts and the Board found this hard to believe in the face of their internal evidence and could not see why even differentiation should invoke the required change of heart; and they could only oppose against abuse and evasion the competence of the Branch within the very restricted limits of their legal powers.

'It is our humble duty,' they wrote, 'to provide facts and figures for the use of others in attack or defence; and if we step aside from the narrow limits of this path it is so far only as may be necessary to correct erroneous impressions which are known to prevail.'[73]

But these conceptions must have seemed somewhat academic to the Surveyor of 1874. He had heard Gladstone appeal to the country

[71] Hansard 19/V/1871 (Chadwick).　　[72] Hansard 19/V/1871.
[73] 'It is our humble duty . . .', Board's Report 1871, p. 52.

CHAPTER VII

Reprieve and Regeneration

GLADSTONE had appealed to the country,[1] as he said, 'on the question of finance and the question of economy', but his party was judged mainly on the later achievements, the earliest spate of reforms being long forgotten. It was not to be expected, however, that the electorate of 1874 would show a fervid enthusiasm for a Liberal-sponsored abolition of income tax which seemed, as Disraeli pointed out,[2] to be something of a death-bed repentance on their part, whereas it had been for long an integral plank of the Conservative platform. *The Times*[3] took a benevolently neutral attitude: 'It is now evident that whoever is Chancellor of the Exchequer when the Budget is produced, the income tax will be abolished.' The following day it was even more emphatic: 'How tame for the Conservative leader, who is nothing, if not original, to have to say "ditto" to Mr Gladstone . . . But there was no alternative. At such a moment as this it would be fatal to bid lower than the enemy . . . We are to have our income tax taken off and our rates lowered, whichever comes in.' In the event, the Conservatives were put in with a faithful working majority which supported them until the end; and the days of income tax seemed, at long last, numbered indeed.

Why then was it not finally extinguished if both parties were agreed that this course was both feasible and desirable? The question seems a dramatic one at this long range, but the answers, for there is no one single reason, are disappointingly mundane. There was no cliff-hanging suspense about the possible fate of income tax; no last minute reprieve, no critical decision. For despite *The Times*, although Gladstone had, in fact, stated that 'at a sacrifice for the financial year of something less than five millions and a half' the country could 'enjoy the advantage and relief of the total repeal'[4] of the income tax, he had not said specifically that it would take place at once or whence the odd two millions in taxation which would be required to balance the

---

[1] Greenwich speech 28/II/1874.
[2] Monypenny & Buckle (*op. cit.*), vol. II, p. 615.
[3] *The Times* quotations are from the issues of 26/I/1874 and 27/I/1874.
[4] See his election address of 24/I/1874.

Budget was to come. To do him justice, many years later he wrote that he would have proposed that death duties should be 'reconstructed and enlarged' as being 'the least of all unfavourable to trade and industry'.[5] Disraeli had been more judicious:

'But, though I think the Income Tax is a war tax and should not exist except when we are in a position of war, we find that tax now in operation and I certainly do not consider I am relieving the country of a burden by abolishing it and substituting for it taxes much heavier and more vexatious; let the Income Tax die naturally. You have a surplus. You need not devote the whole of that surplus to the remission of the Income Tax. A part of it you may apply to other parts of public policy, but everyone feels that in a short time the Income Tax under those circumstances would disappear.'[6]

So, in the first place, the promise of abolition by both parties was to an extent simple electioneering; indeed, a contemporary historian[7] stigmatized it as bribery, as did the Queen[8] herself as far as Gladstone was concerned.

Secondly the point must again (see p. 97) be stressed that income tax, related to its current yield was not an important tax and did not, by any means, provide a major part of the national revenue. In 1873–4, for example, income tax accounted for only £5·7 millions out of a total revenue of £77 millions, whereas customs and excise produced no less than £47·5 millions or nearly two thirds of the total.[9] True, income tax did represent an elastic element in the Budget and it was not expensive to run. But the quantum of its contribution to the Exchequer was comparatively so small that the question of its abolition could hardly assume the proportions of a major issue.

Its impact, too, in the nation at large was inconsiderable. The Schedule A taxpayer laboured perhaps under a genuine grievance in having to pay on his gross income without any deduction, but as rates of tax had been, for some time, so low, the main objection tended to be directed against the inconvenience of paying tax, rather than the actual amount payable. The Schedule D taxpayer was well able to cushion his profits against the incidence of taxation, not only by the admittedly few permissive deductions, but by various types of evasion about which the Board had so often complained (see pp. 104–105). And of course the bulk of the country, being well below the ex-

---

[5] The *Nineteenth Century*, June 1887, p. 935.
[6] See his Aylesbury speech 1/II/1874.
[7] Lecky's *History*, vol. VI, p. 600.
[8] *Victoria R.I.*, Elizabeth Longford, p. 395.
[9] Buxton (*op. cit.*), vol. II, p. 349.

emption limit, did not pay any income tax at all; indirect taxation affected even those who were liable far more.

Such were the main reasons why income tax was not abolished at once. The possibility did genuinely exist in 1874, but when the chance was let slip, the worsening trade conditions[10] gave the new Conservative Chancellor of the Exchequer no opportunity of allowing income tax 'to die a natural death'. Time was running out; the boom was over and a price fall was beginning. The Conservative Budgets from 1874 onwards underline this final reason in the intensifying struggles of the new Chancellor with economic adversity.

The Queen wrote to Disraeli early in 1874 informing him of Gladstone's resignation and asking him to form a government, but he did not complete his task until towards the end of the month. Consequently the new Chancellor, Sir Stafford Northcote, had to introduce his Budget within a few weeks of his assumption of office. Disraeli was naturally anxious. 'If we don't take care,' he wrote to Northcote, 'we shall make a muddle of the Budget. It is indispensable that we should take 1d off the Income Tax.'[11]

There was no need to worry. The finances of the country were in a most flourishing condition and the only problem was how to dispose of the surplus of £5·5 millions. Northcote would have wished,[12] but for the shortness of time for consideration, to overhaul the whole fiscal system;[13] as it was, he spread his surplus in remissions of various taxes, including the expected 1d off income tax, thus reducing it to its lowest rate ever, 2d in the £, a rate indeed economically unsound, if retained for any length of time, since the expense and inconvenience of collection would be out of proportion to the receipts. The Budget, however, 'was extremely well received by the House', a satisfied Prime Minister reported to the Queen.[14] There was very little opposition in Committee, apart from a suggestion to raise the exemption limit to £200 and give an allowance of £100 to all incomes between £200 and £500. This, replied Northcote, would cost 'about £240,000' and he deprecated any attempt to alter the incidence of the tax at this moment, 'until the Government could consider it more at leisure and more in connection with the rest of the financial system'.[15] The disappointed abolitionists[16] then mounted a final attack before the House rose for the summer recess, proposing that 'the continued imposition of the income tax, except in time of war, or some great national emergency, is unjust and impolitic and it is

[10] For a general discussion of trade conditions see Clapham (*op. cit.*), *passim*.
[11] Monypenny & Buckle (*op. cit.*), vol. II, p. 646.
[12] Hansard 18/IV/1874. [13] Hansard 3/VII/1874.
[14] Monypenny & Buckle (*op. cit.*), vol. II, p. 648.
[15] Hansard 23/IV/1874. [16] Hansard 3/VII/1874.

advisable that such tax should be still further reduced and ultimately altogether repealed at the earliest possible moment'. The ensuing debate comprised arguments which had been used in previous debates for differentiation and for a more comprehensive machinery for assessing the tax, but the resolution itself was defeated by a majority of 101.

The Budget of 1875, however, did not fulfil the promise of the expected financial reforms. The surplus had dwindled to a paltry £0·5 million and the enthusiasm of 1874 about the buoyant revenue now became the cautious 'happily (the position was) not such as to cause any great anxiety'. Income tax was held at 2d in the £, but the Chancellor seemed to envisage its use as a steady source of income at a steady rate rather than an emergency tax susceptible of spectacular changes.

'The uncertainty which has attended for many years the use to which the Income Tax was put (for great reforms and great experiments), and the rate at which it was likely to be levied from year to year, made the tax much harder and more oppressive than it would be if it were left low, uniform and, as far as possible, steady. With a prospect before us of a fair annual growth of the revenue, ... we may say that this use of the income tax may be considered to be at an end.'[17]

1874 had opened with high hopes of abolition. Within a year these had diminished merely to the prospect of keeping income tax at a low and uniform level. Now in 1876 even that modest ambition was abandoned and, for the first time, the tax was used simply and solely as a means of meeting the deficiency on ordinary expenditure. The increase was to 3d, but every penny of income tax now produced close on £2 millions[18] and the estimated deficit was less than £1. Coupled with this increase, therefore, was an extension in the limit of exemption and abatement:[19] 'We propose to make the reduction £120, instead of £80 and carry it up to £400 a year. That is to say, all incomes below £150 will be wholly exempt, while those from £150 to £400 will have £120 taken off.'

Both proposals met considerable opposition. Hubbard,[20] not for the first time, opened. 'We had an income tax which, as at present levied, was acknowledged to be one of the most bungling, demoralizing and inequitable taxes that had ever been imposed ... Yet properly levied and collected, an income tax was the best tax a country could have.' It came as no surprise to his listeners to hear

---

[17] Hansard 15/IV/1875.   [18] Board's Report 31/III/1884, p. xxv.
[19] Budget speech, Hansard 3/IV/1876.   [20] Hansard 3/IV/1876.

that the reforms he had so often proposed would put 'income tax on a thoroughly equitable and satisfactory footing'. Another member[21] expressed his 'great disappointment that the Government was departing from what was understood to be one of the leading lines of its policy, the abolition of the income tax . . . The time had now arrived when the Government should deal plainly and fairly with the country in connection with this tax, for there was no security that they would not be asked next year for another 1d with an endeavour to charm the country by increasing the line of exemptions'. Three days later, Hubbard[22] was on his feet again to propose '. . . that taxation when levied upon industrial earnings should be subject to such an abatement as would equitably adjust the burdens thrown upon intelligence and skill as compared with property'. There was little new in his arguments except an ingenious debating point that the reason why the Board did not impose, as they were empowered to do, treble duty 'on those whom they had reason to believe under-estimated their income', was because they knew 'the system they administered was rotten and full of scandalous injustice'. The only cure was 'a system which would appeal directly to the good feelings of the taxpayer'. The back benchers saw to it that the resolution was lost.

There were also two interesting discussions on the liability of wages which, in general, echoed the opinions of twenty years before (see p. 96).[23] The Chancellor emphasized the difficulties of collection; 'and as a matter of fact he was informed by the Inland Revenue authorities that there was no class which avoided payment of income tax so much as the men who were working for wages'. The question was again raised in a later debate and it was suggested that 'the Government might go to employers and not only ascertain the amount of wages paid but, through them, stop the income tax on the weekly earnings of working men in their service'. This projected Pay As You Earn scheme was, however, 'not within the power of the employers and . . . to attempt to carry any legislation of this kind into practice would end in miserable failure'. There were also the theoretical objections to increasing the exemption range.[24] It was a 'dangerous precedent' which might lead to 'progressive taxation'; it might 'ruin the income tax and adopt the dangerous and revolutionary principle of a graduated tax'; even the Chancellor, in the same debate, described a graduated tax as a 'most dangerous policy', but thought exemptions free from the taint of graduation; and the Bill finally had no trouble in gaining the acceptance of the House.

[21] C. Lewis, Hansard 3/IV/1876.   [22] Hansard 6/IV/1876.
[23] Hansard 18/V/1876.
[24] O'Reilly, Hansard 15/5/1876 and T. Hankey, Hansard 18/V/1876.

The Budget of 1877[25] was described by Northcote himself as 'ready-made', for there were no changes in taxation. It marks, however, a watershed in the fortunes of Conservative finance. The long-impending war between Russia and Turkey broke out only a fortnight after the Budget Speech; the trade depression showed no signs of lifting; and the Chancellor could no longer give his undivided attention to the duties of his office since he was, now Disraeli had been translated to the Lords, also Leader of the House of Commons. But he did not take a 'very desponding view' of the situation, regarding it as probable that 'the great consuming power of the people is only temporarily less powerful than it was'.

There was a somewhat half-hearted debate four days after the Budget Speech on a motion proposing the extension of the abatement of £120 to all incomes instead of only those between £150 and £400. Northcote had no difficulty in proving, to his own satisfaction at least, that 'if incomes up to £150 were exempt, it was hardly fair that a man having an income of £151 should be taxed on the full amount. It was for this reason that the exemptions were introduced, but in the case of large incomes, it could not be said that it was necessary to give them the £150 exemption'. Two members, however, came out strongly for a graduated tax; one[26] thought 'the percentage of the charge should increase at a uniform ratio proportionate to the amount of the income so that the incidence of the tax should fall heaviest on the wealthy'. The other was William Chadwick, the accountant (see p. 107); he asserted that 'all the most eminent financial authorities had concurred in holding that a graduated income tax was perfectly possible and attainable'. This was a statement which owed more to imagination than accuracy since graduation was tainted with Radicalism in the view of orthodox fiscal thinking. The amendment was by leave withdrawn.

1878 brought no relief. The ageing Beaconsfield was absorbed in the Eastern Question; and the trade decline was now accompanied by an acute agricultural depression. Northcote had to face a deficit of £5·5 millions and income tax was raised to 5d.[27] 'There will be a general agreement that we ought not to throw ourselves on income tax alone', said Northcote, although the tax was providing over £3 millions of the deficit. There was a further Budget in August which gave more accurate estimates of the defence expenditure, but which provided for no increased taxation; the further liabilities were to be met by further Government borrowing.

But no economic or political crisis could restrain Hubbard in his

---

[25] Hansard 12/IV/1877. There was a subsequent debate reported in Hansard 16/IV/1877.
[26] Morgan Lloyd.   [27] Hansard 4/IV/1878.

self-imposed crusade for differentiation. He rose, as Hansard says, on February 26, 1878 'to call attention to the taxation of the country'. Income tax ought not to be abolished since it 'alone could reach a certain kind of property which, but for that would never be taxed at all. Again, a reason for income tax might be found in its being a tax on absentees.' But it needed reform. 'The process was exceedingly simple. . . . In regard to real property, that amount should be taxed which actually went to the owner; and in the case of industrial earnings, a deduction ought to be made which would put professional and trading incomes upon an equality with the products of real property.' In the ensuing debate,[28] Chadwick spoke in favour of a depreciation allowance and other members supported both differentiation and graduation. Northcote reviewed the various speeches, pointed out the diversity of opinion but, although he agreed with many of the speakers on the various anomalies, clearly had no intention of proposing any reforms.

Later in the year, Hubbard introduced a Bill which proposed his old differentiation scheme[29] of allowing a deduction of one third of a taxpayer's gross earned income before assessment. It has been pointed out that the novelty of this new attempt lay in the proposal that 'industrial and commercial profits had to pay full rate on what was deemed income from capital (estimated at four per cent of the value of capital employed), and at a reduced rate on the rest which was regarded as arising from personal labour'. The Bill was withdrawn after the second reading.

Northcote's last two main Budgets,[30] those of 1879 and 1880, imposed no increases in taxation and met the deficits caused by mounting defence expenditure mainly by borrowing, thus continuing the policy of the previous year. It was not a resolute or incisive policy, although perhaps not deserving of Goschen's criticism that it was 'shabby, flabby and inadequate to the occasion and wanting in that courage which was calculated to secure repute abroad and credit at home'. Northcote himself presented a considered justification of the course he had taken.[31] He could have met the deficit by taxation; but 'trade is not what it should be, agriculture is not in a flourishing state' and 'the condition of the people is one that should make us very careful in putting additional burdens on them . . . the present is not a time in which additional taxation would be borne without distress'. He could add the deficit to the permanent debt; 'and I cannot think of anything more mischievous or enervating than that'. There was, however, a third course.

---

[28] See for example the speech of Sir George Campbell.
[29] Shehab (*op. cit.*), p. 181.   [30] Hansard 3/IV/1879 and 6/IV/1880.
[31] *National Review*, January, 1884, Northcote's own article.

'When you see that your revenue is permanently too low for your permanent expenditure, then it is comparatively easy to add duties which will have to be kept on and to which trade will accommodate itself. But when you have to provide for only one or two years, I think that then it will be found inconvenient. . . . We should do that which is entirely in accordance with the spirit of the proposals we made in 1877–8 when the vote of credit was first proposed, namely that we should extend payment of the debt over one year more.'

This was fair comment, but it was still true that to cover only one third of the deficit by taxation was inadequate by any fiscal canons. It would be interesting to know whether there was a Cabinet decision not to raise rates at this juncture which Northcote had the unenviable task of presenting to the House. For the election was approaching and possibly 'disinclination to increase taxation had got the better of arithmetic'[32] and an election which could have been won on the slogan of 'peace with honour' was lost eighteen months later because, amongst other reasons, the Chancellor had not faced the responsibilities of his office.

The Budgets of Northcote contain all the elements of economic tragedy, the dashing of the high hopes of abolition against the hard facts of depression and falling revenue. The Budgets of the succeeding Liberal Government seem something of an anticlimax despite the fact that the magician again took over the seals of the Exchequer, still a victim to the fascination of figures; and when for the eleventh time he rose to present his Budget[33] the benches, as always, were crowded with an eager and attentive audience.

It was an occasion involving a curious coincidence. In 1853, Gladstone had proposed the abolition of income tax; by 1860, when it should have been liquidated, he was forced to increase it. In 1874 he had again proposed its abolition; now in 1880 he was rising to increase it; the actual increase was one penny but, as following the precedent of 1859, the charge was 'upon one half year of demand', the effective rate was twopence. This was to meet the estimated deficit caused by the conversion of a malt to a beer tax.[34] The following year it was found possible to lower the rate to 5d,[35] partly due to a temporary trade revival. His thirteenth and last Budget[36] 'was as uninteresting in the introductory statement and as unenterprising in its proposals as his first Budget had been remarkable for interest and for boldness of conception'. His final act was to raise the rate in July to

[32] Buxton (*op. cit.*), vol. II, p. 255.
[33] Hansard 10/VI/1880.   [34] Dowell (*op. cit.*), vol. II, pp. 389–90.
[35] Hansard 4/IV/1881 and Buxton (*op. cit.*), vol. II, pp. 276–86.
[36] Hansard 24/IV/1882 and Buxton (*op. cit.*), vol. II, p. 299.

$6\frac{1}{2}$d[37] to finance a vote of credit for the Egyptian Campaign; he then surrendered his post to Childers, hailing him as 'a much better finance minister than myself'.

The new Chancellor could do no better than his master. The initial reduction to 5d in 1883[38] was followed by an increase to 6d in the following year[39] and to 8d in 1885.[40] These increases were directly caused by war charges, and the Government, unlike its predecessor, could at least be congratulated on facing the prospective deficits boldly and covering them lagrely by increased taxation. But the increase of 1885, embodied in an amended Budget proposal the following June, met a hostile reception; the Government declared the division to be a question of confidence; it was defeated by twelve votes and resigned, the second time a Government had done so on this issue, the first being Disraeli's in 1852 (see p. 66).

The fiscal debates of the period were mainly confined to three subjects, agricultural depression, differentiation and the appointment of collectors. The first of these arose because a Free Trade policy finally implied the sacrifice of agriculture to industry;[41] and this process had been intensified by a series of disastrous harvests and pestilences. When the question of special relief was first raised in July 1880,[42] the general tenor of the speeches was that 'the business of farming was becoming more difficult than ever'. Gladstone was at first adamant: 'It was absolutely necessary, if the income tax were not to go down, that the principle of taxation upon owners, who were also occupiers, should continue to be applied as it always had been, namely that persons should be charged as owners on the full value at which their land might fairly be expected to let one year with another.'

The problem was put before the House again in the following year since 'the grievance . . . had become very much aggravated'.[43] Gladstone at first said 'he could not undertake to discuss the question at the present moment', but a few days later he was more sympathetic, if a trifle vague. 'I think I can say that we should be prepared to take the responsibility of framing a measure which will meet the case and we have in the Income and Land Tax Commissioners a body of gentlemen to whom would properly belong the duty of determining whether the loss had been incurred in such a way as to justify the remission.' There was some objection to the idea of giving relief to the agricultural interest only,[44] and one member anticipated the

[37] Hansard 24/VII/1882.   [38] Hansard 5/IV/1883.
[39] Hansard 24/IV/1884.   [40] Hansard 30/IV/1885.
[41] R. C. K. Ensor, *England 1870–1914*.
[42] Hansard 28/VII/1880 (Storer) and 29/VII/1880 (Magniac).
[43] Hansard 23/V/1881 (Magniac) and 26/V/1881.
[44] The opposition was expressed by, for example, Reynolds: Hansard 26/V/1881.

legislation of the early nineteen-forties by claiming that: 'Farmers should be treated like all other traders and should be required to keep books like all other traders and if it was shown they had made a profit, they should pay income tax on that profit and only have relief if they could show they had made no profit at all.'

This was the essential point; as Hubbard put it: 'Farming was as much a trade as any other, although it was specially dealt with on the assumption that farmers did not keep books.'[45] For, as Gladstone pointed out in reply to a further demand for relief, the farmer could pay on his actual profits if less than the assessment.[46] But records were necessary 'and as a result of not keeping their accounts properly, there was extreme difficulty in appealing against the tax'.[47] So the position remained that the farmer had to pay on half his rent, unless he could prove he had made less. The only concession was that if his rent had been abated, then he could return that rent on which the reduction had been based.[48] In addition, there was the question of equity;[49] as one member said: 'He hoped no special treatment would be meted out to farmers seeing that the industrial areas had had quite as long a period of bad trade and losses as the farmers.'

On the differentiation issue, Hubbard found himself face to face with his old opponent again.[50] In Committee on the Revenue Bill of 1880, he put the issue to Gladstone again that 'a barrister depended for income absolutely on his health and strength and the power of his brain. His position was totally different from that of another individual whose income was derived from rents'. He continued, reverting to his proposal of 1878 (see p. 115),

'In the case of a man whose income was created partly by the use of his capital and partly by the use of his industry and intelligence, he should say that in regard to the interest on his capital, he should be charged the full measure of the tax; but as to what was added to that by his industry and intelligence, it was entitled to the same remission as would be given to professional income.'

Gladstone gently reminded him that a recent Committee in which he (Mr Hubbard) as well as J. S. Mill sat, while sharing his feeling, had rejected his scheme as impracticable.

Four years later he moved a resolution requesting not only an 'abatement' on industrial incomes, but the assessment of Schedule A

---

[45] Hansard 30/IV/1885.   [46] Hansard 19/VI/1884.
[47] Hansard 19/VI/1884 (Clare Read).
[48] Board's Circular 27/VII/1879 and Board's Report for year ended 31/III/1879, p. 60.
[49] Hansard 19/VI/1884 (Illingworth).   [50] Hansard 20/VII/1880.

on net income;[51] despite his usual moderately argued, eminently reasonable speech, however, Gladstone countered with the inevitable reference to the findings of the Select Committee of 1861; he went on to admit the many hardships imposed by the Income Tax Acts, but reiterated his opinion that it was 'impossible to reconstruct the income tax on the principle of different rates and allowances in the different Schedules'. This motion may well be regarded as Hubbard's 'last round in the prolonged duel between him and his "right hon. Friend opposite"',[52] for, although he spoke again on the same subject more than once before he went to the Lords in 1887, he must have realized that Gladstone's consistent stand against reform was quite unshakeable.

The pleas for agricultural relief and for the introduction of differentiation were concerned with the principles of income tax. The controversy over the appointment of collectors concerned its administration and was the first overt trial of strength between the Government and the local officials.

Long before land tax and income tax (see p. 15), the local Commissioners had always appointed their own collectors, and this right had been written into successive Income Tax Acts. One of their main duties continued to be the examination of collectors on their arrears. But collection of tax could often be inefficient and dilatory; there were many defalcations; nor was the remuneration sufficient to attract men of the right calibre.[53] In 1864, therefore, the Government sponsored a Bill empowering the Board to appoint collectors, but it failed to pass (see p. 89). There was a second attempt in 1879, the Customs and Inland Revenue Bill[54] for that year proposing to collect Income Tax under Schedules D and E by officers appointed by the Board. This Bill passed its second reading, but there was considerable petitioning against it; the Government did, however, gain a qualified success[55] by securing the passing of a section of the Bill which provided that if the collector for any parish should not have been appointed by May 31st in any year, the Board should have the right of appointment for that and every subsequent year.

Battle was really joined over the sweeping proposal in 1883 that 'the collection under Schedules D and E should be transferred to officers of the Inland Revenue, although not as against existing collectors, but on the voidance of office by them'. National agitation was reflected in the Commons debates. The Chancellor, Hugh

[51] Hansard 25/IV/1884.
[52] Shehab (*op. cit.*), p. 183.
[53] Hubbard Report, Qq. 3909–3912.
[54] The old title for the present Finance Act.
[55] Board's Report for the year to 31/III/1880, pp. 46–47, 63–65, 81.

Childers, in a reasonable and moderate speech,[56] pointed out that the system of transfer had been steadily going on and that, with the recommendation of the Chambers of Commerce, collection ought to be finally transferred 'from the irresponsible collector on poundage to the responsible collector on salary – that is, a public officer'. A further reason was 'the extravagance of the present system, and the very decided economy which will result from the change'. He went on to point out how much more efficient collection was where undertaken by official collectors as against the record of the local official.

The opposition was led by the Liberal member for Manchester, Mr Slagg, who based his objection on any change in 'the constitutional collection of the income tax which was a serious slip in the direction of compulsory centralization'. Some members[57] thought it was a kind of centralization they would not object to, but with Hubbard and Sir Stafford Northcote against the proposal, division prospects looked bleak. W. H. Smith, later Conservative leader in the Commons, clinched the traditionalists' argument.

'The principle on which the income tax was originally established was this – that there should be Commissioners representing the people who should appoint their own clerks, their own assessors and their own collectors and that, on the other hand, the Crown, the Chancellor of the Exchequer and the Commissioners of Inland Revenue should have their Surveyor and their Inspector to see that the Crown received no damage and that the duties, as charged, were realized.'

On the division, the Government was defeated by 167 to 161 votes

The Board's reports for the period[58] exhibit a statistical pattern which faithfully reflected the prevailing economic trends. For the first two years, 1874 and 1875, although there was a steady rise in the total annual value of property and profits charged to income tax, the increases in amounts charged under Schedule D began to show an ominous decline. The year 1877, however, was catastrophic. There was a decrease in amounts charged to Schedule D of over £15 millions and the increase was a very moderate £5 millions in the succeeding year. Admittedly the raising of the exemption limit (see p. 112) was partly responsible for this fall, but it did not wholly account for what was a very real diminution in trading profits. Two more years of decreases followed and the period ended with modest increases averaging about £12 million annually. There had also been legislation to give further relief from tax to industrial profits. The

---

[56] Hansard 10/V/1883 (Childers).
[57] See, for instance, Hansard 10/V/1883 (Rylands).
[58] See, for example, the Report for the year ended 31/III/1882, p. 63.

question of a depreciation allowance[59] had been raised by the Hume Committee (see p. 71), and it seemed that some concession was allowed in this respect by the London Commissioners, which was not granted, for instance, in Birmingham. To regularize the position, an amendment had been moved in 1877 to provide that, in addition to the deduction for repairs and renewals already allowed to traders and manufacturers, a reasonable sum should also be deducted on account of depreciation. This amendment was negatived on a division. Further representations were, however, made to the Government, and in the following year it was provided that

'the Commissioners, for general or special purposes, shall, in assessing the profits or gains . . . chargeable under Schedule D . . . allow such deduction as they may think just and reasonable as representing the diminished value by reason of wear and tear during the year of any plant or machinery used for the purposes of the trade.'

The Board had also been indulging in some quiet propaganda for the Government control of collectors which, as has been mentioned, resulted finally in a Government defeat when a motion to this end was put before the Commons. Where the appointment of collectors was in their hands, the Board said the results were so successful that it 'has confirmed the opinion we have so long entertained that the taxpayers would prefer to pay, or remit their personal Income Tax under Schedules D and E to an authorized Government official at an established public office, rather than to wait for the personal application of a parochial collector'.[60] This, however, was very decidedly not the opinion of Parliament during the period.

The Board also had reason to defend itself against complaints that taxpayers had not been allowed 'abatements or exemptions to which they considered they were entitled and letters to the like effect occasionally appear in the newspapers'.[61] Investigation usually showed that the aggrieved parties had made no returns and, continued the report ironically, 'the mistake which some people make is to suppose that the officers of the Revenue can have a knowledge that they are entitled to exemption or abatement without their having made a claim'. The concluding paragraph on the subject is equally true today.

'The best advice which can be given to the public if they have reason to object to any assessment . . . is to apply to the Surveyor of Taxes for an explanation which will be readily afforded and we

---

[59] Board's Report for the year ended 31/III/1877, p. 54 and C.12 41 Vict. Cap. 15.

[60] See, for example, the Report for the year ended 31/III/1881, p. 65.

[61] See, for example, the Report for the year ended 31/III/1877, pp. 53–54.

ourselves are always ready to attend to any representations which may reach us from persons who think themselves aggrieved by assessments over which we have any control.'

The Board was also very much concerned with the establishment matters of examinations and staffing.[62] The old nomination system did not ensure automatic appointment, as the proportion of vacancies to nominations was very small and it was necessary, first of all, to have a 'test' examination, lasting one day, and then later, for the successful, a more severe competitive examination lasting three days. The institution of the open examination for entry into the Civil Service (see p. 92) was not, therefore, a complete change of procedure as far as the Tax Surveying Branch was concerned. It was followed, however, by the Playfair Commission which had recommended streamlining and staffing economies in some Government Departments. The Board was successful in having the Surveyors recognized as 'belonging entirely to the higher division' since their duties were 'so important and have to be exercised, for the most part, so independently of immediate control'. But under the Playfair formula, by October 1, 1877, it had reduced its complement of officers 'to the lowest possible limits'. These limits turned out to be too low since three years later the Treasury was being asked to sanction an increase in working strength of the Branch[63] and, in fact, a special open competition was held in August 1881, when the candidates were examined in

'higher arithmetic and the geography of the British Isles and . . . in the following additional subjects, viz.:
1. Translation to and from either French, German or Latin.
2. Euclid (the first three books).
3. Algebra up to and including quadratic equations.
4. Bookkeeping by double entry.
5. Political economy (so far as relates to rates and taxes).'

In the decade of Disraeli's first government and Gladstone's second, income tax came of age, although it was still very different from the complex mechanism of today. Its only concession to graduation was the exemption of all incomes under £150 and the allowance of the abatement of £120 to all incomes between £150 and £400 (see p. 112). The basic principle of differentiation had made no progress since its first suggestion in 1848. There were no family allowances or reliefs and no deductions under Schedule A. Schedule D[64] had the advantage

[62] Report for the year ended 31/III/1877, p. 63.
[63] Board's Report for the year ended 31/III/1882, p. 73.
[64] Board's Report for the year ended 31/III/1877, p. 55 and Rule 3, 1st case Schedule D.

of the deduction for repairs and the recent concession on depreciation, and under Schedule E[65] there had been introduced, in 1853, the familiar rule which permitted the allowance of expenses incurred 'wholly, necessarily and exclusively in the performance of the duties'. Equally familiar is the further allowance for 'keeping and maintaining a horse to enable him to perform the same' which possibly for sentimental reasons still appears in the consolidated Income Tax Act of 1952. Cases where dissatisfaction had been expressed with the decision of the General Commissioners[66] were now beginning to find their way to the Courts, and judgment had already been given on the first of what was to be a long line of tax cases on the question of allowable deductions for repairs, as the Act stated only what was not permissible. The Board, however, reviewed all such cases where the Surveyors had expressed dissatisfaction 'and we do not allow a case to be demanded by them unless we concur with their views, or the matter involves doubt or is of sufficient importance'.

The competitive examination was beginning to produce a different type of staff. The days when City Surveyors were well-known men about town, belonging to the same Hunt as the Chairman of the Board, were disappearing. So too were the characters such as the Assistant Surveyor, who was still of that rank and still in the Branch at eighty, or the Surveyor, who drove to his office in a carriage and pair and before settling down to receive his callers, adorned himself in a handsome frock coat and a beautifully embroidered smoking cap. Double-entry bookkeeping and political economy began to exert their influence on the side of orthodoxy against the picturesque. Perhaps it was some of the latter who, finding the new atmosphere not so congenial, wished to retire on the Playfair reorganization; but the Board 'had to refuse the application of several officers who desired to retire, but whose services we did not think it convenient to dispense with'.

Income tax had emerged with four most significant characteristics. It was, in the first place, an elastic element in the Revenue. Then it was important as a defence measure: 'Foreign countries should know that by raising that tax 3d or 4d in the £, without disturbing trade, without a sensible strain on ourselves, we could raise a larger sum to carry on war than other countries.'[67] Thirdly, it had been used in 1876, for the first time, simply as a means of making up the deficit on ordinary expenditure. And, finally, there is also emerging dimly the concept of income tax as a social instrument. 'The imposition of the tax had greatly contributed to a fair adjustment of taxes between the

[65] 15 Sec. 14 Vict. Cap. 15.
[66] Board's Report for the year ended 31/III/1877, p. 55.
[67] Hansard 23/III/1874 (Gladstone).

CHAPTER VIII

Taxation as a Social Instrument

THE mid-eighties marks the halfway stage between the birth of income tax and its present development; and this halfway stage has a more than merely chronological significance. The campaign for differentiation, although it had been fiercely waged, was fought mainly on an academic level. Its weapons were the speech, the report, the committee, the pamphlet; its battleground was the Commons; and no one particular class would benefit from the proposed reform. But now a second principle was being advocated, with its origins in a decidedly radical source, a principle far more practical and of far more immediate advantage to the manual wage earner. This was graduation, mention of which creeps into Hansard from time to time during the 'sixties and onwards, but usually in unfavourable terms (see p. 113). Gladstone supplied his usual forthright condemnation.

'All persons know that one of the great dangers by which the income tax was beset was the exemptions by which it was accompanied . . . When Mr Pitt introduced the income tax he proposed a variety of graduations . . . (but) it is wise to get rid of graduations and simplify distinctions as much as possible.'[1]

The principle of a graduated income tax – the final condemnation – 'tended to communism'. But this line of criticism was being rapidly outdated by the changing political and intellectual theories emerging towards the end of the century.

The Disraeli–Gladstone duel had ended in 1881 on the death of the former; and the English political scene lost much of its drama. It was not long before Gladstone's real influence, both inside and outside the House, was overshadowed by that of two new men, Parnell, the leader of Irish Home Rule movement and Chamberlain, the demagogue of the revised Radicalism. The extended electorate of 1884 distributed its favours with a fair impartiality over the years from 1885 to 1905 in the shape of three Liberal, two Conservative, and two Unionist ministries. It was a period bedevilled by the Irish question and shocked by the Boer War, a period which saw both the death of

[1] Hansard 27/V/1853. [2] Buxton (op. cit.), vol. II, p. 319.

Gladstone, the longest serving politician, and the death of Queen Victoria, the longest reigning monarch. Perhaps it was just as well; for neither would have approved the increasing amount of state socialism permeating both parties, the advanced reforms of Chamberlain being paralleled by the 'Tory democracy' of Lord Randolph Churchill. Even more menacing from the viewpoint of the old order was the rise of the 'new Unionism' stimulated by socialist theory and with a militancy which had not only fought a successful dock strike, but had inspired the foundation of the Labour Party. It is against this background that the battle for differentiation and graduation was re-engaged at the end of the last and the beginning of the present century.

The Budgets of the twenty years to 1905 have one feature in common: they all attempted to encompass, with varying success and techniques, the mounting Government expenditure arising from the growth of Government services, a growth which it was becoming increasingly difficult to control; three of these years had the additional complication of heavy military outlay. The disastrous expansion of national expenditure[2] 'was already evident in the two Budgets of 1886[3] when income tax was raised to 8d and the sensational resignation of Lord Randolph Churchill seemed to underline the necessity of the sort of radical changes which he had been contemplating'.[4]

George Goschen, however, who succeeded Churchill, represented a gain to the Government of parliamentary and financial expertize although not of radical spirit, which was equally necessary. There now commenced a run of six Budgets, the presentation of which was often more interesting than the content. For Goschen was a master of statistics, 'but his technical knowledge on such points often only dazzled when it should have enlightened the House of Commons'.[5] Even so, in this aspect at least, only Gladstone had rivalled him.

In the first Budget,[6] he was able to reduce income tax to 7d; and he introduced a further concession to the agricultural interest whereby farmers could be assessed under Schedule D at their option, which was a logical extension of their existing right to have their assessment reduced to the figure shown by their accounts.[7] Only 431 taxpayers availed themselves of the new legislation in the first year and, in fact, the procedure never became very popular.

Goschen's second Budget[8] reduced income tax to 6d, an attempt to relieve 'the struggling middle class', but one of his new imposts, the Wheel and Van tax (nicknamed irreverently the 'Veal and Ham tax'),

---

[3] 30/IV (Childers), 9/VII (Hicks-Beach).
[4] *Lord Randolph Churchill* by Winston Churchill, vol. II, pp. 190–4.
[5] B. Mallett, *British Budgets 1887–1913*, p. 41.   [6] Hansard 21/VI/1887.
[7] Board's Report to 31/III/1887, p. 112.   [8] Hansard 26/III/1888.

introduced to fill the deficit, had to be abandoned. Otherwise there was surprisingly little from a three and a quarter hours' speech, apart from the usual florid statistical dissertation. National expenditure had remained at a reasonably low level, but defence costs increased in the following year[9] and the Chancellor had to confess that the 'prospective surplus' still eluded him. Again he displayed that easy mastery in his analysis of figures, even humour, as in his reference to 'that gloomy but financially attractive subject of death duties'. But his over all view of his functions was at best pedestrian and at worst reactionary: 'I say, and I say it with some trepidation that it is better service to the state to increase the number of sources of revenue than to find simplicity.' No wonder Sir William Harcourt, the Opposition speaker on finance, was alarmed: 'It seems we are to revise the financial policy of many years which has been so beneficial . . . The great object of that policy was to diminish the taxed articles in use . . .'

But for his remaining three Budgets, the produce of income tax per penny was beginning to rise after a fall during the first three. In his 1890 Budget,[10] therefore, Goschen was able to hold the tax at 6d, while conceding a change in the allowance of losses which permitted those incurred under one schedule to be set off against the income assessable under another. It had been a prosperous year in spite of the Baring crisis and 'I thought at one time it might be reasonable to allow every Income Tax payer to deduct £400 from his income before paying Income Tax, but I was staggered to find that this would involve a loss of £4·7 millions out of a total receipt of £13 millions'. He had to content himself with a measure of relief to 'the class that begins to wear the black coat' from the Inhabited House Duty.[11]

The last two Budgets[12] were very much mark-time measures, maintaining taxation as it stood and managing to survive Harcourt's attack that 'ingenuity is not what is most wanted in dealing with finance. You do not want a number of small devices for escaping the fact that you are spending more money than you have.' That was indeed the fundamental criticism of Goschen as a Chancellor of the Exchequer. Certainly he restored the financial reputation of the Conservatives which had been languishing since the days of Peel and, possibly, Disraeli (see p. 66). But, as Harcourt had said, there were too many small taxes and in his passion for figures almost for their own sake, he failed, either through lack of courage, or conviction, to make a root and branch revision of taxation. He had said in his Budget speech of 1891 that the reorganization of income tax alone

[9] Hansard 15/IV/1889.   [10] Hansard 17/IV/1890.
[11] The Inhabited House Duty relief was in the form of graduation – see B. Mallet (*op. cit.*), p. 37.
[12] Hansard 23/IV/1891, Hansard 11/IV/1892.

would need a session.[13] Gladstone, wise in the experience of fifty years, interposed 'A century'. Goschen might well have agreed.

Harcourt, the persistent critic of Goschen, found himself faced with an increase in expenditure not covered by increased revenue and was compelled to raise income tax by a penny.[14] The previous Chancellor accused him of adopting 'the latest automatic invention; he puts a penny in the slot and the thing is done'. This initial clash, in fact, illustrated a basic cleavage in theories of taxation, the liberal tendency being towards direct taxation, although still an imperfect weapon.

It was the Budget of 1894,[15] however, which was the Budget of the period. There was a considerable deficit to be met:[16] Harcourt refused to 'peddle with small taxes' and at long last introduced the expected death duties on a graduated scale, the significance of which will be discussed in a later context. He also put a further penny on income tax, raising it to 8d but there were compensations. An allowance of one-tenth, later one-eighth, in respect of lands and of one-sixth in respect of houses was given as a deduction from the gross assessment and the total exemption limit was raised to £160. There was an abatement of £160 in place of the previous £150 on all incomes up to £400 and of £100 on those between £400 and £500. So Harcourt, instead of discussing plaintively, as Goschen had so often done, the relief he would have liked to grant the middle class, implemented his predecessor's pious aspirations. 'It may seem,' he said, 'a trifling measure of relief, but it affects a vast number of Income Tax payers – over 500,000.'[17] The extension would cost £840,000 in a full year.

Harcourt's third and last Budget[18] was inevitably something of an anticlimax after the stern contest over passing his 1894 measures. Its noncontroversial nature is shown by the fact that it went through both Houses within a month. Almost immediately afterwards the Government fell.

The Budgets, seven in all, of the new Chancellor, Sir Michael Hicks-Beach, fall into two sharply contrasted periods. The first three[19] cover three years of comparative inaction, notable only for the much dreaded £100 million Budget and an extension of the abatement system affording relief on incomes up to £700,[20] which won the commendation of one General Commissioner who said: 'We have constantly before us appeals by small traders and people in a small way in the professions, which show that it is a great injustice and

[13] Hansard 23/IV/1891.   [14] Hansard 24/IV/1893.   [15] Hansard 16/IV/1894.
[16] The deficit was £2.4 millions, Mallet (*op. cit.*), p. 79.
[17] Hansard 16/IV/1894.   [18] Hansard 2/V/1895.
[19] Hansard 16/IV/1896, Hansard 29/IV/1897, Hansard 21/IV/1898.
[20] The amendments of the third Budget – see Mallet (*op. cit.*), p. 374.

hardship that Income Tax should be imposed on them at all.'[21] The country could well afford it; the remissions of 1894 had already been more than overtaken; and the long days of prosperity seemed never ending.

1899 was the watershed. The year started auspiciously enough, for, although expenditure had exceeded the estimates, so too had revenue, especially income tax, and the balance was still on the right side. Despite this, the Chancellor proposed to reduce the provision for debt repayment. This could not, as the opposition speakers pointed out, possibly be defended considering the flourishing state of the nation. But the fact of the matter was that he was totally opposed to the imposition of fresh taxation and indeed to the current trend in favour of state socialism.

'I daresay I am old fashioned in my ideas,' he said, 'but I look with alarm on the tendency of the present day quite irrespective of political opinion . . . to look to the Exchequer and Central Government for superintendence, for assistance, for inspection and for control in all kinds of departments of life, in all kinds of relations between individuals in which, in the old days, the Government of the country was never deemed capable of acting at all.'[22]

By October, however, Parliament was being asked to vote £10 millions for the army in South Africa and from then on 'Black Michael' was faced with the task of raising revenue in amounts which suited neither his training, his ability nor, most important, his convictions.

The Boer war began with a strange optimism in which Sir Michael Hicks-Beach could reasonably share, since he had a large surplus which he proceeded to reinforce by adding a further fourpence to income tax, the rate thus becoming 1s.[23] There were in all four financial statements during the year, the net result of which was to raise more money by borrowing than by taxation, a policy open to criticism in view of the continuing commercial expansion. In the following year income tax was raised to 1s 2d and for the first time in budgetary history, a higher revenue was estimated for from direct than from indirect taxation.[24] But in view of the now waning prosperity of the country, and the waxing cost of ordinary as well as military expenditure, the regimen of borrowing was continued, and this imbalance lasted during the last war Budget; although it is true income tax was increased again by a token penny to 1s 3d and the old corn registration tax revived, which latter clearly had imperial preference possibilities.

[21] Hansard 1/IV/1898 (Broadhurst).   [22] Hansard 13/IV/1899.
[23] Hansard 5/III/1900.   [24] Hansard 18/X/1901.

This was also the last Budget of Sir Michael Hicks-Beach. He had, in the Treasury's opinion, 'a remarkable turn for finance' and on his retirement Harcourt paid tribute to 'the good that you have done and the evil that you have prevented'.[25] But, as many of his contemporary critics, including Harcourt himself, pointed out, he did not defray as much of the war expenditure out of taxation as he could or should have done; the fraction generally accepted as the contribution of taxation to the military chest during the Boer war is between a quarter and a third[26] as contrasted with nearly half during the Napoleonic and Crimean wars. His seven years' stewardship had seen the extremes of both prosperity and fiscal embarrassment; and his retirement marked the end of the Gladstonian conception of finance.

This retirement had been triggered off by the resignation of Salisbury, due to ill-health; Balfour took over the Premiership and C. T. Ritchie became Chancellor. He was a convinced Free Trader, and in his first and only Budget[27] repealed the Corn Duty which Chamberlain had seen as the first step towards 'fair trade'. Direct tax he relieved by reducing income tax by fourpence to 11d. His term as Chancellor, however, was short; in a Government reshuffle during which Balfour managed to drop the extremists on each wing he was, in effect, dismissed.[28]

The new Chancellor was Austen Chamberlain. He had proved himself as Financial Secretary and he sponsored two Budgets in 1904 and 1905. In the first of these,[29] in view of the current financial situation, he raised income tax by a penny to 1s. He was able to hold it at this level the following year,[30] thanks to the gradual revival from the depression subsequent to the Boer war. But housekeeping, which had been the main preoccupation of successive Chancellors, especially Goschen and Hicks-Beach, and of Parliament as well, was now being replaced by an intense interest in the reform of income tax itself which, through discussions on differentiation, and graduation, had been gradually building up over the period.

In the first half of Goschen's six-year period as Chancellor, the supporters of differentiation were comparatively subdued. For one thing an increasing amount of attention was being focussed on the unprecedented growth in public expenditure;[31] for another, Hubbard was now in the Lords and a new spokesman for fiscal reform had not yet emerged. T. P. O'Connor protested that 'so long as the income tax does not make a distinction between the property which has been

---

[25] *Sir Michael Hicks-Beach* by Lady Victoria Hicks-Beach.
[26] Taxation generally during the Boer War: see Mallet (*op. cit.*), p. 201.
[27] Hansard 23/IV/03.   [28] R. C. K. Ensor (*op. cit.*), p. 374.
[29] Hansard 19/IV/04.   [30] Hansard 10/IV/05.
[31] See for example any of Gladstone's Budget speeches.

handed down from father to son for generations . . . and the poor
transitory and uncertain income which the professional man makes
out of his own brain and loses with his death . . . it is an illogical
and unjust tax'.[32] But Celtic fervour was no substitute for Hubbard's
painstaking economic expositions and it was not until George
Bartley[33] emerged from a group of likeminded young reformers that
the differentiation campaign got under way again.

Bartley had, at first, confined himself to what he considered administrative abuses in taxation practice, such as the payment of
collectors by poundage,[34] where he had the support of both the
Government and the Board; and he had made an interesting contribution to the 1889 Budget debate on the burden of taxation upon
various classes.[35] His first full scale attack was mounted two years
later when he proposed

'That in the opinion of this House a Committee should be appointed to enquire into the income tax, the mode of its collection,
the system of appeal, the payment of poundage for collection and
generally to report on the present working and incidence of the tax
as now imposed and whether some fairer system could be adopted by a
different rate being imposed on income derived from realized capital
to that derived from industry.'[36]

His speech is a fair summary of the case for differentiation and he
pin-pointed two current features, one of incidence and one of administration, which clearly needed examination. On incidence, he
held 'the increase in the product of the income tax is that a large
portion of the community at the bottom of the social scale is being
gradually drawn within the operation of Schedule D' and on administration he complained

'The Surveyor of Taxes is paid by salary, but all other officers are
paid by poundage; and the result is if ever you have a difficulty or
complaint, the Inland Revenue turn you over to the local people and
the local people turn you over to the Inland Revenue; and between
the one and the other you can rarely get what is a reasonable
adjustment.'

He was, however, incorrect in citing as examples of inequity a
medical officer being unable to obtain an expense deduction for cost
of drugs or a trader not being allowed depreciation; these matters
had been covered by legislation in 1853 (see p. 121) and 1878 (see p. 123).

---

[32] Hansard 25/IV/1887.   [33] Shehab (*op. cit.*), p. 183.
[34] Hansard 13/II/1890.   [35] Hansard 15/IV/1889.
[36] Hansard 24/II/1891. Employments, it should be noted, were still within
Schedule D.

Bartley won considerable support, but W. H. Smith, speaking in reply for Goschen, who was ill, made the usual defence that reform was not a practical possibility when two Committees had found against it and that clearly to differentiate in favour of all earned incomes would give an inequitable amount of relief to the higher ranges of such income, as against the lower ranges of investment income. The majority against was fifty-five.

In the following year, Bartley narrowed his field of attack by suggesting that earned income should be relieved only up to £400 a year,[37] thus by-passing the argument, which Gladstone had used so effectively (see p. 82), that unlimited differentiation favoured the rich businessman against the poor investor.[38] Goschen himself replied on this occasion and was no more accommodating to this modified plan. 'I would not be responsible for the working of an Act which would relieve a person assessed under Schedule D and at the same time, leave so many persons exactly in the same position without relief.'[39]

After the failure of this attempt at conciliation, Bartley reverted to his old radical plan of pressing for the exemption of earned income altogether. The importance of his suggestion, however, survived for it did represent a genuine solution to the problem of reconciling differentiation with equitable distribution. His own personal contribution to reform now began to fade into the background; for although he was a consistent differentiationist, he had never supported graduation, which he did not consider practicable. His supporters were disappointed. 'I was sorry to hear my Hon. Friend make unfavourable observation with reference to a graduated Income Tax. Many of us believe that a graduated system is not only feasible, but fair, reasonable and just.'[40] From now on the graduationists began to force the pace.

The idea if a graduated tax had been discussed by the Radicals as early as Chartist days, but references to it in Hansard are rare until the fourth quarter of the century. In 1877, for instance, Morgan Lloyd and Chadwick, the accountant,[41] had made a considered plea for a form of graduated tax. Their speeches seem to have had little immediate effect, but the movement gained marked impetus from the publication of Joseph Chamberlain's Radical Programme in 1885,[42] which came out strongly in favour of state socialism and the use of taxation as an instrument of social reform; and this taxation should be on a graduated scale.

His programme did not stay simply 'appropriately bound in the brightest of red covers', but was disseminated up and down the

---

[37] Hansard 26/V/1892.   [38] Hansard 24/III/1863.   [39] Hansard 26/V/1892.
[40] Quoted by Shehab (*op. cit.*), p. 188.   [41] Hansard 16/IV/1877.
[42] *The Times* 15/IX/85, quoted by Shehab (*op. cit.*), p. 190.

country during his electioneering campaign in the autumn of 1885 and before. Early in the year he began with differentiation: 'Is it really certain that the precarious income of a struggling professional man ought to pay in the same proportion as the income of a man who derives it from invested securities? Is it altogether such an unfair thing that we should tax all incomes according to this amount?'[43] By summer he had decided on some form of graduation. 'It need not necessarily be a graduated income tax. It might be more convenient to levy it in the shape of a graduated death duty or house tax. I care nothing at all about the method.'[44] When autumn arrived he had made up his mind.

'Taxation ought to involve equality of sacrifice and I do not see how this result is to be obtained except by some form of graduated taxation – that is, taxation which is proportionate to the superfluities of the taxpayer. When I am told that this is a new fangled and a revolutionary doctrine, I wonder if my critics have read any elementary books on the subject, because if they had, they must have seen that a graduated income tax is not a novelty in this country.'[45]

His opinion was reinforced by Sydney Buxton, the best fiscal historian of his day, who advocated both by his writings and his speeches in the House the principle of graduation.[46] As early as 1891, when Bartley was proposing his Committee, he came out strongly in support of the motion. On income tax itself he declared:

'Let it be fairly graduated from the bottom by means of abatements and, in the same way, be graduated as high up as it is possible to take these abatements . . . I assert that the Government could go a good deal further than they have gone in graduating the tax at the lower end of the scale, and I do not see why we should not have a system of graduation extended up to say £1,000.'[47]

But the most effective advocate of graduation, both in theory and in practice, was Sir William Harcourt.[48] Already in 1890 he was expressing qualified approval of the idea. Speaking on Goschen's reduction of Inhabited House Duty, he commented on the Chancellor's admission that it was not merely the money he considered, but the fact that the rate at which the tax should be levied should be less in the case of persons with small incomes. 'That is a very important principle of finance . . . I believe it is a sound principle of finance . .

[43] Speech at Ipswich 14/I/1885.　　[44] Speech at Hull 5/VIII/1885.
[45] Speech at Warrington 8/IX/1885.
[46] See, for example, *Finance and Politics* (*op. cit.*), vol. I, p. 312.
[47] Hansard 24/II/1891.
[48] Hansard 22/IV/1890; see also Shehab (*op. cit.*), p. 195, footnote on Clapham's somewhat unjust opinion of Harcourt.

I thought it necessary to take notice of this because the principle itself is far more important than the application of it the Chancellor of the Exchequer is making today.'

Four years later he took full advantage of his theories on graduation by introducing the income tax reforms already mentioned and especially by the massive revision of death duties.[49] This consisted of progressively graduated rates ranging from 1 % on estates between £100 and £500 to 8 % on estates of £1 million. It has been said that Harcourt intended also to inaugurate a graduated income tax but on the advice of the Board abandoned it 'not on merits . . . but because it would overload the Budget . . .' Certainly he had declared in the House

'I shall be asked the question: "If you graduate the Income Tax down on the lower scale, why not graduate it up on the larger incomes?" In principle there is nothing to be said against such a system; indeed there is every argument in its favour. The difficulties which lie in the way are of an administrative and a practical nature which, as yet, I have not been able to find means to overcome.'[50]

A radical demagogue, a fiscal historian and a prominent politician made a redoubtable combination in favour of graduation. Theoretical backing was supplied by Professor F. T. Edgeworth[51] who made a close examination of the classic dicta about taxation in the light of the old Beccaria–Bentham maxim of the greatest happiness of the greatest number and 'the acme of Socialism is thus, for the moment sighted'. But he was fully alive to the fact that the strict application of his theory,[52] which meant that 'incomes above a certain point should be cut down to that point; those below that point would be completely untaxed, the point being decided by the amount of revenue necessary to defray the expenses of the year' was hardly practical politics. It would act as a disincentive; people would be unwilling to work and the rich tend to be driven away. Then 'taxation extended beyond its proper objects will be abused'. Thirdly, there was always the danger of evasion. He, therefore, so amended the strict logic of his theories that the progress of industry and the accumulation of savings would not be impeded; this was the basis of his 'minimum sacrifice' conception with which he allied a plan for differentiation and personal allowances.

Edgeworth was not the only economist who defended graduation. Amongst his contemporaries J. Burns should be mentioned, who had

---

[49] James: *Rosebery*, p. 346.
[50] A. G. Gardiner: *Sir William Harcourt*, vol. II, p. 282 and Hansard 16/IV/1894.
[51] *Papers relating to Political Economy*, *passim* and vol. II, p. 103.
[52] Shehab (*op. cit.*), generally, especially p. 200.

a very practical plan for imposing a graduated tax.[53] 'The solution of the difficulty (of imposing a maximum tax in the first instance and giving relief by repayment) can, however, be found in the retention of the present system as a means of obtaining the first quota of taxation and by the direct superimposition of a graduated tax on incomes exceeding a certain sum.'[54] On the very valid point as to whether it would be possible 'to obtain and enforce reliable returns for assessment without undue friction and with any amount of certainty',[55] Burns suggests the submission of all returns for assessment by the Special Commissioners. This was, in fact, the procedure laid down by Lloyd George's supertax fourteen years later.

But although support for graduation was increasing steadily, there was still a very considerable body of opposition headed by C. F. Bastable[56] and the expert on taxation G. H. Blunden.[57] The latter summed up the contemporary opposition by stating three possible policies for income tax: abolition, reduction of the normal level, or its full utilization for ordinary purposes. The second course appeared to Blunden to be 'the easiest and the best. It is recommended alike by the considerations springing from an elevated and far seeing patriotism and by a careful estimate of possible present advantages. Neither of the other two policies combines these merits, whilst the last carries with it the grave disadvantage of encouraging and perpetuating the evils of easy, resourceless and ill-regulated finance . . .' It was the old argument that income tax equalled extravagance.

But far more formidable was the opposition of the Board itself. Bartley thought he understood the reason. 'I have been in public office myself and I know that permanent officials do not like revolutionary change in their Department.'[58] This was a somewhat superficial view to take, for the Board's hostility to reform was rooted in the honest conviction that the Act of 1810 needed no amendment in principle. When Bartley moved his resolution in February, 1891, for the appointment of a Committee 'to enquire into the income tax', the debate provoked the private printing of a pamphlet entitled: 'Some opinions on certain Recently Revived Propositions Suggested with a view to a More Equal Incidence of the Income Tax'.[59] The subject is dealt with under three heads, inequality of pressure,

[53] 'A Graduated Income Tax' originally published in the *Westminster Review*, November 1896.
[54] J. Burns (*op. cit.*), p. 11.   [55] J. Burns (*op. cit.*), p. 13.
[56] *Public Finance*, p. 308.
[57] 'The Position and Function of the Income Tax in the British Fiscal System', originally published in the *Economic Journal*, December 1892.
[58] Quoted by Shehab (*op. cit.*), p. 185.
[59] 'Some opinions . . .', by F.L.R. There is a copy of this pamphlet in the Board's library.

differentiation and graduation, and, by means of quotations from 'eminent statesmen who have held the office of First Lord of the Treasury or Chancellor of the Exchequer', their disapproval of any alterations in the Act and, by implication, the author's also is simply demonstrated. This is significant since the writer, F.L.R., as he signs himself, was F. L. Robinson, the author of the Taxes Management Act of 1880 and a member of the Board. It is equally significant to note that the arguments against reform were based, not on current economic thinking of, say, the Bastable School, but simply on the authority of traditional views.

Robinson would have been on surer ground and would have gained a more sympathetic hearing had he pleaded, as he could justifiably have done, general administrative difficulties. These are nowhere dealt with in the Board's reports for the period which are almost totally statistical, apart from bare comments on changes in the law and a summary of the alterations since 1842 contained in the report for the year ended March 31, 1900. They are, however, reflected in the pages of Hansard and in a miscellany of sources which build up a reasonably complete picture of the day to day running of an ever expanding Department.

In the first place there was a chronic shortage of staff. The Playfair reforms (see pp. 122 and 123) had caused a run-down in numbers which had never been fully made up and complements always seemed to lag behind the ever increasing burden of work. In 1894 the Surveyors, who were the first Civil Service grade to organize themselves, petitioned the Board on their understaffing which had been aggravated by such legislative charges as the availability of losses against other income (see p. 127) and the commutation of the assessors' and collectors' poundage which had resulted in decreased activity on the part of those disgruntled officials. Questions on the matter were asked in the House; for instance, in 1900, a member called attention to the necessity of forming new tax districts and increasing the number of Surveyors 'upon their capacity', he went on, 'upon having proper time to discharge their duties and having intellectual capacities which are not affected by the drudgery and the strain of too much thrown upon their shoulders, depends the successful ingathering of the revenue of this country'. Another speaker mentioned the unsatisfactory nature of the clerical assistants.[60] They were, in fact, all unestablished, their status was that of employees of the Surveyor and their wages would rarely exceed £1 per week. In reply, the shortage of surveying and clerical staff was admitted: 'the Treasury was in constant touch with the Board of Inland Revenue with a view to remedying matters.' There was little immediate improvement; in

[60] Hansard 4/V/1900 (Heywood Johnstone & H. Broadhurst).

1905, a London accountant wrote: 'Surveyors of Taxes have always been, and are still, greatly overworked, frequently having to devote their Sundays, as well as every hour of the week, to their work.'[61]

Conditions of work offered no consolation. 'The doorway which gives access to the Revenue offices possesses the quality of squalor in a more marked degree. Its steps reek with a perpetual moisture; the walls of the lobby within are of a grim nondescript colour; and the staircase leading to the offices winds gloomily aloft until it seems to lose itself in darkness.' That description comes from a novel written by a one-time Surveyor.[62] It was also another one-time Surveyor who wrote a corroborative account of his district.[63] 'I fell, with a most unpleasant bump into a perfectly beastly little set of offices, approached by a mean insanitary staircase, with an outlook on to the stagnant waters of a canal and a general atmosphere of decayed vegetable matter.' Training, of course, was almost non-existent. The hero of the novel quoted briefly above, was informed by his Surveyor: 'We have all far too much to do to teach anybody anything'; there is a parallel remark in the Surveyor's autobiography. 'My Surveyor made it clear to me that, the Board of Inland Revenue in their wisdom, having thought fit to send him a raw assistant, he had neither the time nor the inclination to instruct me in my duties.'

The avowed policy of the Board at that time was 'the wish to provide that the work should be performed by fewer men, harder worked and better paid and at a less total cost to the State'[64] and although this statement referred to the excise service, no doubt taxes was not immune. Certainly one of the Chief Inspectors of the time must have been a grim character. From the Surveyor-novelist again: 'The Chief Inspector's grey eyes shone with a steely glitter, his thin lips were tightly compressed and the voice which came from between them was as cold and keen as the east wind . . .' It seems less like fiction, on reading in the Surveyor-autobiographer:

'I have not in my life met many really cruel men, but for two or three years at Somerset House I was attached as confidential assistant to the Chief Inspector of Taxes of that time, who was undoubtedly a very cruel man. In his ruthlessness he had no use for inefficiency and any poor man who did not come up to his standards was destined to have a thoroughly bad time.'

[61] See A. M. Scarff, F.S.A.A.: 'The Income Tax Problem', p. 11, originally printed in the *Magazine of Commerce*, July 1905.
[62] The quotations from the novel refer to *The Government Official* by A. H. Norway. He did not, in fact, stay in the service of the Board for very long.
[63] The quotations from the autobiography are from *Not So Humdrum* by R. W. Harris. He later transferred to another Department.
[64] Board's Report for the year ended 31/III/1888.

The attempt to administer income tax efficiently and fairly must, it is true, have been frustrating to the Board and their Surveyors alike. In many districts very few accounts would be submitted except those of registered companies or figures, more or less accurate, furnished in support of appeals. If a Surveyor was bold enough to ask for accounts in support of a return and the taxpayer complained, an Inspector might well be sent from Somerset House to interview the complainant and effect a compromise settlement. A Surveyor was entirely dependent on the procedure of his Commissioners when the mechanics of making assessments was under consideration. A question in the House on this very point drew an illuminating reply: 'Commissioners of Income Tax (i.e. General Commissioners) are empowered by law to require such information in such form as, in their discretion, they consider is necessary for the purpose of the Income Tax Acts. It is, therefore, entirely within the discretion of the Commissioners to accept, or not to accept, balance sheets as evidence as well as to determine what other evidence, if any, they may require.'[65]

But shortage of staff, squalid working conditions, unsympathetic management and restricted authority were not quite the whole reason for official opposition to reform. The Inland Revenue statistics themselves seemed to show that a graduated scale rising from 1s to 2s on incomes over £5,000 would only give an increase in tax yield of £3 millions.[66] That these estimates were clearly inaccurate is obvious when the product of supertax for the period 1909–10 is considered, but it was on the strength of them that Austen Chamberlain based his resistance to graduation. For this comparatively trivial amount

'the income tax is ruined as a great engine for procuring revenue and if you superimpose on an assessment at the source a further assessment in the case of wealthy people for the purpose of graduation, this will enormously increase the cost, will entail wholly new machinery, will become excessively inquisitorial and will offend powerful interests. I do not think the House could devise a more ingenious way of making the income tax unpopular, ultimately involving its total repeal.'

The pressure from the graduationists was steadily increasing. Starting with Burns's pamphlet (see p. 134), the conception of a superimposed (hence the prefix 'super') tax had been gradually gaining ground and was beginning to be ventilated in the House, if in a somewhat tentative fashion. In 1902, for example, Charles Trevelyan,[67] in raising the issue said he was aware that 'all the authorities in the

[65] Hansard 17/III/1893 (Sir J. T. Hibbert).
[66] Hansard 1/IV/1904 (Austen Chamberlain).
[67] Trevelyan's speech and the various replies, Hansard 1/VI/1902.

House were against a graduated tax'. He thought, however, that 'if graduation began at incomes of £3,000 or £2,000, the difficulty of collection would be removed'. There was considerable opposition as the speakers had anticipated; 'extraordinary change' was one of the kinder epithets and Hicks-Beach, with an irony peculiar to ex-Chancellors of the Exchequer, questioned the possibility of telling whether a person had made a proper return of his income. 'You have to trust to the honour of men and that is a very great temptation.' Three years later Trevelyan and John Herbert Lewis[68] raised the question again, but Chamberlain refused to have either graduation or differentiation initially included in the terms of reference of the Select Committee which he had now agreed should be set up.

This promise had been made by two successive Chancellors and was eventually redeemed by a third. It must be said that this Committee had been a long time coming; the reformers had systematically interspersed between their demands for differentiation and gradua-tion pleas for a further enquiry into the incidence and administration of income tax ever since the reports of 1851 and 1862 which had so long acted as an excuse for successive governments to say that two investigations within ten years had found no reforms possible. As an excuse this was wearing somewhat thin since Sidney Buxton had pointed out 'they were not *bona fide* enquiries. That of 1851 was an abortive Committee; that of 1862 was appointed against the wish of the Government, strongly opposed by the Chancellor and had not a fair opportunity of enquiring properly into the great questions affecting the tax.'[69] Not that the present Committee was all that had been asked for, being Departmental only, although graduation and differentiation were now to be considered. But it was the first victory by the reformers for forty years and more; if Gladstone had still been alive, it is doubtful whether they would have been able to claim even this modified success.

[68] Trevelyan and John Herbert Lewis, Hansard 23/V/1905.
[69] Hansard 24/II/1891.

CHAPTER IX

Trial by Battle – I

THE thirteen years' period covering 1906 to 1918 begins with a Select Committee on Income Tax and ends with one in prospect, which actually reported in 1920. But between the income tax of 1906 and that of 1918 lay a whole world of difference. A comparatively simple engine of finance which Asquith could say, without laying himself open to a charge of stating the obvious, had just reached the status of 'an integral and permanent part of our financial system' had developed into a sophisticated mechanism making an indispensable contribution to the national income.

This transformation was, of course, only part of the wholesale changes sweeping over both Great Britain and Europe affecting every aspect of social, political and economic life. In this country an obvious example was the Parliament of 1906, probably the first truly middle class Parliament. The Conservative opposition looked at the Government benches with some distaste, especially when Campbell-Bannerman, the new Prime Minister, would have none of their traditional delaying tactics. 'Enough of this foolery!' could well serve as the slogan of the new constitutional attitude. Asquith and Lloyd George were typical representatives of the twentieth century type of politician, the one a man of middle-class origins with a tough legalistic intellect, and the other of more humble family whose initial legal training was overshadowed by his magnetic and popular appeal, as the Lords discovered to their cost.

Such were the sort of men who made the Edwardian era, contrary to the popular conception of its stability, an era of ferment, change and bitter political controversy. Nor was this all; behind the general unrest, 'the thunderclouds were gathering'[1] and the ensuing four years' storm left in its wake a world, a Europe, an England and for that matter, a taxation system that could never be the same again. None of these tremendous developments, however, only a short eight years away, were then remotely suspected by the veteran finance expert Sir Charles Dilke,[2] elected as Chairman of the Select Com-

---

[1] The phrase is Lloyd George's.
[2] Report of the Select Committee on Income Tax, Cmd. 365.

mittee in May, 1906. But for an unfortunate divorce scandal he might well have been the leader of the Liberal Party; his consolation was that by the Report of his Committee he influenced as radical a reform as he could ever have accomplished in office.

The terms of reference were simple:[3] 'to inquire into and report upon the practicability of graduating the Income Tax and of differentiating, for the purpose of the tax, between permanent and precarious incomes'. The Committee sat during May, June and July and its report was ordered to be printed in November. That this report was unanimous owed a great deal to the personality of the Chairman himself who was in attendance at every session. Evidence was taken from various officials of the Inland Revenue Department and from 'several Members of Parliament, bankers, statisticians and others' some of whom had been examined the year before by the Ritchie Committee:[4] this Departmental Committee had, to a certain extent, already covered topics which would normally have been considered by the Dilke Committee.[5]

As far as differentiation was concerned, there was general agreement between the official side and the experts that it could be introduced. 'The classification of permanent and precarious corresponds really very closely with our own classification of assessed at the source and directly assessed',[6] and there would be 'no unsurmountable difficulty from an administrative point of view'.[7] This was the view of the Chairman of the Board, and fairly summarized the official attitude. There would be minor complications over 'mixed incomes where there is an income derived from the employment of capital and the addition thereto of personal exertion'.[8] This point was also touched upon by Walter Gyles, a Special Commissioner.[9] He also foresaw the problem of definition; it was 'a further complication of the income tax law and of the income tax practice' and 'you would have to have very stringent and accurate instructions which should be followed similarly throughout the whole country by surveyors of taxes'. The question of evasion also arose; if a man paid interest, deducted tax from it, but did not disclose it; 'we should tax him at the reduced rate on what appeared to be his earnings and when he paid his interest he would probably deduct at the higher rate and say nothing about it.'[10] He would thus save on the difference between the two rates of tax.

For the suggested mechanism of relief was by applying a lower rate

---

[3] The terms of reference and the witnesses, p. iii, paras 1 and 3.
[4] Report of the Departmental Committee on Income Tax, Cmd. 2575.
[5] The Ritchie Committee and its relations with the Dilke Committee, p. xv (4).
[6] Q. 111.   [7] Q. 115.   [8] Q. 116.
[9] Qq. 2706–2849, 3170–3222, esp. Q. 2725.   [10] Q. 116.

of tax to earned as compared with unearned income. 'You could tax all incomes from property at 1s 6d and all earned incomes at 1s; you could make a rough distinction that would probably answer between the two classes of income.'[11] An alternative scheme – an echo of the old 1861 idea of Hubbard's – was an abatement of one third in favour of earned incomes. 'It is a possible way of doing it,' said a member of the Board, 'and in many respects rather an easy way.'[12] The possibilities of this latter procedure were not, for some reason, explored further by the Committee.

It was on the question of graduation, however, that the real divergences of opinion appeared. The official view was uncompromisingly hostile. The Chairman of the Board estimated that there were only 12,500 taxpayers whose income exceeded £5,000.[13] A supertax, graduated from 3d to 1s would only yield about £3·2 millions.[14] Against this somewhat paltry sum had to be set the cost of collection,[15] the problems of administration[16] and the danger of draining capital out of the country.[17] The Chief Inspector faithfully underlined the arguments of the Chairman. It would be necessary to serve 100,000 forms in the first instance[18] and a staff of experts[19] 'would be needed to deal with these returns' on account of the involved character of many of them. The whole exercise would be attended with a 'great deal of irritation'.[20] The Clerk to Commissioners for the City of London[21] added the weight of his authority to these considerations. He had not even been too sure of the merits of differentiation; he was wholly against graduation. He and the late Lord Addington – originally Mr J. G. Hubbard – had spent hours trying to devise a system of graduation 'but in the end we were absolutely convinced that it was not workable' and with regard to the flight of capital, 'I candidly admit that I should prefer to put my capital in a country where there is no income tax'.[22]

It is easy to understand and sympathize with Somerset House at this stage.[23] The taxation machine, with an efficient staff, if not always adequate in numbers, was functioning in an entirely satisfactory manner. Procedures had been settled, and the whole structure now had a solid hundred years of experience backing it. This organization was now being asked to absorb into its well-tried system two novel schemes which might very well need the introduction of new powers to insist on returns of total income and which might finally

---

[11] Q. 419.   [12] Q. 420 (Mallet).   [13] Q. 41.   [14] Q. 74.
[15] Q. 86.   [16] Q. 92.   [17] Q. 177.   [18] Q. 976.   [19] Q. 955.
[20] Q. 977.   [21] Sir Thomas Hewitt, Qq. 2062–2407.
[22] See especially Qq. 2253 and 2308 on differentiation, Q. 2312 on graduation and Q. 2388 on the flight of capital.
[23] Somerset House and the new system, Qq. 1064 and 2976.

involve the collapse of the fundamental principle of deduction of tax at source. If it had to be done, the Revenue would manage 'of course'; as the Chief Inspector remarked, 'we could do anything, but what (income tax) would be under the system you are speaking of, I hesitate to say'.[24]

But there was a well-informed body of opposition to the pessimistic official outlook on graduation. The Board's statistics were challenged by an Australian statistician; the supertax yield on his figures was nearly £1 million more than that of the Board.[25] Professor Bowley of the London School of Economics had been 'very much struck with the difficulty of getting exact estimates'. 'Bold round numbers' were quoted by official sources and 'not examined again, but quoted again and again'. The result was that this round number given rather hastily 'is received as one of the standard measurements of our national welfare when, in reality, it has no basis'.[26] The flight of capital was a myth: 'Ask yourself the question, Sir; where are they going to take it to?'[27] and in any case not all the potential supertax payers would have large investments. The dangers of evasion had been exaggerated;[28] 'agents and solicitors who make the return and keep the account are reputable' and 'out of £502 millions assessed under Schedule D, about four-fifths is assessed at source'. Even the problem of making full returns should not prove insuperable. As it was, a claim to abatement had to be supported by a full return; 'asking for a personal declaration from a man who has an income of above £700 (the abatement limit), 'is no more inquisitorial than asking for a declaration from a man who has income under £700'.[29]

Bernard Mallet,[30] a member of the Board examined by the Committee, accused its members of approaching their deliberations 'with their minds made up, some in favour of both these devices and disposed to brush aside the technical and theoretical difficulties in the way'.[31] This criticism is hardly justified since the Committee was at pains to point out in its report the reasons for its conclusions.[32] The official estimate of the proposed supertax yield 'may be held to err on the side of understatement'.[33] With regard to the 'emigration of capital',[34] this would only happen 'if a sudden increase of income tax were to take place while there exist countries having less direct taxation than our own'. There had been no specific evidence of a possible increase in evasion; on the contrary, the evidence seemed to show that there was no increase in evasion when the taxation rate

---

[24] Q. 1043.
[25] Mr T. A. Coghlan's evidence, Qq. 1321–1686; Shehab (*op. cit.*), p. 233.
[26] Q. 1158.   [27] Q. 1534.   [28] See especially Qq. 1805 and 1806.
[29] Q. 809.   [30] Qq. 216–473.   [31] *British Budgets*, vol. I, p. 280.
[32] Conclusions: p. xx onwards   [33] Supertax, p. xx (28).   [34] p. xxvii (60).

was increased, as for example, in the Crimean and Boer wars.[35] This was, in fact, not wholly conclusive since the national income was rising continuously throughout the period in money terms. Admittedly 'it was a difficult thing to work differentiation and graduation in one tax';[36] 'many of the difficulties . . . are real though in some cases pushed too far'.[37] The Committee summarized[38] the conclusions by finding that graduation was practicable, but would be better introduced in the form of a supertax and that differentiation was practicable also, especially if limited to incomes below £2,000 or £3,000. Collection of tax at source should be maintained; 'abandonment of the system . . . would be disastrous'.

The Committee had fulfilled its terms of reference and published its findings with admirable dispatch; and the reports of its examination of witnesses give an illuminating picture of two contrasting attitudes to income tax. They form a link between the old conception of a harsh, inquisitorial system eager to strengthen its powers by assuming the right to interrogate taxpayers, examine bank accounts and insist on returns of total income in all cases and the new idea of a tax designed to serve the public welfare. It was a pity that Philip Snowden was not allowed to enlarge on his conception of what should be the fiscal aims of government which the Conservative press had called 'highway robbery'.[39] 'We hold that in assessing for taxation the two ideas should be kept in mind . . . that in exercising taxation for the purpose of raising revenue and also bearing in mind its effect upon the general distribution of wealth and the social condition of the people.'[40] If the findings of the Committee did not immediately effect a 'more equitable diffusion of the national wealth' they did, within a few years, influence a quiet but profound revolution in the whole framework of income tax.

Philip Snowden relates how Asquith once told him that 'the post of Chancellor of the Exchequer was the easiest one in the Government'.[41] The view was doubtless coloured by Asquith's own tenure of that office which was almost entirely trouble free. His first Budget was, as he admitted, 'provisional',[42] but since he was in possession of an adequate surplus and a satisfactory income tax yield, he could afford not to propose any hasty reforms. He did, however, realize the need for an authoritative and searching enquiry into the incidence of income tax; the evidence before the subsequent Committee and its report have already been discussed.

[35] Evasion, pp. xxiii (41) and xxii (50).
[36] Combination of graduation and differentiation, Q. 419.
[37] p. xxvi (56).   [38] Summary, pp. xxxv–vi.
[39] Philip Snowden's *Autobiography*, vol. I, p. 417.   [40] Q. 1697.
[41] *Autobiography* (*op. cit.*), p. 146.   [42] Hansard 30/IV/06.

Never were recommendations so swiftly acted upon. A bare nineteen weeks after Dilke had reported, Asquith was able to propose, in his second Budget,[43] that earned incomes not exceeding £2,000 should be charged at 9d in the £ against the standard 1s chargeable on unearned income. He was well aware that the Select Committee had suggested £3,000, 'but I think that £2,000 is quite as far as you can fairly go'. It would, of course, be necessary to make a return in order to claim the relief. Originally, a pension was not included in the definition but was later brought within the scope 'as part of the remuneration not immediately paid'.[44]

The whole debate makes a fascinating illustration of the revived interest in taxation; especially significant is Asquith's pronouncement that 'the Chancellor of the Exchequer ought to budget not for one year, but for several years'. This, to a great extent, answers the criticisms that there could have been remissions of taxation[45] since it was well known that Asquith was planning his Old Age Pension scheme, for which he needed a nest egg. It was an equally justifiable measure to make a compensatory increase in death duties since the administrative machine could hardly have coped with a scheme for graduation on top of differentiation.

In the event, all turned out well. During the following year, the yield of income tax increased again; differentiation 'had paid for itself'; and a scheme which, ever since 1842, had been considered impracticable had shown itself 'smooth and easy in its operation'. Asquith, by now Prime Minister, was able to introduce his cherished Old Age Pension scheme, without altering the rates of income tax.[46] This scheme was 'the garnered result of the prudent finance'[47] of 1906 and 1907; and although his approach to it may seem to have been overcautious, it was financed from general taxation; more, it was quite clearly the beginning of the Welfare State, although Philip Snowden expressed considerable doubts.[48]

Lloyd George was 'not versed, far less trained in public finance'[49] and the orthodox McKenna is said to have remarked to Balfour: 'If George should ever become Chancellor, he would be a very unsound one.'[50] But by a combination of good sense and good advice, backed by Asquith's unwavering support, he decided on the introduction of the type of supertax recommended by the Dilke Committee. In its

[43] Hansard 30/IV/07.   [44] Hansard 3/VII/07.
[45] Shehab (*op. cit.*), pp. 248–50. See also Snowden's *Autobiography* (*op. cit.*), pp. 158–9 and Spender and Asquith's *Life of Asquith*, pp. 186–9.
[46] (Lloyd George, Chancellor), Hansard 7/V/08.
[47] Asquith's biography (*op. cit.*), p. 252.
[48] *Autobiography* (*op. cit.*), pp. 197–8.
[49] Thomas Jones, *Lloyd George*, p. 36.
[50] Frank Owen, *Tempestuous Journey*, p. 161.

final form it was fixed at 6d in the £ on all incomes over £5,000 'upon the amount by which such incomes exceed £3,000'. There were also three significant alterations to income tax itself. While leaving the rate at 9d in the £ on earned income up to £2,000 a year, it became 1s in the £ for incomes in the £2,000 to £3,000 band and for all other incomes above that line it was raised to 1s 2d. There was also an abatement of £10 for every child under 16 years of age granted to taxpayers whose incomes did not exceed £500, an allowance which had lapsed since the days of Pitt (see p. 29).

Such was the famous '1909 war Budget against poverty'[51] comparable in effect with Harcourt's of 1894[52] which 'not only ranged over the whole field of taxation but was significant for its open and unqualified adoption of the theory that taxation should be used for the purpose of social regeneration'. As a parliamentary speech its presentation was, apparently, a failure; but it sparked off a spectacular constitutional crisis and effectively ensured that the whole domestic history of Great Britain for two years centred round its acceptance or rejection.[53] Whether or not the challenge to the Lords was deliberately provoked is not relevant here; on the face of it, Asquith with his legal training and respect for the constitution would hardly have imagined the Lords would break a tradition which had endured two and a half centuries.

The dramatic events of 1909–10 have, to an extent, obscured the place of Lloyd George's first Budget, not only in the series of Liberal Budgets from the beginning of the century to 1914 but also in the shifting emphasis on social taxation from the Victorian conception of taxation for the sake of revenue only. Strangely enough, however, it was the tax on land values, a sort of capital gains tax at a low rate, which aroused the most vehement opposition, not the new supertax, not only from the opposition benches, but also in the Cabinet. Nevertheless, it was unfair to call the Budget 'a class Budget'.[54] Asquith realized that the 'democratic neoliberalism of the twentieth century had little in common with Gladstonian liberalism'.[55] But all must share in the burden of taxation. 'If we are to have social reform we must be ready to pay for it and when I say we, I mean the whole nation, the working and consuming classes as well as the wealthier class of direct taxpayers.' These words of Asquith were echoed by Lloyd George: 'I have never had any sympathy with the idea that

[51] Hansard 29/IV/09.
[52] Comparison of Harcourt's Budget of 1894 with that of Lloyd George: *British Budgets*, vol. I, pp. 298–9.
[53] The Budget did not, in fact, become law until 29/IV/1910.
[54] Lord Robert Cecil, quoted by Shehab (*op. cit.*), p. 253.
[55] Hansard 18/IV/07.

someone has got to be exempt because he is earning a small amount
. . . The only principle I would lay down would be that they ought to
contribute in proportion to their means.'[56] This was the basis of the
Liberal attitude, to distributional taxation, that most people were
suffering in indirect taxation far more than in proportion to their
taxability.

The Budgets subsequent to that of 1909 were not so much an
increasing development from them as a reinforcement of the *status
quo*. The second Budget of Lloyd George[57] was 'unique in the experience of all of us who are now living in that it makes no change
either by way of extension or of reduction in the existing taxation of
the country', and the delay in the passing of the previous year's
Budget necessitated an elaborate constitutional ritual before the
Revenue Bill was disposed of. The third Budget[58] maintained the
level of direct taxation as before; revenue was expanding, the country
was prosperous and there was no need to impose additional burdens
for the cost of the Coronation estimated at a modest £300,000.

But the pace of social reform, through taxation, was not fast
enough for the Labour Party and an increasing number of the
columns of Hansard was being devoted to the highly critical speeches
of Snowden. He had welcomed the 1909 Budget as 'the first real
effort the Government had made to grapple with the problem of
wealth and poverty'.[59] But he was not willing, on that account alone,
to lend it automatic support. For instance, he spoke against the
proposals for debt redemption[60] in the 1912 Budget, which was remarkable for showing the largest realized surplus then on record;
otherwise there were no changes in taxation. There was, however,
one administrative innovation. Following a successful action against
the Bank of England for deducting tax before the Finance Act embodying the resolution authorizing it had passed into law, it was
announced that in future, there would be a Finance Bill for the
renewal of temporary taxes and a Revenue Bill later embodying
amendments.

There were two more Budgets in this halcyon period of peace and
prosperity. Although there was a deficit in 1913,[61] 'Trade was at its
best, unemployment at its lowest, profits were at their highest' and
the Chancellor confidently relied on the growth of revenue bridging
the gap without any increase in taxation. The debate was notable for
a further extension of socialist theory by Snowden. In an attack on
indirect taxation he challenged the current Liberal theory that any

[56] Hansard 11/XII/11.　　[57] Hansard 30/VI/10.　　[58] Hansard 16/V/11.
[59] *Autobiography*, vol. I, pp. 196–9.
[60] Hansard 2/IV/12. (Lloyd George's fourth Budget.)
[61] Hansard 22/IV/13.

class which had political privilege should make a financial contribution to the State by arguing that the poor created the wealth of the nation and that 'the taxation of the rich is really a payment which has been made by the poor who have been exploited'. To return to the deficit, however, Lloyd George found the optimism justified. When he presented his sixth Budget[62] the increase in revenue, instead of the anticipated £6 millions, was over half as much again. But there was increased expenditure to be met from the revision of the grants system to local authorities and changes in connection with National Insurance. Increases in both income tax and supertax were, therefore, proposed.

Income tax was held at 9d but for the first £1,000 of earned income only. Earned income between £1,000 and £2,500 was divided into three groups; up to £1,500 the charge was at 10½d, up to £2,000 the charge was 1s and up to £2,500 it was at the old standard rate of 1s 2d. Incomes above £2,500 were at a new increased rate of 1s 4d where unearned. The exemption limit for supertax was lowered to £3,000 charged according to a scale of seven graduated steps on a progressive basis. There was, however, a small measure of relief for unearned incomes under £500 and child allowances, still only granted for incomes not exceeding £500, was doubled to £20 for each child.[63] Snowden was still not satisfied. 'In the first seven years of this Liberal Government they had increased the expenditure on the fighting services by a sum equal to the cost of the new social reforms they had enacted.'[64]

The success of the campaigns for differentiation and graduation had momentarily silenced the critics as far as theory was concerned. Attention was now focussed on income tax administration and attempts to obtain further or more generous allowances and reliefs. This phase of interest in direct taxation was partly the result of the stepping up of rates, but was also partly due to the growing complexity of industrial organization and commercial life generally. For in its current, comparatively simple, form, income tax displayed some anomalies in its administrative details as well as an inevitable lack of flexibility.

There was one change of considerable administrative importance during 1908, whereby the Excise Department was transferred to the Commissioners of Customs and Excise,[65] leaving the responsibility for direct taxation in the hands of the Board of Inland Revenue. But this did not seem to cure the chronic shortage of staff which pressure of work covered by new legislation made even more acute.

[62] Hansard 4/V/14.
[63] *British Budgets*, vol. II, p. 27ff.   [64] *Autobiography*, vol. I, p. 243.
[65] Board's Report for the year to 31/III/16, p. 6.

Gayler, the Chief Inspector, giving evidence before the Dilke Committee admitted that repayment claims had been taking eleven to twelve months but now 'they would get it within a month'.[66] The point was also raised of returns being dealt with by 'clerical staff who are not civil servants' and Asquith revealed that the employment of established clerks had been tried but 'was abandoned as being unsatisfactory both as regards cost and efficiency'.[67] There were also complaints that repayment claims were being dealt with by unestablished clerks. The Chancellor replied that 'the examination of repayment claims by clerks in the Surveyor's office is carried out under the supervision of the Surveyor who is responsible for their accuracy and whose advice and help is given to the clerk at all stages of the work'.[68] It was a fact, however, that since the authorized staff was under 500 Inspectors, Surveyors and assistant Surveyors,[69] a good deal of the day to day work of any income tax district was necessarily done by unestablished clerks employed by the Surveyor. They had appealed to the Chancellor in May, 1912, for recognition but their case had, for the time being, been shelved.[70] The question was raised again in the form of a motion on the Revenue Estimates for 1913–14, but after a considerable discussion, the mover was unsuccessful.

Many of the complaints recorded in Hansard arose from the inevitable clash between the amateur and the professional sections of the income tax organization. Despite the far-reaching changes in theory, the Liberal Government preferred to make no administrative changes. To criticisms that men should not be employed as assessors and collectors 'who may be tradesmen and are thus given facilities for knowing the circumstances of rivals in business', Asquith replied that 'no change could be made in the existing system without a complete change in the whole scheme of the Income Tax Administration and corresponding changes in the law'.[71] The point was raised again a month later and this time McKenna stated that 'the employment of local persons as assessor is based on the advantage which their local knowledge gives to them in assisting the Commissioners to make proper assessments . . . no complaint has reached the Board of Inland Revenue that improper disclosures have been made'.

There were also complaints against the professionals. The Surveyors were 'interfering' in 'the examination of statements of accounts of profit made in trade'.[72] Asquith shrugged this one off: 'Surveyors of Taxes, so far as I am aware, confine themselves to the performance of their statutory duties', which he then proceeded to detail. Four

---

[66] Dilke Report (*op. cit.*), Qq. 986–7.
[67] Hansard 1/XI/06.   [68] Hansard 10/VI/12.
[69] Dilke Report (*op. cit.*), Q. 968.   [70] Hansard 3/VII/13.
[71] Hansard 25/IV/06 and 14/VI/06.   [72] Hansard 30/X/06.

years later there was an elaborate query in eight parts[73] mainly concerned with requests issued by the Surveyors for the production of accounts by taxpayers and the same charge of 'interference' 'in reference to the assessment of Income Tax'. Lloyd George gave an equally categoric reply: the request for returns and accounts had been adopted by Surveyors 'not on the express instructions of Board of Inland Revenue, but with their knowledge and approval as a course conducive to the convenience of both taxpayers and officials'. The Revenue was also developing the technique of increasing assessments to force the production of accounts. A debate in 1913[74] produced some very valuable suggestions and Lloyd George seemed to favour the setting up of a Departmental Committee on income tax administration in general.

Industry too was finding hardship 'in the limited and often totally inadequate allowance for depreciation of plant and machinery'.[75] The question of an allowance for wasting assets received a good deal of discussion without any satisfactory solution to the problem being found; the final query whether the Government proposed 'to introduce legislation so as to provide that the exhaustion or consumption of capital shall not be treated as profit' received a curt, 'The answer is in the negative'. There was also a very modern suggestion 'with a view to affording the commercial community some allowance for the depreciation on buildings that takes place from year to year'.[76] This had to wait another thirty-five years for full realization.

The Hansard debates of the period from 1906 to 1918 on income tax and allied subjects occupy almost as many columns as the whole of the debates from 1799 to 1906 so that only the trends of the way income tax was developing can be highlighted. But two final items should be mentioned. The Civil List was made free of tax 'for after all it is not a salary but an allowance made to the Sovereign towards the maintenance of the dignity of the Crown'.[77] Queen Victoria had given a 'voluntary promise' to pay income tax but this was perhaps on the optimistic understanding that it was only a temporary charge. Secondly, in 1912 there was an acrimonious discussion on the expenses of £100 allowed to M.P.s for travelling.[78] Lloyd George refused to have the legality of this deduction contested which, in fact, seemed clearly contrary to the Schedule E expenses rule; and it was

---

[73] Hansard 29/III/10.   [74] Hansard 2/VI/13.

[75] Depreciation allowances for plant and the refusal: Hansard 11/V/06, 4/VII/13.

[76] Hansard 28/II/10. This allowance was finally granted by the I.T.A. 1945 although prior to this there was the so-called 'Mills, Factories Allowance' of S. 18/F.A. 1924.

[77] Hansard 22/VII/10: See also Longford (*op. cit.*), p. 157.

[78] Hansard 9/X/12.

the subject of an ironic comment by Mr Justice Rowlatt many years later.[79]

But all the problems of administration, reform and even of evasion vanished in the eventful days following the assassination of the Archduke Ferdinand at Sarajevo. Within six weeks Great Britain was at war, and the Chancellor's duty changed overnight from that of the regulator and watchdog of national finance to the provider of revenue to meet ever mounting expenditure. The finding of money itself ceased to be controversial; what was now at issue was simply the method.

Thus the financing of the 1914–18 war is divided into two sharply contrasted periods. In the first period there was no thoroughgoing attempt to put taxation on a truly war basis. The first war Budget,[80] it is true, doubled income tax and supertax, but this increase was only effective for a third of the year. There was also an increase in indirect taxation deliberately to raise money from the classes which did not pay income tax; for Lloyd George and his advisors still shied from a complete tax on wages because of the apparently insuperable administrative difficulties. It was perhaps understandable that the first war Budget should not have introduced any sweeping alterations in the peacetime taxation system of the Liberal government; but some greater sense of urgency should have been shown even if the censure of Snowden is not altogether justified that 'the Government had neither the courage nor the moral principles of Gladstone and Pitt, who financed their wars mainly out of current taxation'.[81]

Lloyd George's second war Budget was his last;[82] and it has been called 'the weakest link' in the series. For in spite of the remarkable buoyancy of the revenue and the rapidly mounting cost of the war, no new taxation was imposed. The Chancellor's defence was that it was impossible to forecast accurately the duration of the war; 'this is, therefore, not a suitable moment to attempt a forecast of the probable expenditure upon the war or to submit proposals for that purpose'. This does not appear to be a satisfactory explanation since the attempt had to be made at some date, however fluid the military situation appeared. In extenuation it should be noted that it was generally understood the real Budget would be proposed later in the year, there was a hint of taxing excess profits and Lloyd George was already preoccupied with the question of the actual weapons rather

---

[79] See the tax case of Nolder *v.* Walters 15 T.C., p. 388.

[80] The first war Budget (Lloyd George's seventh): Hansard 17/XI/14. See also *British Budgets*, vol. II, p. 48.

[81] *Autobiography*, vol. I, p. 367.

[82] (Lloyd George's eighth): Hansard 4/V/15. See also Thomas Jones, *Lloyd George*, p. 53.

than the sinews of war. In May 1915, the Coalition Government was formed and Lloyd George was transferred to the Ministry of Munitions.

His successor was Reginald McKenna, 'a banker in blinkers',[83] and he was forced to take the first really decisive action to put taxation on a war footing, since daily expenditure had reached £4·5 millions and was expected to rise to £5 millions, which it did in the following year. Income tax was increased by two-fifths to an unprecedented 3s 6d in the pound, making an increase for the year of one-fifth and the exemption rate was reduced to £130, involving consequent reductions in the abatements. The Schedule B assessment was increased to the amount of the rent paid. New scales of supertax were introduced rising as high as 6s 10d in the pound.

This Budget ushered in the second period of war taxation. By now the ugly word 'profiteer' was current and the taxing of excess profits became a moral as well as a fiscal necessity. McKenna therefore imposed an Excess Profits Duty[84] which was retained until 1921 and which accounted for no less than 25% of the total tax revenue during the period. Critics have regarded it as not as effective as it might have been; it could have been imposed earlier; it was subject to evasion, as indeed is any tax with a high rate which always stimulates avoidance; there was a marked time lag in collection; E.P.D. was still coming in fifteen years after its repeal; and an overworked staff found it difficult to administer. It is said that when the draft Bill came out, Sir John Simon, who had just read it through, remarked to the Chancellor, 'Jolly good, Reggie'. This enthusiasm was not shared by those who had to operate, or pay it. It was based on taxing the excess profit from August 4, 1914, over the standard profits which could be the average of the two best of the three immediately preceding pre-war years. There were concessions for hard cases generally, for instance, businesses with poor standards. Precautions were necessary against artificial transactions and ingenious ways were found later to defeat the legislation by manipulation of stocks and transactions in ships. The rate was fixed at 50% but relief was provided for repairs deferred owing to the war and exceptional depreciation of plant. It was also permissible to set off profits in one period against deficiencies in another.

A second radical departure in the first McKenna Budget[85] was the taxation of wages. Lloyd George had complained that 'he had repeatedly invited the Labour Party to give their opinion on the

---

[83] Thomas Jones, *Lloyd George*, p. 61.
[84] Board's Report for the year to 31/III/17 and F.A. (No. 2) 1915: Ss. 15, 16 and 17.
[85] Hansard 9/XI/15.

subject' and had even suggested the collection of duty 'week by week by means of stamps'. Direct taxation was more fair than indirect taxation, which was Snowden's reiterated point; Arthur Henderson's idea was 'have it collected at source through the employers', and this found a good deal of general support. When, however, the scheme was introduced, it provided for the quarterly assessment[86] of 'manual wage earners' by the Surveyor, the right of appeal to the General Commissioners being retained. The traditionalists were up in arms. 'One of our greatest objections is that the Surveyors have power to assess.' McKenna pointed out that the original Income Tax scheme was never intended for weekly wage earners. 'If we mean to have this tax, let us have it a reality and not a sham; and you cannot have it as a reality unless you have quarterly assessments and collection. It is something entirely new and you must have it carried out by persons definitely appointed.'

McKenna's second Budget[87] could hardly be as dramatic as the first, but he made a brave attempt to compass the ever-mounting expenditure by increased taxation. The deficit had to be met by borrowing. Income tax was increased to 5s in the pound and E.P.D. to 60% with a corresponding increase in mineral rights duty[88] which had also been introduced along with E.P.D. in 1915. A new tax was the munitions levy, designed to ensure that armament firms paid the greater of this tax or E.P.D. Such was McKenna's second and, as it turned out, last Budget. It was criticized in some quarters as relying too much on direct taxation which was said to be as excessive now as it had been deficient under Lloyd George. This controversy may well have arisen from the contemporary political cross-currents, for towards the end of 1916, partly as a result of mounting muddle and procrastination, Asquith was jockeyed out of office to be succeeded by Lloyd George, the man who, for all his shortcomings in character, was the only statesman capable of being the organizer of victory.

Bonar Law, the 'sombre raven amid the glittering birds of Paradise'[89] became the new Chancellor, combining with the post that of Leader of the House. This was palpably an administrative error since it was impossible for one man to perform satisfactorily the functions of two such responsible officers. The result was that no new taxes were imposed in his first Budget;[90] the changes were confined to increases in three existing duties,[91] of which only one was

---

[86] Hansard 26/X/15 (Sir G. Younger).
[87] Hansard 4/V/16.   [88] (2) 1915: S. 43.
[89] The phrase was Beaverbrook's and is quoted by Frank Owen in *Tempestuous Journey*, p. 223.
[90] Hansard 2/V/17.   [91] *British Budgets*, vol. II, pp. 127–8 and 135–6.

direct; E.P.D. and its allied taxes were increased to 80% and provision was made to prevent inequitable repayments to shipping companies. The only glimmer of relief was the extension, to adopted children, of child allowance.[92] This allowance, originally £10, having been raised to £20 for 1914–15, £25 for 1915–16 where incomes did not exceed £500, had been extended to incomes up to £700 in the previous year.

The year 1918 opened with the end of the war seemingly as far off as ever and, following the German offensive, by the spring the prospects appeared even more bleak. A spirit of sacrifice was in the air, which made it easier for the Chancellor to carry his hard-hitting proposals.[93] The standard rate of income tax was raised to 6s; Schedule B was now to be assessed on double the rental value and the highest rate of supertax was fixed at 4s 6d in the pound, the exemption limit being reduced £2,500. The Chancellor, as in the previous year, combined these unpalatable increases with the various extensions to allowances[94] where an individual's income did not exceed £800. An allowance of £25 was granted for a taxpayer's wife, of the same amount to a widower with related housekeeper and for a dependent relative, while child relief was extended to persons with incomes between £800 and £1,000 for any number of children exceeding two. There were also three important changes affecting Schedule D.[95] A 'number of persons engaged in any class of trade' were permitted to apply through the Board for increased rates of wear and tear of plant and machinery to the Board of Referees. An obsolescence allowance was introduced by which a trader could deduct 'the cost of replacing plant and machinery which has become obsolete' less the amount allowed for wear and tear and the sale price. Finally an allowance, known familiarly as 'Mills, Factories Allowance' was given to traders of the difference between the gross and the net annual value of trading premises specifically 'for the depreciation of such mills, factories and similar premises'. The Board's report went on to point out that the demand for an allowance in such cases was thus met; and the possible increase in wear and tear rates and the obsolescence deduction also went far to meet the numerous requests for some concessions in that direction, especially over the past decade.

Thus, in this comparatively short period, income tax changed out of all recognition. In 1906 it was still the Victorian apparatus cherished by Peel and Gladstone with a uniform rate of 1s in the pound,

[92] F.A. 1917: S. 17: the Board's Report for the year to 31/III/16, p. 28 and F.A. 1916: S. 33.
[93] Hansard 22/IV/18.   [94] Board's Report for the year ended 31/III/19, p. 1.
[95] Board's Report for the year ended 31/III/19 and F.A. 1918: S. 24.

abatements at the lower end of the scale giving exemption at the £160 point and a total yield of £34·2 millions. As it stood in 1918, it had admitted both differentiation, in the form of an earned income relief, and graduation in the form of a supertax, with Income Tax rates rising to 6s in the pound and supertax to 4s 6d. Against these increasing burdens should be ranged the progressive reliefs of married man's allowance and those for children, housekeeper and dependent relatives. Nevertheless the total yield, including E.P.D., had attained an astonishing £584·7 millions, an increase of over seventeen times.[96] Whether it could have been wielded more efficiently is a debatable and finally unanswerable point; but there is no denying the intrinsic power of the measures.

Administration, too, had radically altered from the leisured days when the Clerk to Commissioners would write to an appellant asking him to be good enough to send his accounts to the Surveyor for examination; now the Surveyor himself was writing to the taxpayer directly for accounts and information. Going fast too were the requests to Somerset House from the Clerk to Commissioners on doubtful points of law; there was now an ever growing corpus of judical *dicta*. More important, as previously mentioned, the Surveyor now had the statutory power of assessing manual wage earners. In general, as Snowden pointed out:[97]

'Anybody who knows anything about the working of the Income Tax laws knows that 99% of the disputes in regard to Income Tax assessments are settled now by the Surveyors of Taxes . . . and I am sure that any Member who has any technical knowledge of this question will agree that the Surveyor of Taxes, with his practical knowledge, his knowledge of the law and his wide experience is a far better person to deal with the matter than the General Commissioners of Income Tax who know nothing about the Income Tax laws. The work with which the Commissioners are accredited is purely of a nominal character. The real work is done by the Surveyors of Taxes.'

It was fortunate the Board had gained a massive increase in staff during the war period; even so, the work burden was considerable.[98]

Along with the obvious changes in statute and organization was a more subtle change in the contemporary comments on taxation. Reforms of income tax had previously been discussed on the basis of efficiency or equity or both. Now the criticism of Labour partisans, such as Philip Snowden, was definitely tending towards evaluation

---

[96] On financing the war in general: *British Budgets*, vol. II, pp. 350–89.
[97] Hansard 6/XII/15.   [98] Hansard 17/VII/16 (McKenna).

CHAPTER X

Further Reforms and the Depression

BEFORE the end of the war Herbert Samuel[1] had given a welcome to 'putting income tax more upon a family basis than an individual basis'; and he had emphasized the need for 'reviewing the whole of our income tax law and placing it upon a consistent and logical basis'. It was true there had been a good deal of 'piecemeal legislative patching'[2] during the war, but a Commission had already been proposed, although understandably the Chancellor had replied that this could hardly be undertaken during the period of hostilities.[3] A start, however, would be made with a Consolidation Act, 'and, as my hon. Friend will appreciate, the labours of the post-war Committee of Inquiry will be greatly facilitated by the existence of a Consolidation Act'.

The Bill for this purpose was introduced into the House of Lords in February, 1918. The effect of consolidation was, without changing the law in any way, to assemble the existing statutory provisions, amend them in accordance with subsequent enactments and tidy up and re-arrange the wording where necessary. Sir Frederick Banbury, the Hubbard of the period, protested against this 'enormous Bill' being introduced at 11 p.m. on the night of August 6th. Another M.P.[4] prophesied that within a very few years the income tax law would get itself into the same 'confused tangle' as at present. He may have been right; but despite his criticisms the Bill had a remarkably smooth passage and came into force in April, 1919. With its 232 pages, its 239 clauses and schedules, it was a monument to the patience, the care and the skill of Bertram Cox, the Solicitor of Inland Revenue; and it is interesting to note that one of the first acknowledgments made by the Commissioners of the 1920 Report was, as Bonar Law had anticipated, to 'how greatly our task has been lightened by the recent consolidation of the whole of the Income Tax legislation into one comprehensive statute'.[5]

---

[1] Hansard 3/IV/18.   [2] Shehab (*op. cit.*), p. 259.
[3] Hansard 18/X/17 (Bonar Law).   [4] Charles Roberts.
[5] P. 1, para. 4.

The mandate of the Commission[6] was equally comprehensive,[7] 'to enquire into the Income Tax (including Supertax) of the United Kingdom in all its aspects, including the scope, rates and incidence of the tax; allowances and reliefs; administration, assessment, appeal and collection; and prevention of evasion; and to report what alterations of law and practice are necessary, or desirable and what effect they would have on rates of tax if it were necessary to maintain the total yield'. They held fifty sittings[8] and heard no less than 187 witnesses,[9] quite apart from written evidence of various kinds, but 'if there are those who expect us to provide a panacea for all the grievances caused by the existence of an income tax', they were due for a disappointment, for 'our recommendations, though numerous and far reaching, do not amount to a suggestion for any fundamental change[10] in the nature of the tax'.

The story of income tax, so far, has been mainly concerned with its reform in the direction of differentiation, graduation and allowances. The scope of the Commission embraced many further points, but it did devote a good deal of attention to these three aspects and its recommendations here were among the first to be dealt with by legislation.

Differentiation, the first reform to be introduced, had been in operation only a short time when an inherent flaw[11] in the relief became evident. A taxpaper who had income of £320, half earned and half unearned, would be due an abatement of £160. This, however, would be set against the earned half of his income and he would thus gain no benefit from the earned income relief since the balance of his income, being unearned, was chargeable at the full rate. A second anomaly arose from the increase in rates. In 1907, when the rate was 1s in the £, the charging of earned income at 9d in the £ represented a substantial relief of one-quarter. But when the full rate was raised as high as 6s in the £ the relief given by charging the earned portion at 5s 3d in the £ was only one-eighth. The Commission therefore recommended that 'earned income should be diminished by a certain fraction thereof for the purpose of assessment and the income so diminished should be charged at the rate of tax applicable to unearned income. The fraction we propose is one tenth…'

Graduation, too, was found in practice to give rise to inequity in subjecting income to abrupt increases in liability at specific points, which could result in an increase of £1 in income producing a tax bill increased by over £50. This anomaly had, to an extent, been mitigated

[6] Report of the Royal Commission on Income Tax, 1920, Cmd. 615.
[7] P. 1, para. 1.   [8] P. 1, para. 2.   [9] P. 2, para. 6.
[10] P. 3, para. 14.
[11] P. 25, paras. 108 and 111. See also table 24, para. 108.

by a system of marginal reliefs,[12] so that, in general, the increase in his tax bill of such a taxpayer should not exceed the difference between his income and the limit of any particular zone. The change suggested here was proposed by the Association of Tax Surveying Officers and, as expressed in general terms by the Commission, was 'that graduation by reference to the size of an income should be effected solely by a variation of the real effective rate of tax chargeable on that income'.[13] There was a firm conviction that graduation 'was almost universally admitted to be as sound in principle as it is imperatively necessary in practice'.

With regard to allowances, the first debatable point was the limit of exemption standing at £130 for single and £180 for married taxpayers. The left-wing witnesses[14] thought the figure for a single man should be £250 in view of the rising cost of living; and there was general support for some increase, apart from the three diehards[15] from the National Chamber of Trade who believed in no representation without taxation. The Commission looked at the question with the 'most careful consideration', and argued that the pre-war exemption limit was not 'the right starting point. That figure was not arrived at by scientific methods, but as a result of all the financial and political considerations existing in 1894.' Applying the same criteria, 'we find it impossible, at the present time to justify the raising of the exemption limit[16] for the bachelor beyond £150 and for a married couple with no children beyond £250'. These figures, it should be noted, referred to earned income; for unearned income the figures were £135 and £225 respectively. Supertax exemption should be lowered to £2,000.[17]

The Commission then proceeded to the personal allowances. 'The aggregation of the incomes of husband and wife[18] should continue to be the rule'; the allowance for a married man should be £250 and 'where the wife has £50 or more of earned income, the allowance to a married couple should be increased from £250 (earned) to £300 (earned)'. No increase in the housekeeper allowance,[19] standing at £50, was proposed or in the dependent relative allowance,[20] standing at £25. Turning to child allowance[21] 'we suggest that the allowance should be, in terms of earned income, £40 for the first child and £30 for each subsequent child'. Finally, a more intelligible scheme was

[12] 8 & 9, Geo. V: C. 40. S. 24 and Board's Report for the year to 31/III/17.
[13] P. 29, para. 128 and 129.
[14] For example Sidney Webb or Robert Shirkie of the T.U.C.
[15] Thomas Pratt, Charles Aveling and Felix J. Blakemore, p. 55, para. 241.
[16] P. 55, para. 244 and p. 56, para. 246.   [17] P. 35, para. 151.
[18] P. 62, para. 275 and p. 59, para. 261.   [19] P. 62, para. 278.
[20] P. 63, paras. 284–9.   [21] P. 62, paras. 280–3.

proposed for relief in respect of life insurance premiums,[22] the oldest of all the allowances. A general recommendation, covering all personal allowances, was that 'in all ranges of income, some regard should be had to the taxpayers marital and family responsibilities'.

But, as previously mentioned, the marathon sessions of evidence-taking enshrined in two foolscap volumes of questions and answers and a third embodying the report itself covered every feature of income tax law and administration. It dealt with the whole scope of the tax,[23] including the vexed questions of residence and double taxation relief. It paid marked attention to the day to day running of the system and was quick to distinguish between the substance and the shadow of power.

'Gradually, imperceptibly at first, but in later years with increasing rapidity – the local bodies of Commissioners ceased to grapple with the ever increasing difficulties of administration and tacitly allowed a large proportion of the work to be done by the Inspector of Taxes[24] . . . The Inspector has thus become the pivotal figure in the Income Tax administration to the majority of taxpayers who, following the directions on the official forms, consult him in regard to their returns, the adjustment of their assessments and the repayment of any sums to which they may be entitled.'[25]

Finally, it devoted a significant twenty paragraphs to the problem of evasion,[26] a problem not normally discussed in the open with such frankness.

It is well known that the recommendations of the Commission on differentiation, graduation, and allowances were swiftly adopted and it is interesting to observe their translation into the terminology of Finance Acts. It is even more fascinating, however, to trace the subsequent history of some recommendations not immediately adopted. It is extraordinary how many of the changes in the structure and composition of income tax were foreshadowed in the report of 1920, for example the abolition of the office of assessor,[27] the appointment of collectors by the Board of Inland Revenue[28] and the use of the General Commissioners as a purely appellate body,[29] which last re-

---

[22] P. 29, para. 130. It had been revived by Gladstone in 1853.

[23] Pt. 1, pp. 1–22.

[24] The Inspector of Taxes was a change in name for the Surveyor. It has been said that this new title was regarded as a reward to the Surveyors for their wartime efforts, as the Inspector used to be the Supervising Officer for the Surveyors. A similar reward was the use of the title *H.M.* Inspector of Taxes.

[25] P. 83, paras 374–5. [26] P. 135, paras. 625–44.

[27] P. 86, para. 346. [28] P. 87, para. 390. [29] P. 77, para. 345.

form was not effected until the Taxes Management Act of 1964. The changes in capital allowances[30] brought about by the Income Tax Act of 1945 appear in embryo during the discussions on depreciation of plant and machinery and of buildings. There is even a percipient forecast of the form P11D (taxation of benefits in kind) in the opinion that 'an attempt should be made to charge income tax on the true remuneration of employment including subsidiary benefits . . .'[31] But an optimistic attempt to secure a closer definition of trading still awaits legislative action as a long line of tax cases testifies: 'We are of opinion that any profit made on a transaction recognizable as a business transaction, i.e. a transaction in which the subject matter was acquired with a view to profit seeking should be brought within the scope of the Income Tax.' A robust common sense distinguished both its particular and general findings. 'The tax has proved its worth as a part of the fiscal system . . . and should be judged, not by a theoretical standard of possible excellence, but the results which it has achieved . . .; even to some of its defects, the taxpayer has by this time fairly well accommodated himself.' Its exhaustive research and patient investigation have rarely been equalled and never excelled by any similar Commission.

The Royal Warrants for the Commission were issued on April 4, 1919. Three weeks or so later Austen Chamberlain rose to present the first post-war Budget[32] after an absence from the Treasury of fourteen years. Although revenue was still rising and expenditure had begun to fall, the Chancellor could only continue to exploit the wartime best payers income tax, and supertax (the rates of which remained unaltered), and E.P.D., which was retained at half the existing rate. The Opposition maintained that E.P.D. should have been imposed at the full percentage, that if anything income tax rates should have been stiffened and a capital or war wealth levy[33] imposed. Chamberlain had a ready defence. E.P.D. was acting as a brake on industrial revival, income tax could hardly be increased in peacetime and any form of capital levy was not only difficult to administer but would be a hazardous and disastrous experiment. He agreed that taxes in general should not be relaxed and that 'it would be a bad day for everyone, including those exempted, if taxation were so imposed that the mass of the electors were freed from the financial responsibilities entailed by such policies as they supported'.[34] There were some minor amendments suggested and made in personal allowances, but any

[30] Pp. 48–51, Sections II and III.
[31] P. 33, para. 102.   [32] Hansard 30/IV/19.
[33] The suggested levy on war wealth was an 80 per cent tax on the capital of those liable at 1919 as compared with their capital in 1914.
[34] *British Budgets*, vol. II, p. 227.

large scale alterations were to await the deliberations of the Royal Commission.

Chamberlain had no easier task with his second Budget,[35] especially as receipts were showing wide divergences from the estimates and the 'enthusiasm for taxation which had characterized large classes of taxpayers during the war had been replaced by an attitude towards all Government finance which was becoming more and more critical'.[36] The result was a curious amalgam of reaction and reform. E.P.D. was increased to 60% and in addition, a Corporation Profits Tax of 5% was imposed on the total profit of companies, a tax which was originally intended to remain when E.P.D. was abolished. In fact, that tax was retained too long and instead of trapping the expected boom profits, it acted as a mechanism for repaying tax when profits slumped. On the side of reform, the land value duties were repealed on the advice of the Deputy Chairman of the Board of Inland Revenue;[37] they had never been productive and were rapidly becoming unworkable; and the debate on the subject echoed only dimly the uproar of 1909.

The real reforms introduced by the 1920 Budget were, however, the implementation of many of the recommendations of the Royal Commission. The fraction of $\frac{1}{10}$ was introduced as the relief for earned income, with a maximum of £200;[38] the suggested reduced rate relief up to £225 of taxable income at one-half standard rate was adopted;[39] the personal allowances were all revised and given with no limitation as to income in accordance with their findings. Two new terms[40] came into the vocabulary of income tax, assessable income or total income less earned income relief and taxable income, or that part of assessable income on which income tax is calculated. As the Board pointed out, this legislation involved 'a radical alteration of the method hitherto in force for granting relief in the income tax charged on earned income and of the method of graduating the burden of the tax according to the size of a taxpayer's income'.[41] These fundamental changes, which finally made a coherent system out of a patchwork of eighty years' enactments would not have been accepted so readily without the tradition of controversy and debate which had always been a feature of the fiscal scene.

It was just as well the reforms came when they did for by 1920 the uneasy political truce was showing clear signs of strain. The 'coupon'

[35] Hansard 19/IV/20, (the second of this present series; the first two Budgets were in 1904 and 1905).
[36] *British Budgets*, vol. II, p. 231.   [37] *British Budgets*, vol. II, p. 275.
[38] F.A. 1920, S. 16.   [39] F.A. 1920, Ss. 17–23.
[40] Board's Report for the year to 31/III/21, p. 80.
[41] Board's Report for the year to 31/III/21, p. 80.

election had resulted in a decisive victory for the Bonar Law–Lloyd George coalition, but essentially it was a Conservative triumph. Labour, as expected, made an unimpressive showing, but for the Liberals the verdict of the electorate meant an inevitable process of attrition. On paper there was a brilliant Cabinet headed by the man acknowledged to be the master of the art of getting things done. But the boom following the Armistice had collapsed by 1920 with a series of economic crises, especially in the coal-fields, culminating in 'Black Friday';[42] mass unemployment, which was to be the crucial question of the next two decades, began to haunt the economic scene; and as Labour began to achieve a certain degree of unity, the tragic split in the Liberal ranks became ever more patent.

The crisis in party politics came with the Carlton Club meeting of October, 1922, when a comparatively unknown Stanley Baldwin, who had attained Cabinet rank only the year before,[43] shattered the Coalition and reduced Lloyd George for the rest of his career to a helpless spectator on the sidelines. The subsequent election gave the Conservatives a majority of 88; the Liberals, now openly split, numbered 117, 60 following Asquith and the rest Lloyd George. The really significant feature was the Labour vote of 4·2 millions and the Labour representation of 142 members.

Bonar Law did not long retain office; in May, 1923, the onset of cancer compelled his resignation and he was succeeded by Baldwin. Neville Chamberlain became Chancellor of the Exchequer, the post having first been offered to McKenna who could not, however, find a parliamentary seat. The new Prime Minister determined to halt the drift of men like Austen Chamberlain and Lord Birkenhead to the Liberals by announcing a Protectionist programme and appealing to the country. The plan united the party but confused the voters; and the result of 'the leap in the dark' was a House consisting of 251 Conservatives, 191 Labour and 158 Liberals.

As the larger anti-Protectionist party, a surprised Labour formed a Government having first, so the story goes, consulted Whittaker's to discover what offices had to be filled. Existing on Liberal suffrance, the days of the Government were clearly numbered as soon as a socialist course was set. Its sudden end was precipitated by the withdrawal of a prosecution against a Communist weekly.

The General Election of 1924 was a handsome win for the Conservatives which might well have occurred without the intervention of the Zinoviev letter and Churchill became Chancellor. It is said that after twenty years in a Liberal wilderness he had thought the offer

[42] C. L. Mowat: *Britain between the Wars*, pp. 122–3.
[43] Baldwin had become President of the Board of Trade in 1921.

(which he thankfully took) was that of the Chancellorship of the Duchy of Lancaster.

There were two outstanding features of the period from 1925 to 1929. The first was the return, in 1925, to the gold standard, now generally admitted to be a talisman which had lost its power. It caused an overvaluation of the £ which overpriced production and had a critical effect on exports. The second was the General Strike, the highwater mark of militant trade unionism. After 1926 Labour tended to move further to the right and was to reap its reward in the General Election of 1929, if indeed the privilege of forming a government for those years of crisis could be termed a reward.

After the income tax reforms of the 1920 Finance Act, which, in some ways, marked the end of war finance, as well as the beginning of modern income tax, the succeeding Budgets matched neither the creativeness of the first two, nor the pace and violence of political events. The first three chased a fading vision of economy; the fourth was the first Budget produced by a Labour Government, if not precisely a Labour Budget; and the final five to 1929 were the work of Churchill. Although they contained some useful income tax amendments, all the Chancellor's rhetorical skill and fiscal ingenuity, both of which were considerable, could not finally hide the fact that he was fighting a losing battle against an impossible economic situation largely of his own devising.

Austen Chamberlain introduced the first[44] of Sir Robert Horne's two Budgets, since the former had only just vacated the office on succeeding Bonar Law as Leader of the House. It was not a very enterprising speech; income tax and supertax were up on the estimates, but the new Corporation Profits Tax was disappointing with a yield of £0·65 million against a £5 millions estimate. E.P.D. had at last been repealed but the consequent terminal adjustments, especially the valuation of stock, were proving troublesome and creating arrears of tax, while the liabilities remained unsettled. There was the perennial problem of weighing the claims of debt redemption and relief of taxation and the necessity for overall economy which so many of the current speeches stressed without any valid suggestions for how it was to be achieved.

There were, in fact, no material tax changes apart from the abolition of E.P.D. and the Labour spokesman, William Graham confined himself to proposing a capital levy,[45] at that time a recurrent suggestion in Labour fiscal policy and a reduction in indirect taxation in view of falling wages and rising unemployment. In general terms, he advocated such a distribution of taxation 'as will make it easiest and best for all sections of the people, as will contribute to economic

[44] Hansard 25/IV/21. [45] Hansard 26/IV/21.

efficiency and as will maintain some kind of reasonable standard of life for the community'. This was a fair statement of fiscal aims to which any of the three parties could have faithfully subscribed; it was a pity there was such a wide divergence of opinion on how these aims could be realized.

Sir Robert Horne had little more success with his second Budget[46] since he was faced with commercial depression and a deficit in both the income and business taxes. Despite this unpromising position, he decided that he must give some stimulus to industry and to that end reduced the standard rate from 6s in the £ to 5s. Agricultural distress was assisted by the reduction of the Schedule B assessment to the Net Annual Value simply, instead of twice the Net Annual Value. There was, on the other hand, a Schedule A revaluation which would, to some extent, make up the subsequent losses by increased receipts when the new values were assessed in 1924–5. Finally, an administrative change, all employments were now to be assessed under Schedule E, instead of partly under Schedule D.

Criticism of the Budget was somewhat perfunctory. Asquith, for the Liberals, described it as a gamble; the general Labour line[47] seemed to be that it was a 'rich man's Budget' and that greater reductions in indirect taxation were called for. 'There were the usual speeches by the usual people on the capital levy'[48] but again, as in the previous year, the same insistence on the pressing need for economy without any clear indication of where economies were to be made or why they were in themselves necessarily a virtue in view of the stagnation of trade and the tragic unemployment figures.

On the fall of the Coalition in 1922, Baldwin introduced his first and, as it turned out, his last Budget.[49] He had a very considerable surplus to dispose of which he employed in debt redemption. As far as income and the business taxes were concerned, he increased the repairs allowance for Schedule A since the new values were considerably higher, he reduced the rate of Corporation Profits Tax, and he took 6d off the standard rate, bringing it down to 4s 6d in the £. It was this third measure which aroused the anger of the Labour Party. This type of tax remission, Snowden maintained, benefited the wrong class; MacDonald was even more forthright: the relief given by remissions of direct taxation was being spent on 'unnecessary and parasitical forms of luxury'. It was, on the whole, a modest and equitable Budget, typical of Baldwin and orthodox Conservative finance. The real mystery, as Asquith pointed out, was how the estimates produced a surplus of nearly £100 millions.[50] It seemed to

---

[46] Hansard 1/V/22. [47] Hansard 2/V/22 (e.g. J. R. Clynes).
[48] *British Budgets*, vol. II, p. 49. [49] Hansard 16/IV/23.
[50] Hansard 17/IV/23.

show that 'the actual expenditure of the country was swollen to a degree far beyond the national necessity'. Baldwin was able to achieve remarkable economies; in fact the outstanding feature of his Budget, looking back, was that for the last time before the crisis year ahead, a Chancellor had cut public expenditure.

The Budget of 1924,[51] however, was the product of the arch-critic of right-wing finance, Philip Snowden, Chancellor by the grace of the Liberals and the first occupant of that office to have worked in an income tax district.[52] The City, mindful of the policies put forward in *Labour and the New World* and *If Labour Rules*, was apprehensive; but its fears were groundless. Snowden might have felt towards capitalism as Danton felt towards monarchy, but as long as Asquith held the balance of parliamentary power, he was not a free agent.

So, with the Financial Secretary at his elbow with a copy of the speech, ready, as customary, to nudge him if he made a slip,[53] Snowden introduced his Budget after only three weeks' preparation and no experience at all of ministerial office. In his own words: 'The Budget imposes no new taxes. It makes no new additions to existing taxes. It proposes to abolish the Corporation Profits Tax; to abolish the Inhabited House Duty (the successor of the old Chimney and Hearth Duty) . . . to extend the allowance for a housekeeper'. By reducing indirect taxation also, he made 'the greatest step . . . towards that cherished Radical ideal of a free breakfast table'.

In the circumstances, Snowden could hardly have proposed a Socialist Budget. In relieving indirect taxation he was certainly following a Labour (and Liberal) ideal. But there was no 'national scheme of productive work' as promised by the Labour Party manifesto; no nationalization; no capital levy; and no schemes for tapping 'the unappropriated incomes of the very wealthy'.[54] If there had been, he would not have been able to 'appeal for the support of the majority of members of this House'; it was indeed the political taint of Socialism which lost the Government the Liberal vote in the autumn of 1924. Whether he would, in fact, have introduced a truly Socialist Budget if the Labour Party had held an overall majority is open to some doubt. Beatrice Webb[55] recalled how he asked 'with a Treasury Clerk's intonation: "Where was the money to come from?"' during a discussion on public works which he firmly believed should pay for themselves. Certainly there was a marked difference between Snowden in opposition and Snowden in office.

Churchill had four and a half years as Chancellor; it is a curious

---

[51] Hansard 29/IV/24.   [52] *Autobiography*, vol. I, p. 45.
[53] *Autobiography*, vol. II, p. 642.   [54] *British Budgets*, vol. II, p. 122.
[55] Beatrice Webb's *Diaries*, pp. 255–6.

coincidence that Britain's other great war lord also had Treasury experience, although even longer. His five Budgets fall into two sharply contrasted periods. In his first two he had room for manoeuvre both in the fiscal and administrative field; in his second group he opened with the ominous words: 'We meet this afternoon under the shadow of the disaster of last year (i.e. the General Strike).'[56] The following year it was: 'The road has lain continually uphill; the weather has been wet and cheerless',[57] and in his last Budget speech, during a retrospective introduction he had to confess 'the difficulties have been more prominent than the good fortune'.[58]

The Budgets of 1925 and 1926 embodied some important alterations in income tax law. In the former, earned income relief was increased to one-sixth and an equivalent relief was given to taxpayers over 65 years old on investment income not exceeding £500. Professional men were allowed wear and tear on plant used for professional purposes which, of course, included their motor cars and the administratively awkward quarterly assessments on manual wage earners became half yearly, a change most welcome to the Inspectorate. In the latter, the basis of assessment under Schedule D was altered, to the great confusion of Mr Albert Haddock,[59] from the three-year average to the previous year basis. These changes were a further legacy of the 1919 Report and commanded general acceptance.

But the reduction in standard rate by sixpence to 4s in the £ and the decrease in supertax rates in 1925[60] produced the familiar automatic reaction from the Opposition. Snowden would have none of Churchill's plea that he had tried to balance relief fairly 'in the scales of social justice' declaring it was 'the worst rich man's Budget that was ever proposed'. Churchill firmly believed that 'the burden of direct taxation fell with injurious effect upon the enterprise of the nation', but Snowden countered that there was no proof the standard rate decrease would stimulate trade. Sir Alfred Mond, however, exposed one fallacy of the Budget; unemployment was the outstanding problem and the present proposals 'lacked any foundation of constructive idea of finance'.[61] Snowden was quick to seize on this point in the following year.[62] 'Can the Rt. Hon. Gentleman point to a single instance where his reduction of the Income Tax and Supertax has added to employment by a single person?' Churchill brushed aside all criticism.[63] He had never known such a 'weak, discursive, disunited and contradictory opposition'. As for Snowden, he was a man of one idea: 'as long as the money is spent on social services and the greater the burden on the direct taxpayer, the better'.

[56] Hansard 11/IV/27.   [57] Hansard 24/IV/28.   [58] Hansard 15/IV/29.
[59] See Misleading Cases. (A. P. Herbert.)   [60] Hansard 28/IV/25.
[61] Hansard 29/IV/25.   [62] Hansard 27/IV/26.   [63] Hansard 28/IV/26.

The contrast between orthodox Conservative finance, the quasi-socialism of Snowden and the crypto-liberalism of Churchill is reflected in the variety of speeches in the House during Budget debates and in the variety of opinions expressed quite apart from any political implications. This current fluidity of taxation theories in general was also illustrated in the Report of the Colwyn Committee,[64] commissioned in March, 1924 and presented in November, 1926. Its duty was 'to consider a report on the National Debt and on the incidence of existing taxation with special reference to their effect on trade, industry, employment and natural credit'. As its members commented, they had been given a 'wide subject matter'.

The Committee came to some significant conclusions on direct taxation which were to play an important part in subsequent Budget debates, although not all those who used Colwyn arguments were agreed on their interpretation, especially as there was a minority report by some of the more left-wing members. For instance, the majority,[65] in fifty pages, came to the conclusion that even if 'there were a prospect of a capital levy being well received, the relief from debt which it offers would be insufficient to justify an experiment so large, difficult and full of hazard . . . Further, unless a levy were accepted with more goodwill than it would be possible to anticipate under present conditions, it would be highly injurious to the social and industrial life of the community.' The minority report, however, still considered that a capital levy was a practical proposition and the Labour Party still continued to press its claims.

The general effect of income tax on the lower levels of income[66] was clearly to influence spending and saving and to the extent that it restricted either, or both, it clearly acted as a disincentive; although the use of revenue for pensions and similar grants clearly increased the workers' purchasing power. It would, however, 'be difficult to maintain the view that as a whole the enterprise of the wealthy business man is seriously damaged' and it had 'no important influence on work and enterprise as far as concerns employments and professions'.

Did income tax enter into prices?[67] Opinions varied from: 'the trader puts a margin of profit for himself and, of course, it is his profit which is subject to the direct income tax and if he wants to get a sufficient reward for his own exertions, he must put on an addition to his price sufficient to cover the profit to the Government as well as the profit to himself', to the opinions of the professional economists: 'income tax is assessed on the profits resulting from trade and industry; and if, as may be presumed, people are already charging the prices that yield them the best profit, the removal by the

[64] The 'Committee on National Debt and Taxation'.
[65] Pp. 246–96.   [66] P. 119, para. 325.   [67] Q. 7297.

State of part of the profit will not tempt them to fix prices differently"[68]

But heavy taxation did present one danger.[69] It acted as a brake on the speculative type of business and prevented the pioneer from risking his capital in an experimental business which might prove of enduring national benefit and it also restricted the supply of capital to established enterprises and stultified their development. Much more was to be heard of this argument in later years.

The problem facing the Chancellor in 1927, however, was that of repairing the damage done by the General Strike. Expenditure was up by £14·5 millions and those once 'stalwart and lively'[70] agents of revenue, income tax and surtax, were down by £17·5 millions; nor had the betting tax of 1926 proved a success. No changes in the rates of direct taxes were proposed; there were, however, some administrative alterations. Schedule E followed Schedule D in adopting the previous year basis of assessment; supertax became surtax and was assigned to the year in which it properly belonged;[71] of more immediate relevance to the balancing of the Budget, however, was the restoration of payment of Schedule A tax by one instalment in January (instead of one half in January and the other half in July), which brought an additional £14·8 millions into the current financial year, proving, in effect, the saviour of the Budget. It was the Lowe technique all over again (see p. 100), and Churchill paid tribute to his predecessor's 'anticipatory plagiarism'. There were a good number of references to the findings of the Colwyn Committee in the subsequent debates, but mainly in connection with indirect taxation without any fundamental criticism of the Budget proposals in principle. Indeed it would have been difficult to find the principle which had inspired the Budget, apart from that of trying to make both ends meet. It was a Budget of expedients; and the Chancellor ended his introductory speech with a warning admission that he had reached the end of his 'adventitious resources'.[72]

The year 1928 opened somewhat more favourably and although the recovery of income tax was not up to expectations, ScheduleA, in one instalment, had proved a marked success, bringing in some £17 millions. The main topic of the Budget was the rating revision which was criticized by Lloyd George and Snowden. The latter had, of course, been conducting a guerilla campaign against Churchill ever since he had become Chancellor. The ex-Chancellor had never allowed his successor to forget his rash promise to economize at the rate of £10 millions a year[73] and constantly prodded him about this

[68] P. 109 (Pigou).   [69] P. 169, para. 451 and p. 167, para. 444.
[70] Churchill's phrase from his Budget of 1925 (28/IV/25).
[71] Part III: F.A. 1927 and Board's Report for the year to 31/III/28, p. 58.
[72] Hansard 11/IV/27.   [73] Hansard 28/IV/25.

and his need to economize in general. Churchill kept his temper admirably, even under the severest provocation of Snowden's 'Billingsgate-ese'. Snowden recalled rather complacently how 'the debates between us became quite a Parliamentary entertainment. They were regarded as the best show in London'. He did, however, appreciate that 'it would be tiresome . . . to deal at length with the innumerable encounters'.[74] Sir Alfred Mond would certainly have agreed. He referred, after a considerable amount of cross talk between the two one evening 'to a rather dreary kind of discussion in which the pot calls the kettle black and in which they compare notes as to why they did or why they did not succeed in reducing expenditure'.[75]

There were no changes in the rates of direct taxation this year or in the following year[76] when Churchill indulged in a retrospect of his five years as Chancellor. He admitted the failure of the Betting Tax 'through the volatile and elusive character of the betting population', but claimed in general a material improvement in the condition of the people. 'His genius', it has been said, 'was particularly adapted to steering the country's finances through depression with an appearance of balance in the Budget, but with a minimum of tax burden'.[77] He preferred revival of industry through remissions of direct taxation to public works financed by surtax or loans, which were the panacea for commercial ills of the two opposition parties. Snowden challenged his reading of the situation at practically every point and concluded that the speech was 'an election manifesto – a bribery Budget'. (This was a reference to the abolition of the tea duty.) The promise to economize had not been redeemed. 'The Chancellor will be judged not by his debating skill, but by the record he leaves behind him.'[78]

But considering the fiscal policy of the period as a whole, there were two problems. The first was pinpointed by the Colwyn Committee: the decline in industrial activity had 'wider causes than taxation, however, and particularly the dislocation of our old export markets must be held mainly responsible for the lack of buoyancy in recent years'. None of the three Chancellors appreciated this. Churchill may be said even to have aggravated it by the return to the gold standard. Secondly, as Mond pointed out more than once, none of the main measures of any of the Budgets directly affected the level of the million and a quarter workless. Snowden and Churchill could enjoy, if they wished, scoring debating points against each other. But why, asked a Labour M.P., himself once a boilermaker, could not something be risked in the solution of the unemployment prob-

[74] *Autobiography*, vol. II, p. 723.   [75] Hansard 25/IV/28.
[76] Hansard 15/IV/29.
[77] Mrs U. K. Hicks: *The Finance of British Governments 1920–1936*, p. 15.
[78] Hansard 15/III/29.

lem?[79] For the fact of the matter was 'the great majority of the working class are getting less and less joy and benefit and pleasure and real help in their lives'.

1929 saw the end of a confusing decade in all aspects of national life and it was to be followed by an even more bewildering period covering another ten years. But, during that first ten years from 1919–29, income tax assumed the form which it was to possess for a generation and more. It was a tax on income, defined in the cases of Schedules A, B, C and E; defined also, in the case of Schedule D, but far more subject, by the nature of the rules applicable to that Schedule, to judicial interpretation. The standard year of assessment, ran from April 6th in one calendar year, to April 5th in the following year. Taking 1929 as a convenient year in which to summarize its provisions, liability to tax was arrived at by first ascertaining total income. This was subject to a deduction of one-sixth for earned income relief, up to a maximum of £250. From this figure of assessable income, a further series of deductions could be made according to the circumstances of the taxpayer. They were the personal allowance of £225 to a normal man, £135 to other persons and £45 where the wife had earned income; 'Housekeeper' (the term was not statutory) allowance of £50; dependent relative allowance of £25; and child allowance of £60 for one child and £50 for each subsequent child (this was authorized by F.A. 1928). The taxable income so arrived at was charged at half standard rate for the first £225 and at full standard rate on the remainder. There was also life assurance relief at varying rates and Dominion income tax relief at a rate dependent on the taxpayer's effective rate. Surtax was levied on income exceeding £2,000 at rates rising from 9d in the £ to 6s. A return of total income was issued by the Inspector and returnable to him; it could, however, on request, be made to the Special Commissioners. The administration was under the 'care and management' of the Board of Inland Revenue which presented an annual report to the Treasury. The staff in 1928[80] numbered 21,000 against 16,253 in 1914, an increase of 28·2%; the revenue collected showed a comparative increase to £331·9 millions or 378%. And, a postscript to this summary, in 1920 the Surveyor of Taxes had become H.M. Inspector of Taxes (see p. 160, note 24). Sir Josiah Stamp, once a Surveyor himself, did not altogether approve of the change. 'Monarch of all I inspect,' he observed, 'is not as impressive as monarch of all I survey.'

Of course there were still anomalies. The continuation of the assessor, despite the recommendations of the Royal Commission of 1929, was archaic and inefficient; only 25% of the collectors in

[79] Hansard 16/IV/29 (J. Gibbens).
[80] Extract from the Second Report from the Select Committee on Estimates.

England and Wales were appointed by the Board although in view of the ill-fated Revenue Bill of 1921[81] the climate was still thought not right for reorganizing this wasteful and expensive system. The Select Committee, however, recommended that 'further careful consideration should be given to the whole matter'. Apart from these main administrative difficulties, the reforms had been absorbed and the taxes machine was running smoothly. The wonder was that no statesman recalled the example and precept of Peel, or paused to consider that if the income tax and business taxes had been used once again to fight a war, they could also have been used for a second time to win a peace.

[81] *British Budgets*, vol. III, p. 22.

CHAPTER XI

Crisis, Evasion and Recovery

THE changes in the principles of levying income tax, that is the introduction of differentiation and graduation, were sixty years or so in coming and then only after tough and persevering debating by the early pioneers of reform, the recommendations of a unanimous Committee and the acumen of Liberal statesmen of Lloyd George's and Asquith's calibre. Once these principles had been established, the detailed amendments, such as those inspired by the 1920 Report, followed far more quickly, so that soon after the end of World War I, the shape of the modern income tax had clearly emerged. Simultaneously a slower, but nevertheless significant, evolution was taking place in the function of the Budget itself. During the Victorian era, the Budget speech was the occasion when the Chancellor of the Exchequer rendered account of his stewardship to the nation by relating the necessary expenditure of the Crown and the Government to his available revenue. Even before 1914, however, it was evident that the Budget had advanced beyond these simple limits and had tacitly assumed the duty, if not the right, of promoting social and economic measures; it was this expanding secondary tendency which Hicks-Beach had looked 'upon with alarm' (see p. 129).[1]

This process was given immense acceleration by World War I and after, when the Government was spending a constantly increasing proportion of the national product; and joined with this paternalism was a third feature, the obligation of managing the necessary deflation when Churchill restored the gold standard in 1925. The sphere of state influence, as shown in the previous chapter, spread wider; there was a growing conviction among the two Opposition parties that it had now become the task of the Government to create employment by the expansion of credit and the promotion of public works, an opinion very much counter to the official Treasury and Conservative view that 'whatever might be the political or social advantages, very little additional employment and no permanent additional employment can, in fact, and as a general rule, be created by State borrowing and State expenditure'.[2]

[1] Hansard 13/IV/1899.   [2] S. H. Beer, *Treasury Control*, pp. 1–2.

173

The increasing complexity of budgetary policy meant that income tax began, by parallel stages, to lose its singleness of purpose. Peel knew exactly why he was reimposing it; Gladstone at least thought he knew why he had to continue it; and throughout the nineteenth century the polite fiction was preserved that it might yet be abolished, since it was not until the succeeding century that the yield of direct taxation overtook that of indirect. From that time it was, along with supertax and the wartime business taxes, the wholly reliable element in the Budget, only wavering in 1927 and never being allowed to fall in rate below 4s in the pound. But from the 'twenties onward it is increasingly difficult to distinguish its overall effects and the motives behind its variations as a separate issue on their own. Listing the changes in income tax only is an arid and artificial exercise; but not if they are seen to an increasing extent in the context of current economic and political conditions.

These conditions were becoming more uncertain and perplexing. Britain's staple industries, coal, steel, ships and textiles had declined as a force in world markets; their traditional homes had now become what the 'thirties aptly termed 'distressed areas', although the primary cause of the decline of exports in general was probably, as Keynes pointed out, the return to the gold standard.[3] It was in this uneasy atmosphere that the General Election of 1929 was held.

For the first time Labour won the largest number of seats but, as in 1924, not an overall majority. Desperate remedies were imperative but with a Cabinet of moderates, Snowden's financial orthodoxy and MacDonald's progressive indecision, desperate remedies were not forthcoming. The May Committee Report threw not only the Government but also the bankers of Europe into a panic, and precipitated *La Crise Britannique* which André Siegfried had diagnosed with Gallic acuteness.[4] Out of this confusion was born the first National Government in August, 1931. Before the end of the year, this became, by a landslide in the General Election, the second National Government, still under MacDonald but committed to a trade protection policy. This forced the resignation of Snowden and the Liberals, leaving the Prime Minister the prisoner of the Conservatives whose Government it virtually was.

The 'thirties were dominated by the joint problems of unemployment and peace. After 1931 and the abandonment of gold, the former was proving less intractable. There was recovery of a sort and the queues at the Labour Exchanges began to decline; but it was an unhealthy recovery based on economy, not expansion, and mainly confined to home industries such as steel and housing. Still, it was

---

[3] 'The Economic Consequences of Mr Churchill'.
[4] André Siegfried: *La Crise Britannique au XX Siécle*.

economic recovery of a sort; and it had not yet merged into an economic recovery of another and more ominous character.

By the time Snowden was ready to present his opening Budget for the second Labour Government, the portents of that first crisis were already visible in the shape of rising unemployment figures[5] and falling trade. Snowden looked at both simply in the context of balancing his Budget; 'the worst economic blizzard the world had ever known'[6] was not yet seen as an immediate menace to Britain. He therefore proceeded to take the orthodox, predictable steps, preserving the balance he thought appropriate between direct and indirect taxation. But he was essentially a realist and had no sympathy with 'the illusion that there was an inexhaustible source of revenue to be drawn upon by further taxation of the rich'.[7]

Consequently, although, as he says, 'I looked to an increase in the Income Tax to meet the greater part of the additional revenue I needed', the proposed advances in direct taxation were comparatively modest.[8] With the raising of the standard rate from 4s in the pound to 4s 6d went a revision of reduced rate relief from the first £225 of taxable income at 2s to the first £250 of taxable income at 2s 6d.[9] This had the 'remarkable effect' of relieving 'about three-quarters of the whole number of income tax payers of any increase and to concentrate taxation on the small minority who already bore the brunt of direct taxation'. There was also an increase in surtax rates and a steepening of the scale.

He had placed, he maintained, 'the burden on the shoulders best able to bear the weight'. If, however, as he continued, 'I abate not one jot or tittle in my life-long advocacy of great schemes of social reform and national reconstruction; but our immediate concern is to make those things possible out of a revived and prosperous industry', the Opposition critics were not slow to point out that he had made no contribution whatever to reviving commercial prosperity; while his own party declared that 'as an instrument of Socialist financial policy it is a defective instrument, a timid instrument'.[10]

The proposals were fought clause by clause, to Snowden's bitter resentment, by the Opposition,[11] from motives of political strategy.

[5] Snowden's *Autobiography*, vol. II, p. 853, quotes figures of 1,222,700 to 1,660,000.

[6] The phrase is Churchill's and is quoted by Snowden, *Autobiography*, vol. II, p. 853.

[7] Snowden's *Autobiography*, vol. II, p. 845.

[8] The 1930 Budget, (Snowden's second): Hansard 14/IV/30 and *Autobiography*, vol. II, p. 855.

[9] *British Budgets*, vol. III, pp. 286–7 and Snowden, *Autobiography*, p. 856.

[10] W. J. Brown quoted in *British Budgets*, Vol. III, p. 290, and Snowden, *Autobiography*, vol. II, p. 858.

[11] Snowden, *Autobiography*, vol. II, pp. 859–62.

Far more constructive was Samuel's telling use of the findings of the Colwyn Committee regarding the effects of high taxation on capital and saving. Snowden was aware of this to a limited extent; he had made and had quoted against him a remark taken from a broadcast to the United States[12] that English taxation was the highest in the world, adding, 'With such a burden as this on our shoulders . . . is it any wonder that we have suffered industrial depression?'

It was argued later in the debate that some relief should be given to limited companies, first for sums put to reserve or, alternatively, for sums paid out of reserve for re-equipment.[13] Both schemes were felt to be administratively difficult and the second Snowden thought would be enormously expensive.[14] Perhaps some relief might be given in the way of increased capital allowances. It was a pity this eminently sensible suggestion was not followed up at once.

Snowden could and did make the classic reply of Chancellors down the years to their critics that, if they could not suggest economies, increased taxation was inevitable. This inflexible and unimaginative attitude blinded him to the possibility of an alternative course, the course of trying to encourage, by selective, and in some instances, lighter taxation an industrial revival; the possible upsurge of profits and fuller employment might even result in a greater all-round yield of taxation. He could not indeed foresee the completeness and the duration of the coming collapse; but he should have paid more heed to those who maintained: 'We should economize in every form of expenditure which was not essential to increasing output' and 'turn our whole energies and attention to the search for new markets and new forms of production to replace the old forms which are lost'.[15]

The first Budget of 1931[16] was a little later than usual as Snowden had been ill during March. Before he underwent his operation, he had agreed to the setting up of an 'economy committee' at the insistence of the Liberals. Since the Government took office, he observed, they had 'set up seventy-two of these committees and one more will not hurt'.[17] But this was the famous May Committee and, while it was gathering its evidence, Snowden was proposing a Budget which he knew and admitted was only a 'stop-gap'; a second Budget[18] was

[12] *British Budgets*, vol. III, pp. 293-4.
[13] Hansard 1/V/30 (Stanley) and 7/VII/30.
[14] *Autobiography*, vol. II, p. 863.
[15] Hansard 25/VII/30 (Sir E. Hilton Young) and *British Budgets*, vol. III, p. 312.
[16] Snowden's third Budget: Hansard 27/IV/31.
[17] *British Budgets*, vol. III, p. 315.
[18] Snowden, *Autobiography*, vol. II.

already scheduled for the autumn. There was no increase in direct taxation, but for a third time the 'accelerated payment'[19] technique was used to bridge the deficit. Income tax under Schedules B, D and E was normally payable in two equal instalments, on January 1st and July 1st respectively. The tax under these three schedules would now be payable as to three-quarters in January and the balance in July. The Chancellor then issued a warning that if the world depression failed to lift 'reduction of expenditure will be the only alternative to increased taxation'. This challenge would have been more effective had he not then plunged into his doctrinaire proposal to tax land values,[20] undeterred by the fate of the Bill in the previous budgetary session and the unproductive legislation of Lloyd George in 1909. This scheme was quite irrelevant to the worsening economic situation and the grim fact that, with the unemployment figures now over the two and a half million mark, borrowing for unemployment insurance had got completely out of hand.

The second Budget of 1931 inevitably centred round the May Committee's suggestions for economy, especially the alterations in unemployment insurance benefits and contributions which accounted for £66½ millions out of the aggregate recommended savings of £96 millions. The Cabinet split on this issue and Snowden eventually found himself presenting his fourth and final Budget[21] as the Chancellor of the National Government. Borrowing for the Unemployment Insurance fund was to cease and stringent economies were enforced all round, the most drastic still being in Unemployment Insurance. The remaining deficit Snowden proposed to make good in characteristic fashion, by increases in direct taxation, both by advancing the standard rate by 6d to 5s in the pound and drastic changes[22] in personal reliefs including reduced rate relief. Surtax payers had to face a 10% jump in their scales in addition. The burden on industry was somewhat lightened by an increase in wear and tear rates of 10% and a more liberal allowance for obsolescence on plant and machinery. The ordinary wage earner was compensated for the lowering of the exemption limit by an increase in earned income allowance from one-sixth to one-fifth. Snowden managed to ensure that 70% of the increased taxation was direct and 30% indirect[23] and, undeterred by cries of 'Dick Turpin!' from the Communist group, concluded with an emotional stanza from Swinburne.[24]

---

[19] The 'accelerated payment' technique had been first used by Lowe (p. 100) and later by Churchill (p. 169).

[20] Taxation on land values: Snowden, *Autobiography*, vol. II, pp. 905–16.

[21] Hansard 10/IX/31.   [22] *British Budgets*, vol. III, p. 367–9.

[23] Snowden, *Autobiography*, vol. II, p. 369.

[24] Reception of the Budget: Snowden, *Autobiography*, vol. II, p. 370.

It is difficult to pass a final judgment on Snowden. His early record as a financial critic was very different from his later record as a Chancellor. Certainly, as he grew older, his fiscal thinking became more rigid and more orthodox; and inevitably, being Chancellor in minority governments dependent on Liberal goodwill left him little opportunity of proposing a truly Socialist Budget even if, by 1924, he had wished to. By 1929 he was in the grip of economic furies which he did not understand and for which his temperament, training and experience had not prepared him. He was not the dupe of a 'bankers' ramp'; rather the innate conservatism of the bankers appealed to his own evangelical devotion to economy; and never was there a more willing victim to the call for a second Geddes axe.

At the opening of this chapter, the changes in income tax and the Budget itself were discussed. There was, however, a third feature of taxation which was evolving also, namely the practice of evasion. Taxation and evasion are complementary twins, and in England resistance to taxation had a long and not always dishonourable history from Wat Tyler to John Hampden. But when parliamentary control over the assessment and collection of revenue had been established, the word evasion gained a more sinister connotation. Income tax in 1799 was, in some ways, the product of 'the evasion, the fraud and the meanness' (see p. 27) which, as Pitt complained, had defeated the Assessed Taxes; but this evasion applied the comparatively unsophisticated method of either omitting assessable items altogether or scaling down their amounts. These techniques were revived along with the reimposition of income tax when evasion again consisted mainly of the concealment of profits or the failure to notify liability.

Although Victorian taxation stayed at rates which now seem mythically low, it is surprising how many complaints of evasion arose even from the early days of the reimposition of income tax. 'I believe no man,' said Lord John Russell, 'who had been concerned in the collection of this tax will deny that his experience has shown that great frauds are practised under this tax . . . those who wished to evade the tax, either found the means of doing so, or entangled themselves and the Government in the most expensive proceedings.'[25] The Hume Committee (see pp. 68–9) heard a good deal of evidence of evasion, especially from the Somerset House officials and the Surveyors, but in general it was not thought seriously to distort the yield in view of the surcharge system and the voluntary rounding up of profits. Some interesting figures were, however, revealed in claims for compensation when true profits were needed as evidence. 'Two years ago,' said Sir Stafford Northcote, 'I was employed in investiga-

[25] Hansard 17/II/1845.

ting claims for compensation in consequence of the abolition of their offices . . . When I came to compare some of the claims with the returns which the claimant had made to the Income Tax, I was astonished by the most painful disclosures.'[26] He proceeded to give examples of 'one gentleman, who stood very high in his profession' returning £3,000 with an income of £9,000; a 'very respectable firm' had made £31,432 but admitted to only £8,800. The same point arose some years later when the Metropolitan Board of Works was in the position of having to pay out compensation (see pp. 104–5).

Meanwhile the Hubbard Committee in 1861 (see pp. 85–6) had also discussed the evasion problem, but neither that body nor the Hume Committee, ten years before, had concentrated on its prevention. A general opinion expressed before the earlier Committee was that since income tax was intrinsically unfair, taxpayers were bound to try and avoid it; while witnesses before the later Committee, agreeing that inequity produced evasion, thought that revision by differentiation would ensure the automatic disappearance of evasion, a theory, as the official witnesses pointed out, which did more credit to their faith in *laissez-faire* than their commonsense. Chadwick, the accountant, put the matter most forcibly when he said that 'there were innumerable cases of fraud in the returns made and . . . such general dishonesty could only be accounted for by a sense of gross injustice'.[27] Perhaps, however, there was a certain *arrière pensée* in his suggestion that 'as the falsification of returns could easily be prevented by requiring verification, professional accountants might be employed to examine them with a view to the detection of fraud', Sir Stafford Northcote could not agree. 'It is said that if you were to do away with some of the irregularities in the assessment of the tax, you would practically do away with or diminish fraud. That is a view which we can hardly accept.' On the employment of accountants, he pointed out that 'any investigation would be of a highly inquisitorial character. This plan could only be rendered effective by arming the gentlemen in question with very stringent powers and that would not increase the popularity of the tax.' This indeed was the heart of the problem; evasion could only be countered by granting greater authority to the Board; and, in general, any increase in the authority of the central Government was counter to current political thinking. In any case, as a matter of practical economics, if not of public morality, the lowness of the rates meant the actual loss of revenue was inconsiderable.

The Boer War, however, when the rate of income tax rose as high as 1s 3d in the pound, forced the problem of evasion into the open and there was a marked increase in informations being laid before

[26] Hansard 23/III/1860.   [27] Hansard 26/II/1876.

the General Commissioners where, as the Act phrased it, there had been a failure 'to have delivered a true and correct statement in writing containing the amounts of the profits or gains arising'. It was a cumbersome procedure and only the most heinous examples would normally be accepted by the Commissioners; for instance, where a return had not been made for many years. Even then the Commissioners often imposed only a mitigated penalty of a few pounds. The maximum penalty of £20 plus treble tax was only exacted when no extenuating circumstances were present such as the Manchester jeweller about whom the Surveyor complained that his returns were so inaccurate as to amount to no returns at all. The appellant could give no excuse beyond 'his desire to reduce his liability as much as possible'.

But even with the apparent increase in evasion, there was, as yet, little advance in technique.[28] There were still only four main methods of evasion; by omissions to make returns, resulting either in escape from assessment altogether or in the making of an inadequate assessment, by fraudulent returns, by appeals against assessments, supported by deliberately inaccurate accounts and by incomplete accounts or erroneous deductions put forward in good faith. The omission to make returns was by far the most prevalent and was strongly criticized by Ritchie in presenting his Budget for 1903–4.[29] In the following year the Association of Tax-Surveying Officers[30] published a pamphlet entitled *Evasions and Fraudulent Returns with Suggested Remedies for Dealing with Them*,[31] which proposed a considerable extension to the powers of Commissioners and Surveyors in view of the 'numerous instances of persons making Returns of £2,000 to £3,000 while their profits were from ten to thirty times those amounts'.

Government as well as official opinion was now moving strongly in favour of at least some enquiry into evasion and the Committee of 1905, the Chairman of which was Ritchie himself, had as the first of its terms of reference to enquire into 'the prevention of fraud and evasion'.[32] The Committee found that there was 'abundant evidence to show that in the sphere in which self assessment is still requisite, there is a substantial amount of fraud and evasion . . . serious enough to demand some amendment of the law and practice'. The Committee proposed, as the Surveyors had done, more severe penalties and an extension of the time limit for making surcharges from the

[28] Techniques of evasion, Ritchie Report (1905), p. vi, para. 20.
[29] Hansard 23/IV/03.
[30] Now the Association of Inspectors of Taxes.
[31] See p. 47 for examples.
[32] Introduction, p. III and p. V, para. 17.

quite inadequate twelve months to three years.[33] One example of evasion from the evidence deserves to be quoted. 'One of the Surveyors came to the Commissioners and said, "Here is Mr So-and-so, who never sends in a Return. We have assessed him at £3,000 a year for the last two or three years and he has always paid on his £3,000. Do you not think we might put him up now?' 'The Chairman said, "Yes, I do." He said, "Well, what shall we call it? What would you put it at – £4,000 or £5,000?" 'The Chairman said, "No; make it £50,000.' He happened to know something about the man, who paid without a murmur.'[34]

The Select Committee of 1906, as previously mentioned (see Chapter IX), was appointed primarily to enquire into the two principles of graduation and differentiation, but the fifth of its summary of conclusions was that 'a compulsory personal declaration from each individual of total net income in respect of which tax is payable is expedient and would do much to prevent the evasion and avoidance of income tax which, at present, prevail'.[35] Many witnesses agreed that the present penalties were ineffective as a deterrent, although it was equally clear the Revenue, for their part, would have to be much more stringent in their checking of returns.[36] There was a good deal of evidence concerning the now familiar evasion by omission;[37] but for the first time the phrase 'legal avoidance'[38] as distinct from mere evasion makes its appearance, instances being the free exchange of coupons on foreign securities and virtual direction from this country of companies situated abroad.

Asquith,[39] with his trained legal mind, was quick to seize on this phenomenon, that ominous signs were appearing of an ingenious avoidance of the fair share of the tax burden by a form of legal evasion, a far more subtle technique than simple omission of profits; he was, however, pessimistic about the chances of preventing it. 'Income tax under the present law,' he said, 'and probably under any improvement they could make in the law, could be evaded to a large extent. Facilities for fraud and concealment and illegitimate exchange of wealth as between man and man were so great, that an income tax which would operate fairly and justly between all classes of the community was an ideal which could never be fully attained.' Austen Chamberlain was equally clear about the new development, but

[33] Ritchie Report (*op. cit.*), p. VIII, para. 36.
[34] Ritchie Report (*op. cit.*), Q. 2104.
[35] Report of Select Committee (1906): On returns: p. IX.
[36] Report of Select Committee (1906): On penalties: Qq. 3345–3348 (Primrose).
[37] Qq. 2014–2031 (Snowden).
[38] The evidence of Sir Thomas Hewitt is in point here, but this was taken in camera.
[39] Hansard 2/VII/07.

failed to see the underlying menace of the technical difference between evasion and avoidance. 'Evasion was an illegitimate denial of
the tax and avoidance was a legitimate denial of the imposition of the
tax. The hon. Gentleman spoke of avoidance as if it were a refusal to
recognize a moral obligation. I do not think there is any moral
obligation on the part of any taxpayer to pay more taxes than he was
legally liable to pay.'[40] These words have a curiously modern ring and
even in this early expression can be taken to justify any scheme of
legal avoidance shading from the innocuous to wilful distortion
of intent.

There was no real attempt to legislate against evasion before
World War I. The general opinion on avoidance and the method of
dealing with it was well put by Lloyd George on the Committee stage
of the last pre-war Budget when discussing the liability of partnerships carried on abroad. People were not going to transfer their
businesses from this country just to avoid income tax. 'It is perfectly
true,' he continued, 'that you can make legal arrangements . . . to
evade taxes. I am perfectly well aware of that . . . The moment it is
done, the Inland Revenue can submit a scheme which will stop all
that kind of spider's web . . . I considered whether it should be
stopped this time and the only reason why it was not done was because I was advised that at the present moment it was not worth
while.''[42]

The immensely high rates of E.P.D., however, required built-in
safety precautions against avoidance especially as it was a temporary
tax which can always be exploited by packing in as much expenditure
as possible during the high level period, in the hope of increased
profits when lower levels come. Hence there was legislation (see
p. 152) against artificial transactions, against increases in the remuneration of Directors and Managers and a general tightening of
'administrative discretion'.[42] This was preventive legislation; it was
also necessary to bring in defensive measures against the sale and
exchange of ships at inflated prices which did not attract tax since
it was a capital transaction and against the disposal of stocks in
bulk (see p. 154).

Fortified by sharpening their craft on the complex legislation of
E.P.D., the evaders received very serious consideration by the 1920
Committee[43] and some alarming, although happily unsubstantiated,
statistics were quoted of the amount of revenue lost,[44] ranging from
a figure of £5 millions in 1913 to that of the Association of Tax-
Surveying Officers of as much as £100 millions 'during the last few

[40] Hansard 3/VII/07.   [41] Hansard 16/VII/14.
[42] Hicks, Hicks, & Rostas: *The Taxation of War Wealth.*
[43] Paras. 625–44.   [44] Para. 627.

years'. The recommendations of the Committee were, in some instances, so strict that they still await legislation, but many have been
included in Finance Acts, as late as that of 1952.[45] The general intent
of the proposals was mainly against simple evasion: 'the hands of the
authorities must be strengthened in this difficult task of discovering
inaccuracies'.[46] Countering avoidance was a different and more
difficult matter but they did suggest:

'it would strengthen the position of the authorities in their dealings
with the taxpayer who seeks to avoid the tax by so arranging his
business that the intention of the law is defeated, if power were given
similar to that now existing under the provisions of the E.P.D. Act,
that is to say, the power of ignoring, for the purposes of assessment,
any fictitious or artificial transaction entered into for the purpose of
evading or avoiding income tax.'[47]

The members finally wished to put on record that views expressed on
the necessity for stringent administration[48] were 'even more vigorous
and far reaching' on the part of witnesses not connected with the
Revenue than those from the Revenue officials and concluded that
a policy of severity with equity would be welcomed by the 'well
affected portions of the community'. This may, in fact, have been so;
indeed it is, presumably, still the case; with the rider that it is only
human to assume the rigour of the law is something which only
applies to the other man.

The struggle between the Revenue and the avoiders in the immediate post-1918 period was mainly over the repayment provisions of
the E.P.D. legislation and the amount of the total tax refunded, put
at approximately £450 millions,[49] must have owed a good deal to
ingenious interpretations of the law as well as the current general
diminution in profits. A start was made on the general problem in
1922 when legislation was provided against the failure by a company
to distribute, in the opinion of the Special Commissioners, a reasonable part of its income in a reasonable time. In the following year
Baldwin, after prolonged consideration of the Royal Commission's
recommendations, adopted the suggestions of increasing penalties
and extending the existing three years' time limit for making income
tax assessments and surcharges and the recovery of statutory penalties, to six years. Churchill, however, took, possibly, a more tolerant
view of avoidance and pointed out that 'the highest authorities have
always recognized that the subject is entitled so to arrange his affairs

[45] E.g. S. 29 F.A. 1952 which makes it obligatory for banks to render returns
of interest over £15.
[46] Para. 633.   [47] Para. 635.   [48] Para. 644.
[49] Hicks, Hicks & Rostas (*op. cit.*), p. 88.

as not to attract taxes enforced by the Crown so far as he can legitimately do so within the law'.[50] Nevertheless he assured the House the Revenue and himself were 'on a continuous watch for loopholes' and his period of office was marked by reinforcing the 1922 legislation dealing with supertax avoidance and attempting to control a device concerning sales cum dividend; it was not until ten years later, however, that this mode of avoidance was fully checked. The Opposition was not convinced of the Government's wholeheartedness in the matter, although it had no positive contribution to make towards solving the problem. Meanwhile, as Dalton said, 'the rich are not only getting richer, but many of them are living longer and some of them have gone to Jersey'.[51] But by the time the Labour critics had regained office, the Government was fighting for its economic life and the anti-avoidance clauses of the draft 1930 Bill were not as decisive as they were originally intended. The Attorney General was forced to admit 'the way of the man who tries to stop up the holes of the tax evader without hitting the innocent is extraordinarily difficult'.[52] This may well fairly summarize the position of the anti-avoidance campaign as it stood in the early 'thirties.

The first Budget of Neville Chamberlain,[53] after the translation of Snowden to the Lords, was, in effect, a prolongation of the austere policies of his predecessor. Indeed, *The Times* commented on its 'puritanical severity'.[54] This was a virtue conditioned by hard fiscal facts; since although income tax and surtax showed a surplus of nearly £20 millions, the estimates for both these taxes were down due to trade conditions and the increased wear and tear allowances. No relief in respect of direct taxation was, therefore, possible and employers were encouraged to continue their voluntary scheme of paying their employees income tax and deducting it in monthly instalments from their remuneration.[55] Some comfort might, however, have been drived from the Chancellor's observation that the country 'had approached the practical limits of the return from direct taxation', and, a point which had aroused political controversy for some time, a Committee was to explore the question of taxing co-operative societies.[56]

---

[50] Hansard 11/IV/27.   [51] Hansard 26/IV/26.
[52] 'The way of the man . . .' Quoted in *British Budgets*, vol. III, p. 303.
[53] Hansard 19/IV/32.
[54] *The Times* quoted in *British Budgets*, vol. III, p. 399.
[55] Employers and tax deductions: *British Budgets*, vol. III, p. 405.
[56] Co-operative societies had been made liable to C.P.T. which was regarded as the thin end of the wedge of income tax itself and from time to time the columns of Hansard are full of Conservative – Labour exchanges on the merits of taxing or not taxing co-operative profits. See for example Hansard 7/III/16 (Currie) or 4/IV/16 (Tickler).

In his second Budget, Chamberlain was still arguably under the shadow of Snowden, whom he greatly admired,[57] and certainly of current economic conditions which were still critical.[58] There were again no material changes in direct taxation,[59] apart from bringing within the orbit of income tax the undistributed profits of co-operative societies;[60] this did not, however, upset the normal exemption of mutual social clubs. On the wider issues, the occasion was notable for the Chancellor's flat refusal to unbalance the Budget deliberately. 'That proposal had been supported by eminent economists, powerful journalists and, if my information is correct, by some hon. Members of the House.' He could have particularized[61] and said Keynes, *The Times* and Harold Macmillan had he wished. Admittedly, everyone was unbalancing their budgets, 'yet they do not produce those favourable results which it is claimed would happen to us . . . By following a sound financial policy we have been enabled to secure low interest rates for industry and it would be the height of folly to throw away that advantage.'

Chamberlain's third and fourth Budgets should be regarded as complementary. In matters of finance, like Snowden, he had always dominated his party and he was now beginning to achieve an equal mastery of Parliament. In this process he was aided by a slight but distinct economic revival showing rises in both prices and output, so that in his 1934 Statement he was able to budget at long last for no fall in Schedule D tax yield,[62] a clear indication of some measure of recovery. He did not need the Archbishop of York to tell him how to allocate his surplus.[63] Sixpence was to come off the standard rate, an indication of his confidence in increasing profits; all the unemployment cuts were restored and half the reduction in the salaries of State and local government officials. Income tax payers had made by far the largest contribution to extra taxation in 1929 to 1931; the case for remission was overwhelming and 'I rejoice to think it has at last been possible to afford them some relief'.

Labour criticism in the person of Clement Attlee was mainly on the well-worn theme of the shifting of the tax burden from direct to indirect taxation; and subsequent Labour speakers took their cue from the Leader of the Opposition. Major Nathan,[64] however, raised

[57] Keith Feiling: *Neville Chamberlain*, pp. 202–3, 234.
[58] Economic affairs in 1933: Feiling (*op.cit.*), p. 220.
[59] Chamberlain's second Budget, Hansard 25/IV/33.
[60] See now S. 444 (originally S. 31 and S. 32, F.A. 1933) ,and on the mutuality principle: Hansard 22/V/33.
[61] Ian Macleod: *Neville Chamberlain*, p. 167.
[62] Chamberlain's third Budget: Hansard 17/IV/34.
[63] The Archbishop of York: Feiling (*op. cit.*), p. 233; Macleod (*op. cit.*), p. 165.
[64] Hansard 18/IV/34.

the more interesting technical question of further relief on capital expenditure for re-equipment, before going on to say that the cuts in allowances should now be restored, instancing the plight of the £500 a year married man with one child whose sacrifices had not yet been compensated. In general, the official line that the Budget could not give rise to general controversy was justified as was the Chancellor's own comment that 'Bleak House' was closed and 'Great Expectations' opened.

Industry had been relieved; in the 1935 Budget it was the turn of the individual taxpayer.[65] The advance of trade was continuing and the revenue receipts were nearly £16 millions up on the estimates, mainly due to income tax. Chamberlain turned to allowances. 'The old reliefs were never scientific nor are they sacrosanct . . . I want this year to see the smaller taxpayer have his turn.' Reduced rate relief became £135 at 1s 6d instead of the old £175 at 2s 6d, thus, as the Chancellor pointed out, assisting the £500 taxpayer whose cause Major Nathan had pleaded a year ago; in addition, the married man's allowance was raised to £170, Child Allowance was fixed at £50 for each child and the exemption limit drawn at £120 for both earned and unearned incomes. Attlee admitted the justice of these revisions but regarded them as overdue. Morgan Jones[66] returned to fundamental Labour criticism: there was still a 'steady drift' to indirect taxation and away from direct taxation and 'behind this picture of prospective prosperity is the grim spectre of unemployment'. The general run of speeches, however, was on general principles; Duff Cooper wound up the day's debate by maintaining the restoration of industry was the only cure for unemployment and Chamberlain echoed this on the following day.

In a period dominated by two strong Chancellors and a fiscal crisis, as well as the increased emphasis on countering avoidance, the Board had an exceptionally busy seven years. Behind the apparently barren figures and the deliberately formal reports lay an organization to which any Chancellor would automatically turn in an emergency. Not less than 70% of the additional revenue raised in 1931 had come from income tax[67] by a simple adjustment of rates and allowances bringing, as the Board commented with an unusual flash of the picturesque, 'more into the met'.[68] The 1920 Committee had reported 'the general efficiency of the work carried on by the Board and by the officials for whom they are directly responsible';[69] addi-

---

[65] Chamberlain's fourth Budget, Hansard 15/IV/35.
[66] Hansard 16/IV/35.
[67] Feiling (*op. cit.*), p. 236.
[68] Board's Report for the year ended 31/III/32, p. 47.
[69] 1920 Committee Report, p. 74, para. 335.

tional duties only served to emphasize the Board's ability to absorb them.

The 1920 Committee had also expressed the opinion that 'all the collectors throughout the United Kingdom should be appointed by the Board of Inland Revenue',[70] and as a corollary that the Board should also be responsible for 'the general management of the collection of the tax'. Collectors should also become 'whole time Civil Servants'. This had long been a cherished wish of the Board which had been lying dormant for nearly fifty years since the narrow defeat over this issue in 1883 (see pp. 119–20). Admittedly a modified success had been achieved in 1879 (see p. 119), whereby the Board could appoint the Collector for any parish where the General Commissioners had failed to do so by May 31st; but even so, in 1920 four-fifths of the Collectors had been appointed by the General Commissioners, although remunerated by the Crown.[71]

Now by the 1931 Finance Act, the appointment of all collectors of Taxes in England and Wales, excluding the City of London, was vested in the Board. It was pointed out that centralized collection was in operation already for seventeen large areas in England and Wales and for practically the whole of Scotland and Northern Ireland. ''ware bureaucracy!' was no longer the rallying cry it had been in the 'eighties. The Board even circularized collection areas asking the General Commissioners specifically if there were any complaints about the new arrangements. Manchester, for example, expressed no opinion as the Board had been making the appointments there for many years, ever since the scandal of a defaulting Collector; and the changeover generally took place smoothly without any real challenge from the Opposition. Indeed the reform had been too long delayed. The final establishment of control came in two instalments; in 1942 all collectors in Scotland and Northern Ireland were to be appointed in future by the Board; and in 1945 the City of London was assimilated to the rest of England.[72]

And so, as the nation began to enjoy a limited recovery, Chamberlain's first four Budgets, pitched as they were in a minor key, played a vital if unspectacular part in restoring '80% of our prosperity' by a delicate combination of inflatory and deflatory measures.[73] Income

---

[70] The 1920 Committee Report, p. 87, para. 390 (*a*), (*b*), and (*c*).

[71] Collectors in 1920: The 1920 Committee, p. 86, paras. 387–8.

[72] The appointment of collectors: S. 37 F.A. 1931: in Scotland and Northern Ireland Tenth Schedule, F.A. 1942, para. 9: in the City of London S. 60, F.(No. 2)A. 1945.

[73] The general effect of Chamberlain's first four Budgets is summed up by Feiling (*op. cit.*), p. 236 and MacLeod (*op. cit.*), p. 169. The latter contains Chamberlain's own summary (Hansard 15/IV/35) and an interesting contradiction in Mowat (*op. cit.*), at pp. 432 and 455.

tax itself had not altered in principle since 1929, although it was a comparatively new development for the Board to be continually on the watch for avoidance devices; as for the yield, Peel and Gladstone would have congratulated Chamberlain on succeeding in enhancing the revenue from reduced rates of taxation. 'Given peace abroad', full recovery should be possible. It is an ironical thought that the Board would soon be considering a new business tax with the ominous title of National Defence Contribution.

CHAPTER XII

Trial by Battle – 2

BEFORE the 1935 Budget the real life of the Government had faded out and the revitalization of an election was needed. After the poll it was seen that Labour had recovered ground to the extent of 154 seats from the 46 of 1931, but there was still no effective opposition to the Conservative Government of Baldwin. That was indeed the tragedy of British politics in the 'thirties, the frustration of not being able to make any impression on the still overwhelming Conservative majority. It may well be that their impervious security in the House induced both a contempt of criticism which, as in the case of Churchill's warnings,[1] they would have done better to heed, and an inability to appraise the menace of totalitarianism. The House of Commons' life was young, it has been said, but the Government seemed old and the country itself was disunited. The 'two nations'[2] of Disraeli had now become the four nations of Priestley;[3] old-world England, prosperous and sometimes elegant England of suburbia, northern and midlands industrial England and England on the dole. The rate of industrial recovery, fostered by a long delayed rearmament programme, was increasing in tempo; but despite this, when Chamberlain succeeded Baldwin in 1937, he had started on a fruitless errand which was to end in another National Government facing an even graver emergency than that of 1931.

The British tax structure of 1929 (see p. 171), steeply progressive at the upper end with a standard rate only 1s below 1920 and surtax considerably higher and equally steeply regressive at the lower end, especially after the amendments of F.A. 1935 (see p. 186), did not alter greatly in form during the decade to 1939. There was, however, a certain shift in the balance between direct and indirect taxation,[4] the adoption of Protection by the National Government causing a relative increase in the latter, perhaps even to the extent of 'a sub-

---

[1] For example, *The Gathering Storm*.
[2] The subtitle of Disraeli's *Sybil* is 'The Two Nations'.
[3] See J. B. Priestley's *English Journey*.
[4] (*a*) *Taxation under Capitalism* – New Fabian Research Bureau, 1934, p. 11; (*b*) Mrs U. K. Hicks (*op. cit.*), p. 16.

stantial restoration of the pre-war (1914) relation between direct and indirect taxes'. This increase would, in some degree, be balanced by the poorer classes enjoying a greater amount of social services than they paid in taxation.[5] Chamberlain had ridden out the economic storm in his first two Budgets with the help of a reimposed tariff; he had made a further contribution to recovery in his second two Budgets by granting relief to industry and individual taxpayers. But his progress was halted in 1936 when, for the first time, defence expenditure[6] rose from £137 millions in the previous year, to £187 millions.

Chamberlain's 1936 Budget,[7] therefore, was inevitably circumscribed and he grumbled privately 'that four years of fruitful finance were to be undone'.[8] It was necessary to raise the standard rate of income tax to 4s 9d in the £, despite a general increase in yield from rising prosperity, and to put a further penny on the reduced rate, making it 1s 7d in the £. As a compensation to the smaller taxpayer, the allowances for a married man and for children were raised by £10, making them £180 and £60 respectively. To be forced to ask for these sacrifices so soon after the 'Great Expectations' of 1935 was a bitter disappointment to the Chancellor, but his duty seemed plain, especially as he was doubling with his office that of Premier-designate.[9] To opposition critics of the defence votes, he retorted that 'no man hesitates to set his firefighting appliances in readiness when already he can feel the heat of the flames on his face'. Apart from the re-armament expenditure, the Budget was almost unopposed.

But raiding the Road Fund, 2d on tea and 3d on income tax were not sufficient to meet the mounting deficiency. In the following year, Chamberlain was compelled to bring the standard rate up to 5s in the £ by an additional threepence;[10] he 'could not resist this' since he had been so advised by two ex-Chancellors, Horne and Churchill. There was a further penny, too, on the reduced rate which thus stood at 1s 8d in the £. He also mentioned the further advice which any Chancellor receives from the lunatic fringe incorporating 'a large number of suggestions with a view to assisting me to find new and hitherto untapped sources of revenue'.

There were, however, two further Budget features of some importance. The first was an intensification of the drive against avoid-

---

[5] Redistribution of income: S. Pollard: *The Development of the British Economy 1914–1950*, p. 207.

[6] Pollard (*op. cit.*), p. 214; Macleod (*op. cit.*), p. 191; Feiling (*op. cit.*), pp. 283–4.

[7] Chamberlain's 1936 (fifth) Budget: Hansard 21/IV/36.

[8] Macleod (*op. cit.*), p. 191.   [9] Macleod (*op. cit.*), p. 191.

[10] Chamberlain's 1937 (sixth) Budget: Hansard 20/IV/37.

ance which had been initiated in the previous year. To legislation against fictitious settlements were added measures against 'bond-washing', a device for evading tax on interest arising from securities by a temporary change of ownership, and against one man companies, a contrivance largely for escaping surtax. There was a general warning in this context that 'if people persisted in devising these ingenious contrivances for defeating the intention of the legislature, they must not expect that they would escape retrospective legislation'. These measures commanded universal acceptance and in improving them Parliament was expressing the common morality of the country and the steadfast opinion that the heavy burden of taxation should be borne according to an individual's capacity to pay and not according to his ability to cloak that capacity in a legal form which makes it different from what it is.

The second measure was the new business tax, to be named National Defence Contribution,[11] which Chamberlain had embarked upon 'without taking wide counsel on an immensely difficult proposition: to tax not profits, as such, but their rate of expansion.' The rates of change varied according to the percentage of growth. A minimum return of 6s on capital was exempt; between 6% and 10% the expansion was taxed at 20% with higher percentages of growth being taxed up to a maximum of $33\frac{1}{3}\%$. He 'could not expect members to grasp it at the first hearing' which was not surprising as there were further complications, such as the requirement of a full capital computation in every case.[12] Pethick-Lawrence[13] said, not unfairly, 'it was our old friend, E.P.D., resurrected from the grave and given new clothes'.

Despite Chamberlain's motives,[14] which were not only the raising of revenue, but the prevention of profiteering, the results were a near disaster,[15] including a Stock Exchange slump, an unholy alliance between the City and Keynes, and a spasm of international monetary unrest. The Opposition 'wished him luck in his endeavour to put salt on the tail of the profiteer',[16] but the very day he kissed hands as Prime Minister, his party was begging him to drop the tax,[17] which he did on the understanding that an alternative business tax would be found with a yield of £25 millions.

[11] Chamberlain's personal responsibility for N.D.C.: Feiling (*op. cit.*), p. 293 and Mrs U. K. Hicks (*op. cit.*), footnote, p. 19.
[12] The original (abortive) N.D.C. in general; the clearest account is by Hicks, Hicks, & Rostas (*op. cit.*), pp. 90–1.
[13] Hansard 21/IV/37.   [14] Feiling (*op. cit.*), p. 292.
[15] The reaction to N.D.C.: Feiling (*op. cit.*), pp. 292–3 and Macleod (*op. cit.*), p. 192.
[16] Hansard 21/IV/37 (Attlee).
[17] Government reaction to N.D.C. (Mark I): Feiling (*op. cit.*), p. 293.

The new Chancellor in the new Government was, as expected,[18] Sir John Simon. He had 'a critical brain of the first order'[19] and temperamentally was well fitted to that side of the Chancellor's duties which involve working within the framework of hard financial facts and nice legal considerations; on the other hand, the independence and initiative which a Chancellor had scope for did not appeal to him, which was just as well since he had an exacting and experienced master.[20] His first duty was the moving of the Second Reading of the Finance Bill which Chamberlain had introduced.[21] He defended the original N.D.C. 'largely out of loyalty to its author',[22] but eventually replaced it by a much simpler tax.

This took the form of a levy on the profits of bodies corporate and similar bodies from April 1, 1937.[23] This profit was normally computed by taking the adjusted profit for income tax purposes, adding the net annual value of premises owned and occupied for the trade, investment income not received from bodies corporate liable to N.D.C. and excess directors' remuneration if the company was director controlled; and deducting annual charges from which tax is legally deductible and wear and tear allowances for the accounting period. The resultant figure was taxed at 5% and the duty was an allowable deduction in arriving at the amount assessable under Case I of Schedule D. The first full year of the Contribution was less than £200,000 short of the anticipated £25 millions and from it was to emerge the Profits Tax[24] of ten years' hence.

Simon's first Budget[25] imposed a further sixpence on the standard rate (hence the Scriptural description of the Budget – 'Simon, a tanner'), the third rise in three successive years, to provide for the ever-mounting cost of rearming. To lessen the impact on industry, Wear and Tear rates were increased by 20% in place of the 10% which had been Snowden's cushion against his 1931 increase in the standard rate (see p. 177). He also continued his predecessor's campaign against avoidance which he defined as 'the adoption of ingenious methods for reducing liability which are within the law but which none the less defeat the intention on which the law is founded'. He thought, however, that 'these devices are resorted to by few; the great majority accept the full and natural burden and discharge it without any attempt to avoid it'. Attlee was not so sure. 'It seems to me,' he

---

[18] *Retrospect; The memoir of The Rt. Hon. Viscount Simon*, p. 227.
[19] Feiling (*op. cit.*), p. 296.   [20] Simon (*op. cit.*), p. 275.
[21] Simon (*op. cit.*), p. 228.
[22] Defence of N.D.C. (Mark I): Simon (*op. cit.*), p. 228.
[23] N.D.C. (Mark II): F.A. 1937.
[24] N.D.C. in effect changed its title to Profits Tax at the beginning of 1947.
[25] Hansard 20/IV/38 and Simon (*op. cit.*), p. 230.

said in reply, 'that tax dodgers are always a few moves ahead of any given Chancellor of the Exchequer.' Pethick-Lawrence was in no doubt about the real nature of the proposals.[26] 'This,' he said, 'is not a peace Budget.' Even so, it is a remarkable illustration of the fatalistic atmosphere of those days that even when the imposition of charges almost amounting to the scale of a war Budget were being debated, the House was nearly counted out.

Simon's second Budget[27] proposed an increase in surtax[28] but none in the standard rate which remained at 5s 6d in the £. Even so, as he pointed out, he was budgeting for an expenditure nearly twenty times greater than Gladstone had had to provide for in 1853. With regard to tax avoidance, the evil still persisted although 'recent legislation has worked well and checked to a considerable extent abuses against which it was directed'.

The reception of the Budget was not as favourable as in the previous year. Sinclair, for instance, the Liberal leader, who had found the 1938 Budget 'austere and honest', thought the present proposals 'unimaginative'. Attlee accused the Chancellor of not facing the problem of expenditure fairly; he was simply passing it on. Pethick-Lawrence made the constructive suggestion that now was the time for the mobilization of weatlh; and he proposed a capital levy which, he argued, should be imposed annually. The Opposition might well have spared its censures. The Budget proposals were in effect still-born, for the prologue to World War II was now working up to crisis pitch, and within three weeks of the declaration of hostilities, Simon 'was ready with an Emergency Budget'.[29]

World War I had taught two primary fiscal reasons; the sooner finance is placed on a war footing the better, and as much as possible of the excess of incomes over necessary living expenses should be hived off in taxation. 'Finance,' as Simon declared in opening the first war Budget, 'is the fourth arm of defence.' Proposals for increasing direct taxation were suitably drastic. Standard rate was raised to 7s 6d in the £ and reduced rate to 2s 4d although the zone was amended from the first £135 of taxable income to the first £165. Personal allowances were all reduced including earned income relief from a fraction of one-fifth to one-sixth.[30] Surtax was also scaled up[31] and a new business tax was imposed, based on the abortive Arma-

---

[26] Hansard 27/IV/38.   [27] Hansard 25/IV/39.
[28] Board's Report for the year to 31/III/40, p. 18, para. 19.
[29] Hansard 27/IX/39, Simon (*op. cit.*), p. 233 (Simon's third), F.(No. 2)A. 1939.
[30] Reductions in allowances: Board's Report for the year ended 31/III/40, pp. 18–19, paras. 23–7.
[31] Board's Report for the year ended 31/III/40, Table 24.

ment Profits Duty of 1939,[32] entitled Excess Profits Tax, chargeable at 60%. In addition, 'It was,' said the Chancellor, 'a duty to search out for means to avoid wasteful outlay.'[33] Provision was made, finally, for relief to any individual whose actual earned income for 1939–40 had, owing to circumstances connected with the war, fallen 'substantially' short of his earned income as assessed to tax.

The Opposition[34] was in substantial agreement that 'it was right to start at once with heavy new taxes', but there was some objection to the increased burden on earned as opposed to unearned income, to the reduction of allowances and to the net result that 'the poor taxpayer has to meet the largest proportion of the increase'. More positive suggestions were for a capital levy and for the administrative reform of transferring the General Commissioners' assessing powers to the Inspector. The basic criticism was that the country was still meeting, by direct taxation, only a small fraction of the total expenditure and the Budget represented 'the first step only in our war finance'.

There were some speeches away from the main stream. There was, for instance, a thoughtful contribution by Sir George Schuster[35] on the need for retaining a profit incentive to some extent in which he quoted Stamp's opinion on the point with approval. Some Members thought the limit of taxation had been reached;[36] some thought E.P.T. had been levied at too low a rate;[37] and one Member at least advocated the now old fashioned idea that no one should be exempt[38] and there should be a graduated tax on all incomes: 'sweep away all allowances,' he declared. In general, apart from a universal acceptance of the need for substantially increased tax burdens, the debates took a remarkably party tone, with each side automatically adopting the accustomed attitudes.

Simon's fourth Budget[39] was presented after the 'winter of illusion' when the 'phoney war' seemed to have set in a perpetual stalemate. After giving some comparative figures of income tax and surtax yield, £390 millions and £69·75 millions respectively, as against a mere £59 millions and £10 millions in 1914, he revealed that the two taxes were to remain unchanged for 1939–40. A liability to tax under Schedule D was imposed on rents under short leases to the extent that

[32] See F.A. 1939; repealed by S. 20, F.(No. 2)A. 1939, before any assessments made, it was based on the E.P.D. of World War I days: Board's Report for the year ended 31/III/40, p. 46, para. 58.

[33] Cf. Hicks, Hicks & Rostas (*op. cit.*), p. 5.

[34] Opposition criticisms: Attlee (Hansard 27/IX/39), Pethick-Lawrence (Hansard 28/IX/39), Wilmot (Hansard 28/IX/39), Dalton (Hansard 2/X/39).

[35] Hansard 28/IX/39.　　[36] E.g. Hansard 27/IX/39 (Hammersley).

[37] E.g. Hansard 27/IX/39 (Adams).　　[38] E.g. Hansard 27/IX/39 (Southby).

[39] Hansard 23/IV/40.

they were not adequately taxed under Schedule A, or, as it was popularly called, an 'excess rents'[40] assessment was raised in such cases. Dividends were limited and a prohibition placed on the issue of bonus shares. The Chancellor could survey his work with justifiable pride; 'out of £1,817 millions spent in the previous twelve months, more than £1,000 millions had been found out of revenue'.[41] As he remarked to the House: 'Nothing on that scale has ever been approached before.'

There was little detailed criticism of the Budget, apart from complaints about the increased Post Office charges. The general line of attack[42] was against the Government's failure to attain total mobilization of the national war effort. 'The problem that confronts the country is how to turn a peace economy into a war economy'; or, as a future Chancellor more forcibly put it, 'the war effort of this country, at the present time, is gravely insufficient'. The main suggestion for fiscal reform was still a capital levy;[43] if this was, as the Government maintained, administratively difficult, the total poundage of income tax and surtax 'could be pushed up to 25s or 30s or even £2 in the £'. It was not surprising, after such a flight of fancy, that a more moderate Member observed,[44] 'how very easy was the task of hon. Members who can get up to criticize or propose plans without the responsibility of carrying them out'; and he pointed out further that if the whole of every income over £2,000 were confiscated, the yield would only be £60 millions.

Simon himself wound up the debate[45] saying that the main complaint about the level of taxation was that 'it ought to have been more'. Members who felt that way were by no means confined to the Opposition. One referred[46] to Chamberlain's 1934 Budget speech, when he had made play with 'Bleak House' and 'Great Expectations'; a good deal had happened since that afternoon, enough, perhaps, to warrant a composite work entitled 'Bleak Expectations'. Another, who was soon to lead the revolt against Chamberlain,[47] welcomed the increase in direct taxation, but warned the House 'that undoubtedly it may have to go higher yet and the minimum at which it begins may have to go lower'. This was certainly a prescient forecast; he followed it up with an even more accurate prediction that the Budget was a stop-gap affair 'which will require to be supplemented before the year is

---

[40] Board's Report for the year to 31/III/41, p. 19, para. 21.
[41] Simon, *Retrospect*, p. 235.
[42] Opposition attitudes: Attlee (Hansard 23/IV/40), Pethick-Lawrence (Hansard 24/IV/40), Dalton (Hansard 25/IV/40).
[43] Dalton (Hansard 25/IV/40).   [44] Schuster (Hansard 25/IV/40).
[45] Hansard 25/IV/40; Simon, *Retrospect*, p. 236.
[46] Hansard, 24/IV/40 (Braithwaite).   [47] Hansard, 23/IV/40 (Amery).

over'. This was also the opinion of *The Economist*[48] which pointed out that the war effort was still below that of Germany.

The five months from April to September, 1940 were perhaps the most eventful in the whole course of World War II. Within that short space of time occurred the ill-fated Norwegian expedition, the *Blitzkreig*, Dunkirk and the Battle of Britain. There had also been a dramatic turn in domestic politics; Chamberlain had been replaced by Churchill, who now headed a Coalition Government. Since this commanded the confidence of both capital and labour, it could and did impose a completeness of control on both manpower and materials which the previous Government could never have approached. The new Chancellor was Sir Kingsley Wood. By profession he was a solicitor; he had been Postmaster-General and behind his somewhat prim exterior lay a logical mind which, when convinced of the need for the most ruthless taxation, led him to propose it without hesitation.

He opened his first Budget[49] in July by stating 'it was necessary to review again our financial position and to take certain immediate action'. There was evidence of a greatly accelerated war effort under the stimuli of isolation and danger, but that in itself had created further financial problems. War expenditure was now running at the rate of £50 millions a week. He would have to raise the standard rate to 8s 6d in the £, the reduced rate to 5s and depress exemption limits; surtax rates would be revised, the peak charges now being 18s in the £.[50] Above all, the E.P.T. rate was fixed at 100%.[51] A prototype P.A.Y.E. scheme was set up by which the Board was given power to make regulations for the assessment and collection of income tax chargeable under Schedule E and in particular for requiring employers to deduct tax from remuneration paid to employees and account to the Revenue for it. There was some fear that a system of refunds might overburden the scheme but, as the Chancellor said: 'What I need is cash and cash out of current income.'

There was no real objection to any of the measures.[52] Some fears, however, were expressed about the rate of E.P.T. both inside and outside Parliament and the fact that so high a level might destroy initiative and enterprise. Indeed, the increased charge had been first announced by Attlee as early as May, 1940, but not until the Budget did it become finally clear that it was to apply to all trades from

[48] April 27, 1940, pp. 759–60: quoted by S. Pollard (*op. cit.*).

[49] Hansard 23/VII/40.

[50] Taxation changes: Board's Report for the year to 31/III/41, pp. 20–21, paras. 29–36; p. 36, paras. 52–7.

[51] F.A. 1940, Part III, S. 26.

[52] Criticism of rate: Hansard 23/VII/4 0 (Wardlaw Milne); Hicks, Hicks & Rostas (*op. cit.*), pp. 100–3.

April 1, 1940; it is possible that there was a divergence of opinion on the matter in the Government.[53]

E.P.T.,[54] as previously mentioned, had been imposed by F.A. (No. 2) 1939. It was descended from the old E.P.D. of World War I, but was more complex as befitted the more complex type of concern it was mainly designed to assess. It was a tax additional to income tax, imposed on trades or businesses, apart from professions. E.P.T. was allowable as a deduction against the Case I profit and was charged as an alternative to N.D.C., which was imposed only when the liability to that tax exceeded the E.P.T. liability.

The computation of the E.P.T. profit was very much on the lines of N.D.C. (see p. 192), which itself might not differ greatly from the income tax profit. The tax was then levied on the amount by which the profit arising in the chargeable accounting period exceeded the standard profit. It was at this point that the complications began. There was, first of all, a minimum standard of £1,000 below which no liability arose; where, however, a company was director controlled, the standard was £1,500 for one 'working proprietor', £3,000 for two, and so on; and there could, in certain circumstances, be an extension to these standards if inadequate having regard, for instance, to the size of the business. Such standards were comparatively simple. More elaborate was the working out of a profits standard. The taxpayer was given various options in his choice of a standard period which could be the year 1935, 1936 or the average of 1935 and 1937 or 1936 and 1937. These profits, or average profits, were to be adjusted up or down to take account of any variation in the capital employed in the business between the standard period and the chargeable accounting period.

At 60% such a tax was penal enough; at 100% it could be crippling from a reserve point of view; and looking at current efficiency the danger was 'not so much that it provides no incentive to make profits, but rather that there is no adequate inducement to avoid losses'.[55] These factors were appreciated early in the life of the tax and their impact softened by such concessions as an allowance for exceptional depreciation in respect of war purpose buildings and plant, the treatment of borrowed money as capital, a deduction for repairs deferred owing to the war, and consideration for terminal expenses. The most important abatement of the severity of the 100% rate, however, was announced by Kingsley Wood in 1941. Dealing with the 'no reserves,

[53] Hicks, Hicks & Rostas, (*op. cit.*), p. 100, footnote 4.
[54] A good summary (to 1941) is in Hicks, Hicks & Rostas (*op. cit.*), pp. 93–117. There is a useful rapid reference compendium by Tolley covering 1939 to 1946. The E.P.T. legislation is spread over the Finance Acts from 1939 to 1953.
[55] Hicks, Hicks & Rostas (*op. cit.*), p. 101.

no reward' line of complaint, he said that wider issues of policy than purely fiscal ones were involved. 'It is directed primarily against taking the profit out of war; but it is quite another thing to tax a business in such a way that it is worse off at the end of the war than at the beginning.' Nevertheless, he proposed to treat 20% of all E.P.T. paid at 100% less Income Tax,[56] as a post-war refund[59] 'to assist industry to undertake the essential task of reconstruction and readjustment and to absorb the mass of the nation, as quickly as possible, into profitable peacetime employment'. The idea was first put forward by the Committee on Financial Risks in 1918 and was revived by a group of Manchester economists in 1941;[58] it is also paralleled by Keynes's scheme of enforced saving,[59] which will be mentioned later.

When E.P.T. was first introduced, one member remarked:[60] 'As the war goes on, this tax will be his (the Chancellor's) main source of income.' It never became that, in view of the astonishingly resilient yield of Income Tax, but, combined with N.D.C. it reached the remarkable figures of £98 millions in 1940–1, £269 millions in 1941–2, £377 millions in 1942–3, £501 millions in 1943–4 and £508 millions in 1944–5. There were, inevitably, complains of evasion and the E.P.T. legislation is concerned with such techniques as artificial transactions and elaborate avoidance schemes the 'main purpose, or one of the main purposes of which was the avoidance or reduction of liability to E.P.T.'.[61] The word 'main', incidentally, was a Committee stage amendment which the Revenue could well have done without. Simple evasion was principally through the well worn method of inflated expenses;[62] as the 'hard faced men who had done well out of the war' used to say in the 1914–18 days, 'Let us have some fizz; it all comes out of E.P.D.'.[63]

'The year 1941 was certainly a watershed in the conduct of the war, producing firm policies of taxation, of free and forced saving . . . The whole economic situation was illuminated in that year by the new statistical analysis contained in the first White Paper on national income and expenditure.'[64] This new spirit was exemplified in

[56] 'Less Income Tax.' Because of course the original 100% E.P.T. had been allowed as a deduction in computing the Case I profit. The point seemed to puzzle a good number of the Members when the Chancellor first broached the point.

[57] Hansard 7/IV/41.　　[58] Hicks, Hicks & Rostas, (*op. cit.*), pp. 83 and 105.

[59] J. M. Keynes: *How to Pay for the War.*　　[60] Hansard 2/X/39 (Boothby).

[61] See F.A. 1941, S. 35; F.A. 1944, S. 33.

[62] Hicks, Hicks & Rostas (*op. cit.*), p. 44.

[63] Hansard 5/X/39 (Williams).

[64] W. K. Hancock and M. M. Gowing: *British War Economy*, p. 152: quoted by Pollard (*op. cit.*), p. 303.

Kingsley Wood's second Budget.[65] He began by paying tribute to the financial front which had stood 'firm and strong', to the gratifying lack of profiteering and to the Englishman's 'genius for co-operating with the tax collector'; the success of the tax deduction scheme was a 'silent revolution'. But despite this, he needed a further £250 millions from new taxation.

Various alternatives had been considered, including a turnover tax and an excess income tax;[66] in the previous July he had told the House that administration difficulties stood in the way of capital levies and land value taxes. He must, therefore, resort to direct taxation again. Standard rate became a record 10s in the £ and reduced rate 6s 6d; the earned income relief was cut to one-tenth and all other allowances were reduced, apart from child allowance. With surtax up, the rate of taxability could be an astronomical 19s 6d in the £. Farmers were also to be assessed under Schedule D where they occupied land of a total value exceeding £300.

There was, however, some slight consolation. It was provided that for every year of assessment for which these reductions in allowances were in force, the extra tax ultimately borne by any individual 'should be recorded and notified to him and should be credited to him after the war at a date to be fixed by the Treasury'. This post-war credit[67] was originally to be placed in a Post Office Savings Bank account, but it was later decided to issue an appropriate certificate.[68]

Criticism, at last, was almost silenced. 'On the occasion of all three previous Budgets,' remarked a Member, 'the House has said to the Chancellor "You are not taxing us enough".'[69] This time no such cry was raised, for the Budget passed the three vital tests of facing up to the facts, delivering the goods and preserving equity. Not only did it raise the taxation required, but it performed the equally vital function of restricting purchasing power. Indeed the theme that 'we should continue to tax and tax' was pursued at such length that it provoked a dignified rebuke from the Chair to a Member who, in self defence, had donned a gas mask.[70] It was, however, a question to be asked whether it would not be advisable to review, as soon as convenient, the effect of the tax system on the 'general stability of business'.[71]

Some credit for the new thinking at the Treasury must go to Keynes who had become its economic adviser late in 1940. Early in that year he had published his *How to Pay for the War*. He pointed out that

---

[65] Hansard 7/IV/41.   [66] Hicks, Hicks & Rostas (*op. cit.*), p. 105.
[67] Board's Report for the year to 31/III/42, p. 20, para. 19.
[68] Hansard 14/IV/42 (Wood).   [69] Hansard 8/IV/41 (Pethick-Lawrence).
[70] The gas mask incident: Hansard 8/IV/41 (Williams).
[71] Hansard 8/IV/41 (Schuster).

'while earnings will be increased, consumption must be diminished'.[72] Therefore, since the size of the 'civilian cake' was fixed, the only way out was 'a suitable proportion of each man's earnings must take the form of deferred pay'.[73] The whole argument was based on taking the national income first, determining its war potential and then the amount of taxation required; so far taxation had simply been based on the burden which it was thought the taxpayer would tolerate. The plan was violently opposed by Labour,[74] especially the plan for an 'iron ration' and family allowances.[75] The shock of the fall of Europe in 1940, however, concentrated the minds of the public wonderfully and, as has been mentioned, the post-war credit system was adopted for both E.P.T. and income tax.

Kingsley Wood's last two Budgets continued the mode of calculation and format laid down in the great Budget of 1941. In 1942[76] rates of direct taxation remained unchanged; the only material alteration was the inclusion of farmers having lands over the annual value of £100 within Schedule D. The modified P.A.Y.E. system was working well and was proving a great advantage to the clerical staff of the Inland Revenue which was chronically undermanned.[77] There was, however, a suggestion that deductions should be put on the current year basis which, so far, the Chancellor, with the approval of both the T.U.C. and the British Employers' Federation, had found 'neither desirable nor practicable'.[78]

In the first of his last two Budgets, he was able to announce that the income tax receipts had topped the £1,000 millions mark and that 44% of expenditure was being met from current domestic revenue. As in the previous year, he was now holding direct taxation at unchanged levels;[79] there was even a minor concession by granting an extension to the so-called housekeeper and doubling dependent relative allowances. The increases were, again as last year, to be in indirect taxation. Normally the Labour critics[80] would have seized on this point, but in view of the burden of direct taxation, they were inclined to say: 'Not guilty, but don't do it again.' More than one speaker took up the point of revising the Schedule E deduction system to an actual payment basis which had been broached in 1942;[81]

---

[72] J. M. Keynes: *How to Pay for the War*, p. 17.   [73] *Ibid.*, p. 30.

[74] Labour opposition – 'The Keynes Plan – its Danger to the Workers' – Labour Research Dept., 1940.

[75] *Ibid.*, pp. 31–4.   [76] Kingsley Wood's third Budget: Hansard 14/IV/42.

[77] Shortage of clerical staff: Hansard 15/IV/42 (Financial Secretary to the Treasury).

[78] P.A.Y.E. and the current year: Hansard 15/IV/42 (Pethick-Lawrence).

[79] Kingsley Wood's fourth Budget: Hansard 12/IV/43.

[80] Hansard 13/IV/43 (Pethick-Lawrence).

[81] Hansard 13/IV/43 (Pethick-Lawrence).

technical difficulty was not now a convincing excuse since the United States had developed a 'Pay As We Go' procedure. In general, however, most Members would have agreed that the Chancellor's department 'was now so well "tooled up" that the production of his Budget has become almost an unskilled or semi-skilled repetitive operation'.[82]

But the comparative failure to find a true Pay As You Earn[83] system rankled; research continued and by September the problem of the cumulative system had been cracked. The T.U.C. and the British Employers' Federation, which had originally opposed the idea, were talked round; then a White Paper and an appropriate Bill were drafted to launch what has been described as 'the joint brain child' of Sir Cornelius Gregg, the Chairman, and Paul Chambers, the Secretary, of the Board. An arranged Parliamentary Question was put down for September 21, 1943, but in the early hours of that same morning, Sir Kingsley Wood collapsed and died.

He was succeeded by Sir John Anderson, an ex-Chairman of the Board. It was his first duty to put the new system into effect. At first it was intended to apply to weekly wage earners only; then it was extended to salaries under £600, but finally everyone, the collection advantages being apparent, assessable under Schedule E was brought within the scheme, which might almost be called 'Pay As You Receive', whereby the tax deducted from weekly or monthly pay is the actual tax on that pay.

How is this achieved? The system adopted is a cumulative one which, to take the case of a monthly wage earner, works as follows. The total allowances are divided into twelve equal parcels. Then one parcel is given against the first month's wage, and tax on the difference deducted from it. For the second month two parcels are given against the total of the two months' wage and tax computed on the difference again. The tax to be deducted will now be the amount by which this second total of tax on two months' pay exceeded the first total on the first month's pay. This process is exactly the same in the case of a weekly wage earner except that it is repeated weekly instead of monthly with weekly parcels of allowances.

---

[82] The Chancellor's Dept.: Hansard 13/IV/43 (Schuster).

[83] P.A.Y.E.: See Board's Report for the year to 31/III/44, pp. 14–15, paras. 24–7, the Income Tax (Employment) Act, 1943, and the Income Tax (Offices and Employments) Act, 1944.

The story of Sir Kingsley Wood's death is on p. 44 of *A Hundred Years*, by Wyn Griffith.

One of the main reasons for P.A.Y.E. was the substantial increases in wage level of sections of the community who were unused to the idea of saving to meet large half-yearly demands for tax. This had been a considerable problem in the 1914–18 period; it was the prospect of collection difficulties in this type of case which almost forced the introduction of a P.A.Y.E. system.

A wage payment may happen to be so low for one period that the addition of the next parcel of allowances results in the total tax due to that date being less than the tax paid for previous periods. The overpayment is then added to the wage. Whatever the fluctuations in wages may have been, therefore, the cumulative principle ensures that at any time in the year the tax deducted is in step with the wages paid. This is so even on a change of employment. For then the employee is given a 'leaving certificate'[84] by his employer showing his pay and tax to the date of leaving, which he hands to his new employer so that the cumulative figures may be continued in computing the tax to be paid or repaid on the new employment.

Sir John Anderson's first Budget[85] was remarkable for that Olympian detachment which, in the corridors of power, had earned him the nickname of 'Jehovah'. Just after the previous Budget, Sir Kingsley Wood had opened talks with representatives of industry on two main topics, the treatment of profits ploughed back into the business and the treatment of capital expenditure for which there was no allowance under the Income Tax Acts. The new Chancellor put the result of these discussions in the forefront of his Budget speech. On the first of these topics it had been argued that reserves for the future development of the business should be either exempt or bear a lower rate of tax; this idea had not commended itself to the Government any more than it had in Snowden's time (see p. 176). The other suggestion that more accelerated relief should be given for capital expenditure on assets 'which are used up in the making of profits' had won the Chancellor's agreement that 'the appropriate allowances for capital expenditure are of supreme importance in relation to the work of reconstruction at the end of the war'. Among his proposals,[86] later implemented, were an initial allowance of 20% on the purchases of new plant, and an initial allowance of 10%, together with a 2% annual allowance on new industrial buildings.

The House was greatly impressed by this new approach to economic problems which was essentially non-party and which did attempt to lay the foundations of a long-term industrial policy. Admittedly, there could not be any relaxations in the tax burden yet, but it was necessary to consider what would be the position after the war. Perhaps the Budget did dangle 'a sort of prospective carrot before the nose of industry in the country'[87] but its 'wide sweep' was wholly admirable.

Sir John Anderson's second Budget[88] was introduced when, as he

---

[84] Leaving certificate: the form P.45.
[85] Anderson's first Budget: Hansard 25/IV/44.
[86] Hansard 25/IV/44. See cols. 671–80 for full details.
[87] Hansard 25/IV/44 (Greenwood).   [88] Hansard 24/IV/45.

said, 'tremendous events are happening and impending all over the world'. That evening the lantern light outside the House was lit,[89] as a sign the war in Europe was over, after being extinguished 'for five years, seven months and twenty-three days'. There were no major increases or decreases in taxation generally, apart from a further raising of E.P.T. standards, as in the previous year, which had wiped out liability on a good number of the smaller cases. When summing up, the Chancellor could well say: 'It was a very satisfactory debate from my point of view.'[90]

The Income Tax Act of 1945[91] contains seventy sections and three schedules. It represented the most ambitious attempt by any Government and the Board not only to codify the whole range of capital allowances, as they were now beginning to be termed, but to assist industry at the same time. It was an almost unprecedented step for 'important declarations of Government policy' to be made so far in advance. The main outlines of the policy were sketched in during the Budget speech of 1944, but it was not until April 6, 1946, that the final form could be implemented.

Briefly, the Act granted the following allowances and reliefs:

(i) An initial and an annual allowance in respect of industrial buildings, the former allowance being for new buildings;

(ii) An initial and an annual allowance in respect of machinery or plant, the former allowance being for new machinery or plant;

(iii) An initial and an annual allowance in respect of mines, oil wells and other wasting sources of mineral deposits;

(iv) An annual allowance for new farm buildings;

(v) An annual allowance for the purpose of writing off capital sums expended on the acquisition of patent rights, coupled with the charging of such sums on the recipient.

The reason for this legislation was 'to benefit productive and creative industry . . . We should, as an act of conscious policy deliberately weigh the scales in favour of those forms of capital investwent which are most necessary to the industrial strength of the community.'[92]

During any war there is normally unanimity of purpose as far as taxation is concerned; party issues are not influential in determining fiscal policy. Criticism of the course pursued by the Government, which for most of the period was a Coalition Government, consisted mainly on the amount being raised not the method. The lessons learned from World War I were applied throughout the economic

[89] Hansard 24/IV/45 (The Speaker).   [90] Hunsard 26/IV/45.
[91] See, for example, *The Income Tax Act, 1945*, by Mustoe & Rowland.
[92] Hansard 14/III/45 (Anderson).

field in control of labour and industry, in rationing and purchase tax, in agriculture and in the finesse used on the loan market. But nowhere were they more effective than in the sphere of direct taxation.

In the early months of the war, it seemed as if the timidity of the pre-McKenna period in World War I was being re-enacted and the back benchers of all parties continually assailed Simon for the tentative approach to the problems of war finance. Not all this criticism was justified; it is arguable that the harsh regime inaugurated by Sir Kingsley Wood would not have received such ready acceptance had not the way been prepared by Simon's 'speeches to the jury',[93] quite apart from the military shocks of 1940. In addition, it is now an almost classical economic axiom 'that in the early stages of a war, it is wise to leave a good deal of scope to the economic incentive; later on it may be necessary to circumscribe it more severely'.[94]

And circumscribed the new regime certainly was, with income tax at 10s, surtax rising to 19s 6d in the £ and E.P.T. at 100% yielding between them by 1943–4 nearly £1,777 millions.[95] The first two of these taxes are as satisfactory as any for taxing war wealth since they are on the whole equitable and economically innocuous; also, for the years in question they were tempered by the post-war credit system. The idea of an excess income tax was considered, that is surcharging the excess of income over a pre-war standard, but administrative convenience was against it.

E.P.T., however, was the really onerous wartime fiscal measure, possessing the inherent objections of depleting reserves, encouraging evasion and extravagance both in revenue and capital expenditure and setting no premium on efficiency. Despite these undoubted disadvantages, its impact was cushioned by not ungenerous standards, especially when borrowed money was included in the addition for capital, post-war refunds, the later increases in minimum standards, and the lowering of the rate to 60% in 1945. 'There is more than a little doubt whether an equivalent amount of money could have been raised by other taxation which would not have resulted in at least as much restriction of output, particularly if the political implications are considered.'[96]

At the end of World War I, a serious industrial problem in the shape of renewing industrial equipment of all kinds arose; this problem was likely to be aggravated at the end of World War II by air raid damage. The motive behind the 1945 Income Tax Act was to

[93] The phrase is Pethick-Lawrence's (Hansard 13/IV/43).
[94] Hicks, Hicks & Rostas (*op. cit.*), p. 7.
[95] Board's Report for the year to 31/III/44, tables 25 (p. 29), 42 (p. 48) and 46 (p. 51).
[96] F. G. Moult, *Economic Consequences of E.P.T.*

give industry a chance to meet the post-war challenge by granting increased capital allowances, including, for the first time, allowances on industrial buildings and a high rate of initial allowance on capital expenditure.

On the whole, therefore, both in its taxation proposals during the war, including the possibly slow build up to placing taxation on a war footing, and in its taxation provisions for the change to post-war conditions, the Government and its advisors could present a remarkably successful balance sheet; and this success was the result of the degree of consent secured. For war taxation had been imposed by a Coalition Government and on that account was essentially a non-party creation. This was especially true of Anderson's two Budgets which were very much the academic product of a Board's Chairman, turned Chancellor. The pity of it was, as one of the chief Labour spokesmen remarked in 1945:[97] 'This is the last Budget where we shall be talking with one another instead of at one another.'

[97] Pethick-Lawrence (Hansard 25/IV/44).

CHAPTER XIII

Labour Theory and Conservative Practice

THE dangers of writing contemporary history are manifold and manifest; not only are events too near for true historical perspective, but they are often too emotive for detached comment. Even the presenting of the salient facts may be subject to unconscious editing; and many of the memoirs or biographies of the period are as yet unwritten. This last feature may to some extent be an advantage in view of the ever increasing amount of contemporary sources and comment.

It is necessary to bear these reservations in mind when looking at the confused political scene towards the end of the war in Europe. Labour had already published its manifesto *Let Us Face The Future*[1] in April, 1945, one of its pledges being 'taxation bearing less on low income groups'. The German army surrendered in May and, following the Whitsuntide meeting of the Labour Party Conference, Attlee wrote to Churchill urging an October election. Churchill promptly resigned and formed a caretaker Government which held office until June 15th. Polling day was July 5th but the count did not take place until the end of the month to provide for the votes of armed forces being brought to England; then an astonished nation learned that Labour had a majority of 180 seats. Whether this was because the Socialists had become the 'electoral beneficiary'[2] of a twentieth-century radicalism based on successful war planning and an equally successful fight against tyranny is another subject; but certainly the Conservatives had suffered their biggest defeat since the holocaust of 1906.

The economic position was equally confusing and the new Government faced tremendous tasks. The war had forced the country to live beyond its means and disrupted its productive capacity. It was essential to secure a smooth changeover from a war- to a peacetime economy, to overcome the food shortages and lack of raw materials and to reconstruct the export markets. On top of these problems were the

[1] D. N. Pritt: *The Labour Government 1945 to 1951*, p. 16.
[2] The phrase is from R. Miliband's *Parliamentary Socialism* and is quoted by Pritt (*op. cit.*), p. 28.

administrative difficulties arising from a heavy legislative programme and the sudden cancellation of lend-lease. Indeed it would be possible to maintain that the country has still not recovered full economic equilibrium from the shattering six years from 1939 to 1945 which left it with a reputation greater than its resources.

The immediate financial programme was the responsibility of Dalton, a consistent spokesman on the Budgets during the latter war period and now Chancellor of the Exchequer. Within three months he had introduced an interim Budget,[3] which indicated the changes which were to take place from the coming April, 1946. He had gathered a strong Finance Group,[4] as he called it, round him in which were two future Chancellors and his avowed policy was to balance the Budget over a period of years, to create surpluses when trade was good, deficits when it was failing, but to ensure an overall balance.

Psychologically, it was essential to ease the burden on direct taxation. To that end he proposed the reduction of standard rate to 9s in the £, the biggest single drop since 1922,[5] the increase of a single man's allowance to £110 and a married man's to £180 and alterations in the reduced rate relief from £165 at 6s 6d in the £ to £50 at 3s and on the next £75 of taxable income at 6s. There was to be an increase in surtax on a scale drafted by the Chancellor himself against Treasury opposition;[6] post-war credits would now cease, 1941 allowances having been more than restored apart from earned income relief. These were the personal incentive measures. 'One of our great achievements on the Home Front during the war, with the aid of a series of war Budgets, has been a national advance towards economic and social equality. If it was right for wartime, it is not wrong for peace.'

Dalton fully realized the danger of inflation in this transition period so, together with his policy of cheaper money and lower interest rates, he also provided tax incentives for industry.[7] The first was the standard rate reduction; secondly the 'appointed day' for the operation of the new favourable rates of capital allowances (see p. 203) under the Income Tax Act, 1945, was fixed at April 6, 1946; E.P.T. was reduced to 60% with a broad hint of its abolition; and fourthly, the industrial post-war refunds (see p. 198) were to be repaid. But he would have no repetition of the old abuse of the E.P.D. period (see p. 162) when relief for deficiencies was retained

---

[3] Dalton's first Budget: Hansard 23/X/45.

[4] Dalton's *Memoirs*, vol. III, p. 22.

[5] Horne's Budget of 1922 (*q.v.*) also reduced standard rate by 1s (1/V/22).

[6] The surtax increase: Dalton (*op. cit.*), p. 31.

[7] Industrial incentives: Hansard 25/X/45.

far too long; there were to be no E.P.T. repayments for deficiencies incurred after December 31, 1946.

Churchill described the speech as a 'bland, mild and temperate survey of the dark, tumultuous, tortured financial scene'; the Budget 'would do no harm if it does not do any good'.[8] Anderson was more specific;[9] while admitting the role of critic was easier, he counselled the Chancellor 'to watch the spending departments with an eagle eye' and confessed himself, as did the Liberals,[10] dissatisfied with the failure to increase earned income relief. On broad principles he did not agree with using the Budget as an egalitarian weapon: 'social equality has very little to do with the Budget.'

On the whole, however, the proposals were well received by the country and the Press; and on the earned income relief point, Dalton said[11] he had the choice between restoring the 1941 allowances *in toto*, which would have given exemption to 1·6 million taxpayers, or increasing allowances as he had done, which exempted no less than 2 million. He later admitted[12] that it would have been better if he had left standard rate and surtax at their current levels and further increased personal allowances and earned income relief.

After the 'amber light'[13] of 1945, the Budget of 1946,[14] which Dalton thought the most satisfactory of the four for which he was responsible,[15] could give only a qualified green. His opening speech was heavily statistical, so much so that Churchill asked him to go more slowly: 'some of us like to get down the figures.' The income tax cuts announced in the previous autumn had come into operation three days before and 'we must go slow with further tax reliefs this year'. However, he did concede the increase of earned income relief to one-eighth; his 'distant ambition'[16] of one-half was a long way away. Three years' post-war credits, too, were to be repaid to men over 65 and women over 60 years of age. E.P.T. was at last repealed and there was more than a suggestion of a prospective tax on profits and dividends.

Criticism was mainly directed against details, such as the surtax increases coupled with the disallowance of seven-year covenants; Eden, however, found too little encouragement to industry[17] and Anderson was pessimistic about the chance of a profits tax;[18] the effort to formulate one when he had been Chairman of the Board was wholly unsuccessful. Inflation was still a danger: 'I must be careful

---

[8] Hansard 23/X/45.   [9] Hansard 24/X/45.
[10] Hansard 24/X/45 (Clement Davies).
[11] Dalton's defence: Hansard 25/X/45.   [12] Dalton (*op. cit.*), p. 28.
[13] Hansard 24/X/45 (Fletcher).   [14] Hansard 9/IV/46.
[15] Dalton on the 1946 Budget: Dalton (*op. cit.*), p. 109.
[16] Dalton, p. 114.
[17] Hansard 9/IV/46.   [18] Hansard 10/IV/46.

not to release too great a flow of purchasing power too soon.' This was not thought by Gaitskell to be so great a menace.[19] He was more concerned with the disincentive effect of P.A.Y.E., especially on piecework, a feeling which was echoed on the other side of the House, although as Callaghan pointed out,[20] it was not P.A.Y.E. which caused the objections, but the rate of tax.

Dalton agreed with his critics on the question of economy but it must be 'rounded out into a programme of economies in definite directions. It is no good speaking in quite general terms about economy.' He then proceeded to summarize his first two Budgets. He had deliberately put the income tax payer in the forefront of his reforms: 'of all the taxes which were causing irritation, were holding back production and, in peacetime, were increasingly difficult to justify, income tax, particularly on smaller incomes stood easily first.'[21] Of the £500 millions in taxation he had relieved, between two-thirds and three-quarters consisted of income tax.[22]

Dalton's last two Budgets were something of an anticlimax after the high promise of 1945. He admitted himself he was 'much less happy' with the first of these.[23] The reason was the grim reality of the economic position, the focus of which had shifted decisively from the Treasury to the Board of Trade and made the proposals to some extent[24] irrelevant to the main issue. As Sir Waldron Smithers, surprisingly, put it:[25] 'Internally he had juggled with figures and got a so-called balanced Budget, but the external position is still desperate.' The Chancellor was well aware of this, but 'could see no early solution'.[26]

However, he was still determined to persevere with further income tax reliefs, the chief of which was increasing the earned income fraction to one-sixth, the maximum allowable becoming £250 from £150. Child allowance was raised by £10 and the income limit for dependent relative allowance by the same amount; post-war credits for older taxpayers were now released for the whole five years they had been accumulated. These were 'modest reliefs'. Turning to tax increases, he introduced a differential profits tax. This was, in the principles which governed the computation of the amount taxable, essentially the old N.D.C., but instead of the flat 5%, there was a rate of $12\frac{1}{2}\%$ on distributed profits and 5% on undistributed profits. The case for such a profits tax was threefold: additional revenue was needed to

[19] Hansard 10/IV/46, see also Boothby's comments.
[20] Hansard 11/IV/46.   [21] Hansard 11/IV/46 (Dalton).
[22] Dalton (*op. cit.*), p. 123.   [23] Dalton (*op. cit.*), p. 223.
[24] Dalton's third Budget: Hansard 15/IV/47.
[25] Hansard 16/IV/47.
[26] Dalton (*op. cit.*), p. 223.

replace E.P.T.; increased dividends ought to be penalized; and the differential rate 'does rough justice within the field of investment income'. There was now to be no liability on individuals and partnerships; surtax secured equity of treatment here.

This was the longest Budget speech since 1909 and received, on the whole, a tolerably good Press.[27] Its general effect was mildly deflationary. This marked a radical change in the financial side of British economic policy much more in accordance with the planning of Cripps, for Dalton's early policy had been at variance with the policy of self restraint advocated by the President of the Board of Trade. The obduracy of economic facts was now bringing the two chief economic protagonists closer together. Admittedly, as its critics[28] were not slow to point out, there were no economies in the Budget and there was no real help to the production drive. But the battle of the dollar gap was won for the time being and the crisis of 1947 warded off by massive American aid.

If Dalton was not happy about his third Budget, his fourth was a personal tragedy.[29] He had already announced that there was to be an autumn Budget, for the second time in three years, and the measures were to be slotted into the export drive and the reductions in imports; indeed when he opened his Budget, to use the traditional phrase, he began by announcing that its aim was 'to strengthen still further and without delay our budgetary defences against inflation'. Tax increases were to be 'simple and straightforward'; there was to be no capital levy[30] until the spring. There were no changes in income tax but, to check the mounting arrears, interest was to be charged on overdue tax; if the duty were not paid within three months of the due date and it exceeded £1,000 it was now to bear interest at 3%. Profits tax rates were doubled, rising to 25% on distributed profits and 10% on undistributed 'due to a continuing and persistent inclination on the part of many concerns to declare increased dividends'.

The official opposition was comparatively subdued. It was clear that Dalton's efforts were now tied in with those of Cripps;[31] and although, instead of the usual formal speeches ending at about 6 p.m. which usually followed the Budget speech, debating this time continued until very late, there was a general appreciation of the fact that austerity[32] had to be imposed; the danger was, had it been imposed too late?

It fell to Cripps to sum up on November 17th, by which time he

[27] Dalton (*op. cit.*), p. 235.
[28] Its critics: Hansard 16/IV/47 (Eden and Anderson).
[29] Dalton's fourth Budget: Hansard 12/XI/47.
[30] Capital levy: Dalton (*op. cit.*), p. 273 and footnote.
[31] Hansard 12/XI/47 (Eden).   [32] Hansard 12/XI/47 (Holmes).

had succeeded Dalton who had resigned over his indiscreet pre-Budget aside to a trusted lobby correspondent. He was in full agreement with his predecessor's policies and he would not admit that the measures proposed were not drastic enough. 'Too much money chasing too few goods' was only inflationary if the operative word was 'chase'; the cash might well be saved. This, after all, was an interim Budget: 'I believe that it will hold the situation.' At least it was the end of what Churchill had called 'a dichotomy of policies'.

It is necessary now to turn briefly aside from the main narrative and bring the history of the Board of Inland Revenue up to date.

The last extension of the Board's empire had been the establishment of control over the collection service, a process which, started in 1931, was not finally completed until 1945 (see p. 187). During that period there had been, as detailed in Chapter XII, an increase in the nature and yield of taxation unparalleled in any other period during the past hundred and fifty years. The consequent growth in staff at Somerset House was matched by a similar growth in provincial offices. By 1938–9 the Chief Inspector's branch was 15,000 strong; but even this mushroom augmentation was barely sufficient to cope with the continuous rise in numbers of taxpayers as more and more, wage earners principally, were drawn into the net. This posed a problem of public relations. Sir Kingsley Wood particularly was most anxious that income tax should, as he put it, be 'understanded of the people'; to that end he published *The Income Tax Quiz for Wage Earners*, an attempt to explain Schedule E in simple terms; the layout and phraseology of returns was simplified also.

Any simplification was equally welcome to the hard pressed staff of the Inland Revenue. In 1945 Callaghan[33] had drawn attention to the 'heavy overwork from which the staff of the Inland Revenue are suffering'. Two years later Peake[34] pointed out that there were only between 1,600 and 1,800 Inspectors in post, barely as many as before the war, despite the increase in legislation and the general expansion in staff to a figure more than double that of 1939.[35] Quite apart from overwork and shortage of staff, there was also an awkward administrative problem;[36] up to 1948 'there had been almost complete division between the Inspectorial and clerical sides; the Inspectorate had been open only to officers fully trained in technical taxation work; and officers of the Executive class had not been employed at all'.

The roots of this division lay far in the past. From the first days of income tax, and for that matter, before, the Surveyors had always

[33] Hansard 25/X/45.   [34] Hansard 17/XI/47.
[35] Board's Report for the year to 31/III/49, p. 10, para. 21.
[36] Board's Report for the year to 31/III/49, p. 10, para. 21.

been established civil servants; they had, in fact (see p. 90) been the first civil servants to form a Committee with the object of protesting against pressure of work and inadequate pay and promotion prospects. This Committee was the ancestor of the Association of Tax-Surveying Officers (see pp. 90 and 182) which had been so far accepted by 1920 that it gave evidence before the 1920 Committee (see p. 159). It is now called the Association of Her Majesty's Inspectors of Taxes and represents some 2,100 officers.

As late as the beginning of this century, however, the clerical staff were still engaged on a local basis and were employed directly by the Surveyors. They, too, had begun to organize themselves, having a representative committee by 1892 but, said Asquith (see p. 149), the experiment of employing established clerks 'had not proved a success'. Nevertheless, in 1908 some tax clerks were finally established as Civil Servants and by 1914 establishment was the general rule, a rapid and justified change of policy. Their organization was at first called the Association of Tax Clerks, but is now much better known as the Inland Revenue Staff Federation, combining in its 43,000 membership, valuation and collection staff also.

Soon after the end of the last war, reorganization[37] discussions with the two staff associations were started since it was thought that the separation had produced far too rigid a structure. These discussions came to a formal conclusion on July 13, 1948, when an agreement was signed involving a radical change in the staffing of the Chief Inspector's Branch. The Inspectorate was broadened to include non-technical posts and there was introduced a far wider avenue of promotion by which all entrants, whether at Clerical, Executive or Open level, had the chance of promotion to the highest posts; and since then both associations have continued to make efforts towards welding the branch into a truly homogeneous body.

Later in the year,[38] the appointment of an additional member of the Board, of Deputy Chairman rank, was approved, 'to watch the general organization and progress of the work, to enquire into the cause of any deficit or delay and to suggest a remedy' which was a pretty comprehensive brief. The Board also decided to carry out a full review [39]of the organization of the Department; the Committee, known as the de Paula Committee[40] from the name of the accountant-banker who was one of its members, was appointed in November, 1948, and reported two years later. Although it examined 'the basic assumptions and principles upon which the Department had been

---

[37] Board's Report for the year to 31/III/49, p. 10, para. 19.
[38] Board's Report for the year ending 31/III/49, p. 7, para. 7.
[39] Board's Report for the year ending 31/III/49, p. 9, para. 18.
[40] Board's Report for the year ending 31/III/51, p. 14, para. 59.

built up' and was prepared, if necessary, 'to recommend fundamental changes', none in fact was suggested, 'their view being that, in general, the departmental organization was sound in design and efficient in operation'.

This streamlining of the organization was soon to be tested by fresh legislative activity after the comparative quiescence of the last two Dalton Budgets. Not that the ex-Chancellor had failed to provide his successor with his 'Thoughts on the Next Budget'[41] suggesting both a capital levy and further income tax reliefs, particularly on earned income and on the smaller incomes. Cripps was willing to bear these suggestions in mind, but he was determined to discuss the Economic Survey of 1948 with its message of plain living and high productivity at the same time as the Budget. He saw his task as a fourfold problem: he must distribute the burden of taxation fairly, pursue a social policy acceptable to the Party, provide incentives for increased output and yet avoid inflation. Since, therefore, he was dealing with the state of the nation not merely the finance of government, five days were to be allocated for the opening debate instead of the normal three.

He began his first Budget[42] by warning the House that he would detain them 'rather a long time' but 'the new task of the Chancellor of the Exchequer is not merely to balance the Budget – it is a much wider one – to match our resources against our needs'. The Budget was an essential part of the national economic plan; this fact was fully recognized by the Opposition, Churchill for instance commenting on the importance of the Chancellor's 'double duties'.[43] What the back benchers of both sides, however, failed, or refused, to recognize were the true facts of the country's economic position.

The Chancellor went as far as he possibly could in taxation concessions by raising earned income relief to one-fifth, which exempted a further half million taxpayers and the exemption limit to £135. Reduced rate relief was now granted to both husband and wife when the latter was working and the band of income on which tax was chargeable at 6s in the £ was extended from £75 to £200. A welcome administrative change was the dropping of formal assessments in certain Pay As You Earn cases.

To offset these reliefs, all farmers were brought finally within the ambit of Schedule D and liability was imposed on expenses payments provided for directors of companies and the treatment of benefits in kind was tightened up. The most interesting innovation was, however, a mild experiment in capital levy known as the special contri-

---

[41] Dalton (*op. cit.*), pp. 288–9.   [42] Hansard 6/IV/48.
[43] Special Contribution: Part V, F.A. 1948. See also Board's Report for the year ended 31/III/49, paras. 63–7, pp. 16–17.

bution[44] and based on a suggestion of Keynes.[45] It was imposed on individuals whose 'total income' for the year 1947–8 exceeded £2,000 and whose 'aggregate investment income' exceeded £250; the rates levied on investment income were graduated from 2s to 10s in the £.

The debate was far more economic in tone than budgetary and much of the fiscal criticism was almost perfunctory.[45] On the minor income tax reliefs, the Opposition claimed a change in standard rate would have been better; the current reforms 'encouraged workers in industry, but not industry itself'. The Government Left-wing thought the reliefs too small; but in the context of inflation this charge was easily refuted. On the increases, the Opposition reminded the House of farmers' inability to keep accounts and wondered who would be in the greater difficulty, the farmer in preparing, or the Inspector in deciphering them. The special contribution came under sharper attack; it was not worth while, in view of the consquent loss of surtax and death duties and its effect was inflationary. Cripps had already covered this point. 'Some of those who possess large capital assets are already spending them in a matter that is distinctly inflationary.'

Another interesting feature of the debate, apart from its length, was the distinct injection of political animus. The Chancellor, perhaps, started it with his strictures on companies and 'the extravagant way which in recent years they have made allowances to their directors and senior officials'. The right remedy, claimed the Opposition, was the raising of the surtax limit; and the special contribution was a 'piece of party spite and rancour' or 'naked class warfare'. In fact, as *The Times* commented, the Budget generally was 'brave and courageous'; it was also sound and orthodox. The Financial Secretary[46] summed it up as anti-inflationary, surplus-producing and incentive providing: 'surely these motives should secure general agreement?' Macmillan[47] gave qualified assent; it was broadly deflationary; it was a good thing to have 'one conductor in charge of the orchestra'; but, an ominous but, all it would enable us to do was 'scrape through for a year or two'. He was not far wrong.

Cripps's second Budget,[48] which *The Times* called 'stern and even brutal', he himself described as a 'hold-fast' Budget. The direct

---

[44] 'A suggestion of Keynes': *How to Pay for the War.*
[45] Criticisms of the Budget:
    (*a*) Income Tax reliefs: Hansard 7/IV/49 (Crookshank).
    (*b*) Farmers' accounts: Hansard 13/IV/49 (Drayson).
    (*c*) Special Contribution: Hansard 7/IV/49 (Anderson).
    (*d*) Raising the surtax limit: Hansard 7/IV/49 (Hinchingbrooke).
    (*e*) Class warfare: Hansard 12/IV/49 (Lyttleton).
[46] Hansard 7/IV/49 (Jay).   [47] Hansard 13/IV/49.   [48] Hansard 6/IV/49.

taxation changes were confined to the compulsory redemption of Land Tax[49] and the increase of the initial allowance granted on the purchase of new plant and machinery on or after April 6, 1949, from 20% to 40%; and the allowance for capital expenditure on scientific research was raised to 60% in the first year. There was, therefore, little comment on taxation except an Opposition argument that capital allowances[50] were still not high enough, which hardly seemed convincing in view of the machine manufacturers' long order books.

The Chancellor had, however, announced also that there would be 'an enquiry on technical issues which arise in connection with the computation of taxable profits'. This was to be a pilot report for a full enquiry into the incidence of taxation on industry. In June, 1949 a Committee was accordingly set up under the Chairmanship of James Millard Tucker, K.C.[51] The appointment of this body reflected a renewed interest in the theory of taxation which had, to some extent, been dormant since the great battles of differentiation and graduation a generation ago. For not only was this Committee welcomed, but there were far ranging disquisitions on taxation in general, especially from an ex-Chairman of the Board[52] and the Secretary of the Inland Revenue Staff Federation.[53] The former thought the tax authorities were being too inquisitorial in their review of directors' benefits in kind and wondered what the conditions of work in the Inland Revenue were. The latter could tell him. If it were asked 'whether the equipment of the taxing machine were equal to the burdens placed upon it, the answer was "No"'; and he contrasted Pay As You Earn' with what he termed 'pay as you like'. An Opposition speaker was more effective;[54] after repeating Chamberlain's Dickensian old joke about 'Bleak House' and 'Great Expectations', he pointed out that income tax 'came just as much from the tool room as the Board room'. In fact, out of £1,400 millions, £500 millions was paid by those with incomes under £1,000. Perhaps the best summary of the whole state of direct taxation in 1949 came from the ex-Chairman. 'Our tax structure must inevitably reflect to a considerable degree the complexities of our social and economic system.'

Before his third and last Budget, Cripps was to devalue the pound and face the unwarranted charges of bad faith; he was also deeply involved in the 1950 Election when he retained his majority but found on his return to the House the overall Labour majority had

---

[49] Board's Report for the year to 31/III/50, paras. 77–81, p. 17.
[50] Hansard 12/IV/49 (Hutchinson and Mikardo).
[51] The Tucker Committee: Board's Report for the year to 31/III/50, paras. 14–15, p. 9.
[52] Hansard 11/IV/49 (Anderson).   [53] Hansard 11/IV/49 (Houghton).
[54] Hansard 12/IV/49 (Lyttleton).

shrunk to a mere 8. Gaitskell was appointed Minister of State for Economic Affairs, mainly to assist the now ailing Chancellor.[55] This was the occasion of the famous Wykehamist Budget[56] 'a unique event', when all the three ministers presenting it, Cripps, Gaitskell and Jay, had all been to Winchester College. No wonder, on a previous occasion, an old Etonian opposition member had referred to 'a small esoteric, scholastic circle, whose motto is "Manners Makyeth Man", which we may roughly translate that as long as you are courteous you have no need to be convincing'.[57]

This was the second Budget in succession in which there were no radical changes. The minor amendments consisted of a small reduction in reduced rate relief, the continuation of the 'Mills Factories Allowance' (see p. 154) since there had been some difficulty in preparing Industrial Buildings Allowance claims (see p. 203) and a measure of relief from tax for industrial research associations. The measure which caused the most controversy was, however, the making of restrictive covenants by employees retrospectively[58] chargeable to surtax, a proposal which, to do him justice, the Chancellor had threatened in 1948.[59] This was directly aimed at the payments the chairmen of Austin and Standard Motors had received, which deprived them of 95% of the gross amount payable. Criticism turned on the ethics of retrospective legislation which converted what were at the time not taxable items into income liable at a penal rate.

Cripps, in opening, had drawn attention to the halted rise in profits and the decrease in income tax receipts and emphasized that the Budget was a mechanism for influencing or implementing economic policy as well as for determining tax levels. It was his duty to avoid the twin evils of inflation and deflation; there could be 'no tax remission spree'. He wound up the debate[60] by maintaining it was the right time for what the Opposition had called 'a dull and pedestrian Budget'; it would have been dishonest to have a vote-catching one.

The main idea behind the reduction in reduced rate relief had been to lessen the tax on overtime earnings.[61] It did not, however, give any relief to the higher paid worker, or indeed to the lowest paid worker either. Despite this, it had been necessary to find even this limited amount of relief by the increase in petrol tax. In general, however, it was fairly pointed out[62] that the tax reductions over the past four

[55] *The Life of Richard Stafford Cripps:* Colin Cooke, p. 400.

[56] Cooke (*op. cit.*), pp. 401–2; Hansard 10/IV/50.

[57] Hansard 13/IV/48 (Stanley).

[58] This was, of course, the then notorious Lord–Black case.

[59] Hansard 6/IV/48.   [60] Cripps's winding-up: Hansard 24/IV/50.

[61] The effect of the changes in reduced rate relief: See, for example, Hansard 19/IV/50 (Jenkins).

[62] Hansard 21/IV/50 (Houghton).

years should be looked at as a whole; since 1946–7 the tax bill on incomes ranging from £8 a week to £30 a week had been cut by proportions ranging from a half to a third; indeed pre-war levels of direct taxation were, in some income bands, almost within striking distance. Over the whole five days the speeches were, understandably, less against the modest Budget proposals as such than against the general economic policy of the Government.[63] The warning note against increasing military expenditure[64] was only tentatively sounded; and a fair summary was: 'I have had to repeat the dose and I hope the patient will get on with it.'[65]

The years 1947 and 1949 were both years of economic crisis; in 1947 the British economy only survived by being given a massive fix of American aid; within two years its effects had worn off and drastic devaluation was necessary. 1950 was in many ways the end of an era; as an Opposition spokesman put it, 'When Sir Stafford Cripps left the Treasury, his departure coincided with a momentous, a fearsome change in the British economy'.[66] It was the last year of effectve office for another equally dominating character, Bevin;[67] and, incidentally, the year which saw the emergence of Gaitskell and Wilson. It was the former who succeeded Cripps, now seriously ill, in the autumn of 1950. The Korean crisis had imposed an increase of over 50% in the previously determined level of Government expenditure, but even so, it had been decided to postpone until spring, consideration of the means of financing rearmament.

The problem, therefore, that Gaitskell had had to face before presenting his first and only Budget[68] was how to fit a 'massive new defence programme' into the economy; and with this he had to combine a maximum limitation of consumption. He proposed to depart from the practice of his predecessors by not discussing the Economic Survey; even so, he had to sketch the economic background and Churchill asked him to go a little slower when discussing these 'complicated matters'.

His direct taxation changes each had a specific objective. The initial allowance of 40% of the cost of new plant was suspended from April 6, 1952 to be reintroduced when the rearmament period was over; the purpose of this was 'to reduce the pressure of home demand on the engineering industry for plant and equipment for civilian purposes'. Secondly, while recognizing that 'in an economy three-

[63] 'Over the whole five days . . .': Hansard 24/IV/51 (Gaitskell).
[64] Hansard 24/IV/51 (Fernyhough).   [65] Hansard 20/IV/50 (Davies).
[66] Hansard 11/IV/51 (Eccles).
[67] Bevin in fact did not resign until 9/III/51, but he had been ill for some time before then.
[68] Hansard 10/IV/51.

quarters of which was run by private enterprise, it is foolish to ignore the function of profit as an incentive', he could equally not ignore the 14% rise in dividends over the previous year; the profits tax rate was, therefore, increased to 50% on distributions with a 10% rate on undistributed profits. Lastly, despite increases in indirect taxation, there would still be a gap; 'in the circumstances' (the phrase has a familiar ring), I must turn to Income Tax'. The three rates of 9s, 5s and 2s 6d in the £ were all raised by 6d; but as part compensation, the allowances for married men and for children were raised by £10 which meant, to cover a criticism of the previous year's Budget, a slight decrease for the lower levels of taxpayers.

Criticism of the Budget ran very much to pattern. 'All the old Budget-puncher has to do is pick up the old arguments, add a little pepper and salt and go on with the dishing out.'[69] The increase in profits tax rates came in for the sharpest censure, 'the most evil thing in the Budget',[70] but the Chancellor had an almost unanswerable reply: if profits were rising he must take some decisive action in view of the Trade Union attitude. The two most searching strictures were on points of principle. 'The tax burden should be imposed as much as possible on the point at which money is spent rather than the point at which it is earned',[71] which was the modern version of the old Conservative principle of direct rather than indirect taxation. Even more searching was[72] 'I am criticizing not only the tax plan, but the policy of the Government which presented him (Gaitskell) with this Budget problem'. It was the case of 'a good Chancellor presiding over a bad situation'.[73]

The high drama of the Budget, however, centred round the ceiling of £400 millions imposed on Health Service expenditure which led to the resignation of Bevan, Wilson and Freeman. Attlee was ill during this internal crisis and might otherwise have prevented the private views of the two opposing interests hardening into public attitudes which left neither room for manoeuvre. The strain on both the King and the members of the Government[74] was intensified by this division within the party and the logical way out was a General Election. This decision may have been a tactical error; in the first place, Gaitskell's policies had been given no chance to prove their efficiency; the party itself was left wide open to the charge of internal factiousness and fiscal incompetence; and, most ironic of all, a slow economic recovery was beginning. The country's verdict on the

[69] Hansard 16/IV/51 (Follick).   [70] Hansard 10/IV/51 (Williams).
[71] Hansard 11/IV/51 (Maudling).   [72] Hansard 12/IV/51 (Salter).
[73] Hansard 10/IV/51 (Hinchingbrooke).
[74] Joan Mitchell: *Crisis in Britain*, on p. 226, uses an *Observer* article by Attlee as evidence for this.

merits of the two main parties was almost as indecisive as in 1950, only this time a Conservative majority of seventeen replaced a Labour majority of five. It was, however, the beginning of thirteen years of Conservative rule.

The choice of Chancellor was not easy; Stanley was dead; Anderson was out of the Commons and on his way to the Lords; and Lyttleton was thought, despite his desire for the office, not to be an easy House of Commons man.[75] The appointment, therefore, went to Butler, a considerable speaker in recent Budget debates, but by training and inclination more academic than Dalton and Gaitskell, who were professional economists. He was the first Conservative post-war Chancellor; he was the longest in office; and he was 'probably the best (leaving Maudling out of account)'.[76]

In November, 1951, he took emergency measures by cutting imports and raising Bank Rate; he then announced that the Budget was to be brought forward a month earlier than its usual date. When he presented it in March,[77] he opened with an oblique thrust at his predecessor's policy: 'the country has taken on far too much at once.' It was necessary 'to reduce Government expenditure and make a significant start in reducing taxation'.

The first tax measure was the imposition of an excess profits levy,[78] designed to cream off 'the excessive profits made as a result of the injection of rearmament into the economy'. It was to be charged at a net rate of 30%, that is to say, it was not a deduction in arriving at the Case I profits, so that the agreement of the liability would not be held up; at the same time the rate of profits tax, to which E.P.L. was an addition, was reduced to a net $2\frac{1}{2}\%$ on undistributed and a net $17\frac{1}{2}\%$ on distributed profits. The new tax was to last 'during the period of the emergency' and was a less elaborate version of the war-time E.P.T. Briefly, liability arose on the profits in excess of the average of a company's profits for any two of the three years 1947, 1948 and 1949, adjusted up or down by 4% of the increase or decrease in borrowed money and 12% of the increase or decrease in share capital and undistributed profits. Alternative standards were provided and in any case there was no liability where profits were below £5,000. A novel feature was the 'overriding limitation', the levy payable being 30% of the excess profits or 15% of the total profits over the whole period of charge.

The plan for income tax was centred round Butler's belief that 'the present weight of direct taxation is a very positive discouragement to extra effort'. He therefore proposed the increase of personal

[75] See Samuel Brittan: *The Treasury under the Tories*, p. 164 and footnote.
[76] Brittan (*op. cit.*), p. 166.   [77] Hansard 11/III/52.
[78] E.P.L.: Board's Report for the year to 31/III/53, p. 35, paras. 115–21.

allowances, a process which was to continue throughout his Chancellorship, and the raising of earned income allowance to a fraction of two-ninths, where it was to remain. The reduced rate relief bands were widened and increased to £100 at 3s, £150 at 5s and £150 at 7s 6d. The effect of these changes was to concentrate relief at the lower end of the scale and to provide the incentive of increased take-home pay.

Labour critics[79] argued furiously that it was a 'change in the distribution of existing burdens only' and the net relief was negligible when the cut in food subsidies was taken into account. E.P.L.[80] too was a tax which, like E.P.T. encouraged waste and put a premium on inefficiency; it was 'a disincentive, demagogic device'; and even Government supporters agreed it was economically harmful if politically necessary. There was also one all-out attack on directors' expenses,[81] but in general there was very little to criticize because there was no net change in the tax burden. Butler had been given a 'Treasury Advisory Committee' to 'assist' him; but 'he and the Treasury knights[82] were more than a match for 'those old battle-axes' and in his winding up he paid tribute to 'the high quality of the advice which I received and finally accepted'.[83]

The eight years covered by 1945 to 1952 began and ended in a flurry of increased allowances and reduced rates. Between these two dates the British economy, always vulnerable to world crises, was the victim of three critical situations, each increasing in intensity, at two yearly intervals, in 1947, 1949 and 1951; and for the control of these, direct taxation could not be a primary mechanism. Whether it could have been better handled than it was, and whether, if a more expansionist policy had been adopted, it would ultimately have had any marked effect on the main problems are questions which no economist seems clearly to have answered. Certainly the advent of Butler and the end of cheap money was not the break in policy it appeared to be at the time; the most that can be said is that his 'restriction and austerity are not enough' coincided with, if it did not cause, a period of recovery; and with it went a renewed interest in the theory of income tax.

---

[79] See Gaitskell (Hansard 12/III/52).
[80] E.P.L.: Dalton (Hansard 17/III/52), Assheton (Hansard 12/III/52).
[81] Directors' expenses: Houghton (Hansard 17/III/52).
[82] Brittan (*op. cit.*), p. 166.   [83] Butler (Hansard 17/III/52).

CHAPTER XIV

Reforms, Reductions and Avoidance

IN his Budget Speech of April 10, 1951, Gaitskell had referred, in passing, to the just published Tucker Report,[1] but he would 'await the reactions of industry before coming to any final conclusions'. Butler, however, did not mention the report when opening his first Budget in the following year, nor did it receive any special discussion during the debate. It was, of course, being restricted to the consideration of the taxation of trading profits, only intended to be 'the first stage in a general review of the whole system of the taxation of trading profits and income'.[2] The second stage[3] appeared somewhat out of time table order, consisting of a report on the problem arising from the current basis of taxation of United Kingdom concerns carrying on trading activities overseas, prepared at Butler's specific request; this report made three recommendations which were almost immediately put into practice. There followed the second report in April, 1954, and the final report in June, 1955; these last three reports comprise what is known as the Radcliffe Report.

'That mine of useful suggestions'[4], the Tucker Report, came out in April, 1951. The Committee had heard 83 witnesses, 35 of whom were associations, besides 'the lengthy and detailed written representations',[5] but by its terms of reference,[6] it was somewhat restricted in the scope of its review. It was, however, possible to adduce three general principles[7] to guide its deliberations; the allowance of expenditure at present not permissible, must logically be followed by the assessment of receipts not previously liable; it is necessary to draw a distinction between expenditure incurred in the course of earning profits and expenditure which is simply the application of

[1] Cmd. 8189.   [2] Tucker Report, p. 6, para. 6.

[3] The Radcliffe Report, so called because of its Chairman, Lord Radcliffe, who succeeded Lord Cohen, the original Chairman, 28/IV/52, was published in three parts, Cmd. 8761 (February, 1953), Cmd. 9105 (April, 1954) and Cmd. 9474 (June, 1955).

[4] Butler (Hansard 14/IV/53).

[5] Tucker Committee's evidence: Report, pp. 5 and 6, paras. 3–5.

[6] Its terms of reference: Report, p. 5, para. 1.

[7] Report, p. 7, paras. 8, 9 and 10.

those profits after earning; and the incidence of taxation was outside the terms of reference. The Committee also observed, as a practical matter, that there were roughly 1·5 million liabilities under Cases I and II of Schedule D;[8] of these, 200,000 were companies and 200,000 partnerships, leaving 1·1 million assessments on individuals; so that a reform which might well be satisfactory for a company could well be inequitable when applied to a small taxpayer. Schedule D assessments were indeed a pretty mixed bag.

The Committee's recommendations[9] are conveniently divisible into four main categories; and within these categories are suggestions of major or minor importance. Many of them were incorporated in the legislation of the succeeding three years; some were considered and rejected as being impracticable; while still others await implementation, for a variety of reasons often involving the question of manpower in the Chief Inspector's Branch.

The most important recommendations came under the heading of basis of assessment.[10] On a change in the constitution of a partnership, the cessation provisions ought to be applied unless the continuing basis was claimed; this proposal would also close a loophole where the constitution of a partnership changed more than once in a comparatively short space of time.[11] There ought to be unlimited carry forward for losses;[12] and in the last year of business a loss should be permitted set off against the assessments on that business for the three preceding years.[13] Capital allowances should be allowed to create or augment a loss by statute not merely by concession.[14] These reforms were all incorporated in the Finance Acts between 1952 and 1954. But, after a long discussion on the pros and cons of substituting an accounting period basis for that of the previous year,[15] it was held that not only were there considerable transitional difficulties, but it was a basis suitable possibly for companies, but not for individuals and partnerships.

On the question of basis of computation of profits, after emphasizing the anomaly 'that the Income Tax Acts themselves contain no rules which lay down affirmatively what sums are to be treated as receipts and what as expenses',[16] the Committee commented drily that 'on receipts,[17] naturally enough, there were few representations

---

[8] Report, p. 8, para. 14.
[9] Summary of recommendations: Report, Ch. X, pp. 107–11.
[10] Report, Ch. II, pp. 9–35, paras. 19–93.
[11] See now S. 19 (1), F.A. 1953.   [12] See now S. 27, F.A. 1952.
[13] Terminal losses: See now S. 18, F.A. 1954.
[14] C.A. added to losses: See now S. 15, F.A. 1953.
[15] Report, p. 15, para. 41.
[16] 'that the Income Tax Acts . . .': Report, p. 47, para. 134.
[17] Report, p. 48, para. 139.

from outside bodies'. On deductions, the most important recommendation was a suggested alteration to the judicial dictum that[18] 'it is not enough that the disbursement is made in the course of, or arises out of, or is connected with, the trade or is made out of the profits of the trade. It must be made for the purpose of earning the profits'. The Board, however, demurred to this proposal.[19]

With regard to depreciation, they recommended further allowances for mines, oil wells and tunnel undertakings which the 1952 Finance Act took care of. But neither they nor the Radcliffe Committee later could break down the Board's opposition to giving an allowance for commercial buildings, which had been suggested as long ago as the 1920 Committee (see p. 161).[20]

Finally the Committee did consider a number of miscellaneous items,[21] including the vexed question of stock valuation, where they indicated the main reason for dispute would be over facts not principles.[22] Indeed a sturdy practical commonsense imbued the whole of the Report; they admitted they were making 'no startling contribution to the universally desired simplification'.[23] In fact, at some points, their proposed minor amendments might have had the effect of providing confusing exceptions to long established rules; and in suggesting a depreciation allowance for commercial buildings, they had lost sight of the original purpose of the 1945 allowance which was specifically 'for productive or creative industry'. Nevertheless, it was a practical report, as might have been expected from a K.C. specializing in taxation, an ex-Chief Inspector of Taxes, a Chartered Accountant and a prominent trade unionist. The same practicality is manifest in the second Tucker Report on the Taxation Treatment of Provisions for Retirement.[24]

The two Radcliffe Reports[25] were more elaborate and more theoretical. Their terms of reference were much wider, 'the present system of taxation of profits and income, including its incidence and effects', and two of its members were the well-known economists and taxation experts, Hicks and Kaldor. The reports were published in April, 1954 and June, 1955, the first being concerned with the Pay As You Earn system and the familiar themes of graduation and differentiation and

---

[18] Strong and Co. of Romsey *v.* Woodifield, 5 T.C. 215 at p. 220.

[19] The Board's attitude: See Final Report (Radcliffe) Cmd. 9474, p. 43, para. 127.

[20] See Report, p. 67, para. 204 and Final Report (Radcliffe) (*op. cit.*), p. 118, paras. 381–2.

[21] Pp. 98–104, paras. 298–317.   [22] Ch. VI, pp. 92–5, paras. 280–8.

[23] Report, p. 8, para. 13.

[24] Cmd. 9063 (February, 1954), Hansard 6/IV/54 (Butler).

[25] Second Report, Cmd. 9105 (April, 1954), Final Report, Cmd. 9474 (June, 1955).

the second (final) report with every other aspect of the direct taxation system.

The April, 1954 Report has not yet been superseded as providing the best available account of the practical operation of Pay As You Earn; and after considering its full details, the Committee concluded that 'whatever discouraging effects P.A.Y.E. may have, we are not satisfied that they are of such magnitude as to justify the upheaval of a system which has been conducted to the general satisfaction of employers and workpeople'.[26] The justification for ignoring the disincentive effect of P.A.Y.E. was derived from evidence in Appendix I.[27] This consisted of a report based on data collected for the Commission by the Social Survey during February 18 to March 20, 1952. This concluded that 'few productive workers had any detailed knowledge of the way they were affected by income tax',[28] that there was no evidence from the enquiry of 'productive' effort being inhibited by income tax' and that 'an attitude towards income tax' was a minor factor in productive effort as assessed by hours of work. Nor did the Committee find it possible to recommend, as had been suggested, a measure of integration of income tax and social security,[29] or that 'it would be advantageous or conducive to equity to substitute some simpler form of tax' in place of the progressive income tax applied by means of the P.A.Y.E. system.

On the twin principles of graduation and differentiation,[30] the Committee regarded the various personal reliefs, the reduced rate relief, graduated surtax and the earned income relief as securing these in adequate measure. It considered, however, that some modification of these reliefs would render graduation and differentiation even more effective. Thirteen recommendations,[31] therefore, were put forward, the most important of which were a graduated exemption limit in favour of the smallest incomes, a child allowance varying with the size of the claimant's income and tapering off with the child's own income instead of ceasing at an arbitrary figure and an increase in earned income relief. The influence of these recommendations is perceptible in subsequent legislation affecting allowances generally such as the exemption limit itself, for example, but not in any one specific instance.

There was, however, a minority report,[32] two of the signatories of which were Kaldor and Woodcock. This reservation arose from the

[26] Second Report (*op. cit.*), p. 31, para. 100.
[27] Second Report, pp. 91–124.   [28] Second Report, p. 92, paras. 9–11.
[29] Income Tax and social security: Second Report, Ch. II, pp. 9–17.
[30] Graduation and differentiation: Second Report, Pt. II, pp. 31–65.
[31] Thirteen recommendations: Second Report, pp. 69–71, para. 224.
[32] The minority Report: Second Report, pp. 72–80.

question of 'whether, in dealing with changes in the structure of taxation, we should put our present recommendations in a form which entails loss of revenue to the Exchequer', the practical issues[33] being the question of the exemption limit and personal allowances, especially for children, and differentiation. This report might have been criticized as impractical; but it did display an originality which, to an extent, was lacking in the somewhat pedestrian proposals of the main Report.

The final report of the Radcliffe Committee, published in June, 1955, considered for the first time for thirty-five years every aspect of income and business taxation including 'any profit ranking as a capital profit under the existing law'.[34] Expenditure taxes[35] were, however, specifically excluded, as were the all embracing topics of direct taxation as a means of controlling the economy and its main distributional effects. There was a mass of evidence,[36] including statements or memoranda from upwards of four hundred individuals and representative bodies, a hundred and twenty memoranda from the Board of Inland Revenue itself and twenty-one days of oral evidence taking. On account of expense, 'this great volume'[37] of representations was not published but complete sets were deposited in various libraries.

With this vast amount of material, it is surprising that the report is not more unmanageable than it is, but the reason is partly the clarity of writing and arranging and partly the careful preservation of historical perspective. It contains ninety recommendations, some involving a loss and some a gain to the yield of revenue, which are arranged under various subheads. These subheads may involve only one recommendation or, as in the case of Schedule A, administration and evasion, ten or more. Broadly speaking, however, there was no proposal to make any basic change in the current income tax code, namely taxation at the source coupled with the division of sources of income into four schedules (Schedule B was to be abolished).[38] This conservatism is in some way surprising in view of the forcibly expressed opinion that taxation of the company and of the individual[39] had long gone their separate ways for there was no attempt to develop the consequential criticism of the hampering link through standard rate between companies and individuals.

[33] The 'practical issues': Second Report, p. 72, para. 1.
[34] 'Any profit making . . .': Hansard 6/II/51 (Gaitskell).
[35] Expenditure taxes: Final Report, Cmd. 9474, p. 2, para. 2.
[36] On the Radcliffe Report in general, see: (*a*) *National Provincial Bank Review* (1956), F. A. Cockfield; (*b*) *The Solicitor*, September, October, November, 1955, A. Farnsworth.
[37] 'this great volume': Final Report, pp. 3–4, paras. 11–12.
[38] Recommendation 59, p. 339.   [39] Final Report, p. 133, para. 436 (2).

This general preservation of the *status quo* did not, however, mean that the proposals lacked practical value. As with the previous reports, such as that of 1920, the results of its comprehensive inquest pervaded subsequent legislation, as, for example, in the provisions regarding compensation for loss of office,[40] hobby farming,[41] responsibility for making assessments[42] and penalties.[43] The members of the Committee, on the other hand, were no more fortunate than had been their colleagues on the Tucker Committee in gaining official support for a revision of the rule regulating deductible expenses under Schedule D, for amending the strict Schedule E expenses rule, for granting capital allowances to commercial buildings. And behind all this patient interrogation lay the perennial quest for equity, for the fair distribution of the burden over the different classes of society.

But the members who signed the minority report, while accepting the aims, could not accept the means. They felt unable to sign the final report 'because of a fundamental difference of view as to the basic requirements of an equitable system of taxation'.[44] In effect they could not agree that 'the tax base itself', that is the definition of income for tax purposes as it had evolved from Finance Acts case law and commercial and Inland Revenue practice, even with the modifications produced by differentiation and graduation, succeeded in achieving an equitable standard of real wealth. They argued that the ability to expend capital, which Cripps had pinpointed (see p. 214), to create capital profits,[45] sometimes by dubious means and to profit from the difference between 'Pay As You Earn' and Pay As You Like' made it necessary to reconsider the orthodox definition of income. It was these considerations which led them to propose not only a capital gains tax, but a corporation profits tax also.[46] This minority opinion, to which the Board was also opposed, at first aroused little interest; but some of the apparent heresies were taken up in the early 'sixties under the heading of income distribution and social change[47] and by the April, 1965 Budget they had really come into their own.

But this final report of the Radcliffe Committee was still in draft when Butler rose to present his second Budget,[48] intended to be 'an incentive Budget'. His first had benefited the individual; now when 'a sort of ebb tide in the economy' had developed, it was the turn of

---

[40] F.A. 1960, Ss. 37–8, 4th Sch.   [41] F.A. 1960, S. 20.
[42] Taxes Management Act, 1964.   [43] F.A. 1960, Pt. III.
[44] Minority Report, p. 354, para. 1 (included with Final Report).
[45] Minority Report, p. 369, paras. 46–7.
[46] Minority Report, pp. 365–89, paras. 34–107.
[47] See R. M. Titmuss's book of that title.   [48] Hansard 14/IV/53.

industry. The first step was the restoration of the initial allowance, at 20% for plant and machinery, 10% for industrial buildings and 40% for mining; the higher rate for the last category is an example of the use of allowances for a specialized purpose, a practice which is still comparatively rare in the income tax code. The second relief was a reduction in standard rate by sixpence to 9s in the £, which would give immediate help to industry. Finally the excess profits levy was to end on January 1, 1954.

There were, in addition, three other reforms of administrative importance to Schedule D. The procedure for claiming loss relief under S. 341 was simplified;[49] the cessation basis became automatic on a change in partnership[50] unless a contrary election was made and the system of subvention payments[51] was introduced, a mechanism for relieving losses within groups of companies.

The individual was not completely forgotten. The standard rate reduction also applied in this sphere; age allowance and the dependent relative relief were increased; and at the lower end of the scale, all reduced rates were decreased by sixpence.

The main theme of the Opposition was not so much the reduction in taxation, amounting to over £400 millions, but 'the unfair distribition of largesse'.[52] It would have been better to increase the earned income allowance and help the more lowly paid. 'We regard taxes as a way of redressing the other distortions, anomalies and injustices of the economic situation.'[53] The Government maintained that 'the main way in which the Budget helps imports is by stimulating the expansion, re-equipment and modernization of British industry'.[54] The 'psychological effect of a direct frontal attack on the main burden of direct taxation'[55] was the best incentive possible. The Opposition, by imputing political motives to the tax changes intended to provide such a stimulus, was only confusing the issue. An impartial conclusion was that the Chancellor had, in fact, 'lifted the Budget out of the restrictive rut'.[56]

The following Budget of 1954[57] was, he said, a 'carry on' Budget and his comparatively brief opening speech was more philosophical than economic. 'We must not be frightened of a little more ease and happiness, or feel that what is pleasant must necessarily be evil.' Almost the only word of warning was that 'industry must beware of excessive distribution of profit'. The warning was perhaps necessary because of the new incentive to industrial development of the invest-

[49] S. 15, F.A. 1953.
[50] Partnerships: S. 19, F.A. 1953.
[51] S. 20, F.A. 1953.
[52] Hansard 15/IV/53 (Gaitskell).
[53] Hansard 16/IV/53 (Wilson).
[54] Hansard 16/IV/53 (Maudling).
[55] Hansard 16/IV/53 (Maudling).
[56] *Financial Times* (16/IV/53).
[57] Hansard 6/IV/54.

ment allowance,[58] a percentage of the cost of new assets; this unlike the initial allowance which in some cases it replaced was not deducted in arriving at the written down value of the asset concerned.

The Opposition called the Budget 'dull'[59] and in default of any detailed criticisms went back to first principles and declared: 'There is a certain difference in our attitude towards high taxation because we, on this side of the House, do not regard taxation merely as a means of raising revenue.'[60] There was general praise for the investment allowance,[61] which ought to pay for itself out of expanded production provided the plant it underpinned was used economically and efficiently. There was a note of caution[62] sounded by the Labour spokesmen; the allowance was a straight, unconditional subsidy; perhaps it should have been made discriminatory – 'we argued this last year'. This lack of discrimination may well have been the basis of the Revenue's alleged objections to it;[63] certainly it was hardly intended to give a tax free bonus to juke boxes or pintables. The position about increasing Government expenditure generally, as the Chancellor said when winding up, was simply that to support an armed welfare state 'frankly we are all in it'.

1954 marks the high water mark of 'Butskellism';[64] 1955 showed a fall from grace. At first sight the Budget of that year, Butler's fourth,[65] seemed as he claimed himself 'of classical purity and simplicity'. He had always held 'the sheer burden of taxation' was too great, echoing a phrase used two years ago. He had a Budget surplus of some £300 millions and proposed devoting half of this to reducing the standard and reduced rates by sixpence and threepence respectively and to an increase in allowances including relief to small incomes under £300. He wanted, as he said on the second reading,[66] to give 'as much advantage as possible to the people at the lowest points' as recommended in the Radcliffe Report. Other recommendations which did not feature in the Budget were not on that account, he assured the House, forgotten.

It was easy for the Opposition to label the Budget simple electioneering and some did.[67] Other members welcomed the reductions in taxation but said they were of advantage to the wrong section of the community; the companies were once again 'the favourite children'[68]

---

[58] F.A. 1954, S. 16 and 2nd Schedule.

[59] Hansard 7/IV/53 (Gaitskell).   [60] Hansard 7/IV/53 (Crosland).

[61] Investment Allowances: Hansard 7/IV/53 (Crosland).

[62] A note of caution.

[63] The Revenue's alleged objections: Brittan (*op. cit.*), pp. 167–8.

[64] 'Butskellism': A word coined by the *Economist* to denote the common features of both parties' fiscal policy.

[65] Butler's fourth Budget: Hansard 19/IV/55.   [66] Hansard 25/IV/55.

[67] Hansard 19/IV/55 (N. Smith).   [68] Hansard 20/IV/55 (Gaitskell).

and 'the larger the income the greater the benefits'.[69] Some felt uneasy at the reductions in principle; there was no evidence to show whether this was right; it was an 'unjustified gamble with the nation's economy'.[70] The debate was often thinly attended[71] and tended to concentrate more on the export situation. The papers were reasonably congratulatory, apart from the *Observer*; its acute forecast was that by the summer holidays 'the country would be in the midst of a balance of payments crisis'.[72]

The Chancellor had been in something of a dilemma. As the *Economist* put it: 'To have given nothing would have proved Mr Butler too much of an economist to survive in politics; to have given the lot would have shown him too much of a politician to have charge of the national economy.'[73] There was certainly 'a background of an odour of dissolution'[74] to the Budget and the General Election was held in the following May. The Conservatives strengthened their majority to 345 seats against Labour's 277, but whether the Budget contributed largely to the result only the psephologists can say.

It has been said that Butler resumed office after the election 'full of fury with the bankers who had misled him'[75] in his give-away Budget of a few months before, although there is no such implication in a contemporary semi-official biography.[76] The *Observer's* prophecy had indeed been amply justified and Butler's last Budget was forced upon him in the autumn.[77] A dual policy of incentive and restraint was needed. The latter was provided by increases in purchase tax and profits tax which was increased to $27\frac{1}{2}\%$ on distributed income; the idea of a flat rate was rejected and the arguments for a capital gains tax were 'far from convincing'. The incentives provided by the increased allowances of the spring were retained: 'I do not propose to single out personal incomes for further taxation or for some reduction of the relief from taxation which I have already given them.'

The Opposition had a field day of moral indignation;[78] the newspapers joined in. "This is the consequence of leaving things too late and trusting too much to luck.'[79] Butler himself did not reply to the debate but his chance came later in the censure motion of October 31st when he delivered 'one of the most effective speeches'[80] he had made in the House. The truth is that in this confusing period when many politicians were economists, or forced to debate as if they were,

[69] Hansard 20/IV/55 (Houghton).　　[70] Hansard 22/IV/55 (Fletcher).
[71] Hansard 21/IV/55 (Houghton).　　[72] Hansard 24/IV/55.
[73] *Economist*, May, 1955.　　[74] Hansard 22/IV/55 (Wilson).
[75] Brittan (*op. cit.*), p. 179.
[76] Ralph Harris: *Politics Without Prejudice* (1955).
[77] Butler's fifth (and last) Budget: Hansard 26/X/55.
[78] See e.g. Hansard 27/X/55 (Gaitskell), Hansard 28/X/55 (Jay).
[79] *Manchester Guardian* 26/VII/55.　　[80] *Manchester Guardian* 1/XI/55.

when the Harrods, Clarks and Hobsons could not agree whether deflation, disinflation or inflation would be the most disastrous, when one month the economy was over-extended and the next not extended enough, no one even now could secure general agreement on what should have been the correct policy. At least, during the Butler period, there was a coherent, mainly expansionist policy; when he made way for Macmillan in December, 1955 it became increasingly difficult to trace any consistently pursued policy for any length of time.

The principal reasons for this apparent lack of fiscal pattern seem, at this short range, to be quite simply having five very different Chancellors in office from 1956 to 1964 and the replacement of expansion by varying degrees of caution. 'What the economy most lacks is a firm indication of the real view of the Government as to the kind of economy and society which they want to create.'[81] In the field of income tax itself, this deficiency was reflected in a policy of spasmodic remission and retrenchment in both allowances and rates.

Macmillan confessed his surprise at becoming Chancellor, especially as he considered Budget day to be, rather like Speech Day, 'a bit of a bore, but the parents and old boys like it', and there was a long speech before 'the fortunate prizewinners' were announced. Certainly there was a long speech; and, as the Opposition unkindly put it, a very small Budget.[82] Essentially it could be claimed to be one of saving and of anti-inflation. The direct taxation measures were of minor character only; the recommendations of the second Tucker Committee were implemented in setting up retirement provisions for the self-employed; investment allowances were suspended, apart from shipping, scientific research and fuel saving equipment; savings bank interest up to £15 was declared exempt; and in the sphere of profits tax there was legislative amendment[83] arising out of a recent tax case; and its rate was increased to 30% on distributed and 3% on undistributed income.

An Opposition spokesman[84] claimed it was the most muddled and least clear Budget statement he had ever heard; but Opposition criticism in general was no better, which possibly explains the meagre attendance on some days and a press complaint that 'the Budget debate was dying of inanition'.[85] This criticism had ranged from the Chancellor's failure to tackle the system of direct taxation,[86] root

[81] 'What the economy most lacks . . .': Hansard 18/IV/56 (Grimond).

[82] Macmillan's Budget: Hansard 17/IV/56.

[83] Legislation: Income Tax, Profits Tax: Board's Report for the year to 31/III/57, pp. 40–41, paras. 133–46; p. 42, paras. 147–8; also Universal Grinding Wheel, T.C. 35, p. 551.

[84] Hansard 18/IV/56 (Jay).   [85] *Manchester Guardian* 18/IV/56.

[86] Hansard 18/IV/56 (Wilson).

and branch, which was something of a tall order, to detailed points of income tax procedure. There was a general tendency to use the recommendations of the Radcliffe Report as sticks to beat the Chancellor with, the emphasis being on the lack of relief to the small fixed income group[87] and of course the failure to introduce a capital gains tax[88] (to which Macmillan might not have been averse)[89] and a flat rate corporation profits tax.

Macmillan had not claimed the fiscal omniscience of some of his critics. 'There was no true science which can give us certainty in this uncertain field'; and in his winding up comments he brushed aside all criticism in his usual cavalier fashion.[90] His Budget was 'sound, sensible and likely to be popular'. The Opposition had decided to call it 'flash, irrelevant and squalid and let it go at that'. His vignettes of some of the Opposition speakers were equally diverting; of Wilson, for instance, he remarked that sometimes he was driving a tumbril and sometimes had his eye on a Government Humber. But quite apart from his entertainment value, the Chancellor did secure greater statistical accuracy in official statements; and in the context of the economic situation he had produced a justifiable Budget.

Before the year was over, however, the Suez crisis had put Eden out of 10, Downing Street, and Macmillan in. His successor was Thorneycroft, who had been a faithful and lucid apologist for Government finance over some years. Like Macmillan, he was responsible for only one Budget; but unlike him, he left office for the comparative if temporary obscurity of the back benches, along with his Financial and Economic Secretaries, over the issue of government expenditure.

That less than ten months would see such a crisis over economy could hardly have been visualized from the new Chancellor's cheerful Budget.[91] For industry, although there could not yet be any general restoration of the investment allowance, it was increased in the case of shipping to 40%; the exemption of overseas trade corporations was also proposed.[92] For the ordinary individual there was an increase in earned income allowance from a maximum of £450 to £1,550, a revision of child allowances depending upon age and an extension of small income relief. Thirdly, for the surtax payer, there was the allowance against his income of the amount by which the total of certain income tax reliefs exceeded the single personal allowance of £140.[93] The Chancellor had attempted to steer a middle

[87] Hansard 18/IV/56 (Wilson).   [88] Hansard 17/IV/56 (Gaitskell).
[89] Brittan (*op. cit.*), p. 183.   [90] Hansard 23/IV/56.
[91] Thorneycroft's Budget: Hansard 9/IV/57.
[92] Overseas Trade Corporation: F.A. 1957, Ss. 23–8, 30–7 & Schs. 4–6 & 8.
[93] Surtax relief: F.A. 1957, S. 14.

course; while 'rejecting unequivocally' the view that 'his sole duty was to remove taxation at whatever risk to the economy', he held that the other extreme 'covered elements of almost equal folly'.

The Opposition was willing to give qualified approval to the increase in allowances, but the concession to the surtax payer was a universal target. Criticism ranged from a mild 'the sympathy for the rich is rather overdone',[94] to a forthright 'this is a class Budget',[95] a 'shameful Budget'[96] which 'pampers the greedy rather than ministers to the needy'.[97] More considered judgments were that the proposal represented an 'assignment with inflation'[98] and that the investment allowances should have been restored on a selective basis.[99]

The opinion of the Press[100] was that 'the tax changes were well advised and well balanced'. Thorneycroft himself regarded his measures as 'part of a steady process of lightening the burden of taxation'[101] which since 1951 had meant that 'almost every income has received some tax benefit'. There was a good case for relief, in theory: 'I do not object to the reliefs which the Chancellor has given on their merits, looked at in isolation as studies in fiscal equity or in suitable incidence of taxation; but where the Budget can go wrong is in not keeping the balance at the right time.'[102] This was the real basis of the Opposition's charges.

The job of Chancellor was in truth proving 'a political graveyard',[103] but Heathcoat Amory survived to introduce three Budgets; for he carried the administrative skills he had learned at the Ministry of Agriculture to the Treasury and continued the fiscal caution which Thorneycroft had developed after the run on gold in the summer of 1957. His three Budgets[104] were, in turn, neutral, mildly expansionist, then neutral again and may conveniently be looked at together, since they serve as an illustration of what has been called 'the brake or the throttle technique', or, less kindly, 'Derick or Little by Little'.

The story of the three Budgets, as far as allowances and reliefs are concerned, is comparatively straightforward. His first was a part of the 'continuous battle against inflation'; it would be wrong, he warned

[94] Surtax sympathy: Hansard 9/IV/57 (Hynd).
[95] Hansard 9/IV/57 (Rankin).
[96] Hansard 9/IV/57 (Short).
[97] Hansard 9/IV/57 (Moody).
[98] Hansard 10/IV/57 (Wilson).
[99] Investment allowances: Hansard 10/IV/57 (Jay).
[100] The Press: *The Times* 10/IV/57.
[101] Hansard 15/IV/57.
[102] Hansard 11/IV/57 (Houghton).
[103] Hansard 10/IV/57 (Grimond).
[104] Amory's three Budgets: Hansard 15/IV/58, Hansard 7/IV/59, Hansard 4/IV/60.

the House 'to remit substantial sums of taxation'. There were, in fact, three minor changes in allowances affecting small incomes, age relief and dependent relatives; industry benefited from an increase in the initial allowance. Amory's second Budget was 'not full steam ahead, but steady ahead with confidence'. To this end he reduced standard rate by ninepence and the three bands of reduced rate by sixpence in the £; besides the standard rate change, industry also gained a bonus in the shape of the restoration of the investment allowance at its original rates; despite these concessions, costing £229 millions in a full year, this should not be regarded as 'a spending spree Budget' The age limits for post-war credit repayment were also reduced and other conditions (hardship involved) for repayment introduced. The third Budget, in 1960, was one of 'moderate restraint',[105] making only two minor amendments in the housekeeper and dependent relative allowances. With regard to profits tax, Amory had already introduced in 1958 a flat rate of 10% instead of the old dual rate on distributed and undistributed profits; this rate he raised to 12½% in 1960.

In each of the Budget debates, Wilson was the chief speaker for the Opposition and his criticisms followed fairly predictable political lines. Much play was, of course, made with the tough Budget of 1960 following the pre-election give-away Budget of 1959 when the Conservatives had come back into power with a majority of over a hundred, but this was normal political ritual. More serious was the amalgamation of the profits tax rates which had already been labelled a 'mistaken move';[106] it would lead to increased dividends and should have been coupled with a capital gains tax[107] 'which had a prominent place in the demonology of the Conservative party'. As for the expansionist Budget of 1959,[108] this stimulation had come too late; such measures might have prevented the recession of 1958 and led to a smoother advance into the 'sixties. Labour critics in general stressed the lack of relief to Old Age Pensioners and the 'chequered history'[109] between 1946 and 1959 of the initial and investment allowances, which, owing to their indefiniteness could make industrial planning more difficult, especially in view of the Chancellor's remark when restoring the latter that 'it could be equally appropriate to reverse the action I am taking now'. Perhaps the sense of the Opposition's feeling was best expressed in the charge that the Budgets 'served no social purpose whatever',[110] as exemplified by the neglect of the Old Age Pensioners already referred to.

[105] Hansard 5/IV/60 (Maudling).   [106] Hansard 15/IV/58 (Gaitskell).
[107] Hansard 5/IV/60 (Cronin).
[108] Hansard 8/IV/59 (Wilson; and see also Brittan (*op. cit.*), p. 203).
[109] Hansard 8/IV/59 (Houghton). See also *British Tax Review* for 1959, p. 158.
[110] Hansard 13/IV/59 (Robens).

Amory on the whole had little difficulty in defending himself and his measures. The Opposition in 1958 'had directed its fire less against specific taxation proposals than against the general economic policy of the Government'. In 1959 it was generally agreed that the measure of remission was about right; at issue was merely the sort of stimulus required and its distribution; while as for 1960 'if the Budget had been agreeable and popular, I doubt whether it would have secured its purpose'. Amory's final cause for gratification was his attainment of that pantheon of Chancellors, Madame Tussaud's.[111]

When he resigned in July, 1960 he is said to have advised Macmillan that an incomes policy was essential for economic stability,[112] but it was in fact his successor, Selwyn Lloyd, who managed to secure its acceptance as a recognized feature of Conservative policy. This was possibly his major achievement as Chancellor for, although he introduced, as a summary of his Budgets will show, at least three other notable reforms in this field, their timing could have been managed with a far greater degree of political tact.

The 'broad effect' of his first Budget,[113] he announced, 'must be counter-inflationary' and to achieve this end, he introduced economic regulators giving him power to vary indirect taxation between Budgets, some minor administrative Schedule E changes including the restriction of capital allowances on luxury cars, together with the raising of the percentage assessable as a benefit and the increase of the profits tax rate by $2\frac{1}{2}\%$. But the really controversial proposal was the uplift of the surtax limit, in effect, to £5,000 on earned income; this would have 'a dynamic effect upon the initiative and effort of individuals'.

The Opposition was aroused; there was no room for surtax relief 'when immense capital profits continue to be made';[114] it was 'class legislation of the most blatant type'.[115] Quite apart from the equitable aspect 'there was no evidence to substantiate the idea that high taxation was in fact a deterrent to incentive and hard work';[116] the Radcliffe Committee (see p. 224) had certainly not found it so; and a contemporary article was equally emphatic. 'Whatever may be the important causes behind Britain's post-war economic difficulties, a lack of incentive to work because of high income taxation was not one of them.'[117] The proposal was also criticized on purely fiscal grounds: 'I hope we are seeing the end of the period when successive

[111] Hansard 21/IV/58 (Amory).   [112] Brittan (*op. cit.*), p. 206.
[113] Lloyd's first Budget: Hansard 17/IV/61.
[114] 'There was no room . . .': Hansard 17/IV/61 (Gaitskell).
[115] 'Class legislation': Hansard 18/IV/61 (Wilson). See also Hansard 17/IV/61 (Allaun).
[116] Hansard 19/IV/61 (Diamond).
[117] Professor Break: *British Tax Review*, 1957.

Chancellors seem to think that any reliefs they give in the Budget can be recouped by putting an increased tax on Company profits.'[118]

The Government emphasized in reply that for an increase in productivity and exports 'the only course of action . . . is in the sphere of personal taxation and incentive'.[119] The surtax limit was 'grotesquely out of date'[120] and 'the scarce commodity is good management' which was being insufficiently rewarded. The cost of the relief was some £83 millions which was practically offset by the profits tax increase of £70 millions, but much play was, of course, made with the National Health increases in the February; the juxtaposition was, to say the least, unfortunate. The fact of the matter was, however, that most of the taxation experts on both sides of the House would have admitted privately that the starting point of surtax was far too low and compared most unfavourably with rates abroad, but both were frozen in fixed ideological postures which made the discussion more extreme than it should have been; this was equally true of the discussions on expenses.[121]

But scarcely was the ink dry on the 1961 Finance Act, than Lloyd produced his 'little Budget'.[122] This was wholly concerned with indirect taxation but the Opposition soon registered its protest again against the surtax concession, which should be suspended, and to suggest a capital gains tax should be imposed at once instead of merely being forecast. Popular reaction, however, fastened on the notorious 'pay pause' which Lloyd considered 'essential as a basis for continued prosperity and growth'. The statement in general had a bad press and the Opposition was quick to say so. Macmillan's winding up mollified them not at all.

By the time of his next Budget,[123] which, contrary to all precedent, he opened on a Monday, Lloyd may well have known he was fighting a losing battle. 'Unpopular though our actions have been, we have gone some way to compel the country to face up to this problem (of wage restraint) – in many ways the central problem of the 'sixties.' He increased small income relief, promised the abolition of Schedule A and introduced a short term gains tax which taxed the profit on shares sold within six months of purchase and land sold within three years of purchase. The net result was a 'no change Budget' with neither an increase nor a decrease in revenue.

It is recent history that the Budget proved the Opposition to have been more correct in their judgment than the Government and that

[118] Hansard 19/IV/61 (Thatcher).   [119] Hansard 17/IV/61 (Leather).
[120] Hansard 18/IV/61 (Maudling).
[121] Hansard 20/IV/61 (Houghton), Hansard 18/IV/61 (Wilson), Hansard 17/IV/61 (Gaitskell).
[122] Hansard 25/VII/61.   [123] Lloyd's second Budget: Hansard 9/IV/62.

the capital gains tax, for instance, intended to secure 'a greater sense of fair treatment' and not a heavy yield offered in too many ways 'an invitation not to pay'.[124] But Lloyd's realism on the question of wages and surtax underlines his *credo*: 'I think there is one very sound rule for Chancellors of the Exchequer. They should not pay any attention to by-elections, or to the morale of political parties. They should do what they think is right and that is what I have done.'[125]

If Lloyd's last Budget had not been sufficiently expansionist, no such complaint could be made against the ebullient proposals of his successor, Reginald Maudling.[126] 'The theme of this Budget,' he announced, 'is expansion' and expansionist it certainly was. Callaghan[127] could no longer complain that personal allowances had not moved for ten years, since there was a round of increases,[128] a simplification of the reduced rates and the introduction of a tapered child allowance.[129] Schedule A was at last abolished for owner occupiers and a new Case VIII substituted to charge rents.[130] Capital allowances were simplified and in some cases increased, investment allowances increased by 50%, except in the case of shipping, and luxury cars were again allowed a total write off, but in effect at a modified rate.

Individuals and companies had been taken care of by the increases in personal and capital allowances respectively. The spectacular innovation was the provision of 'free depreciation'[131] for capital expenditure incurred after April 3, 1963 on new machinery or plant, excluding mobile equipment, provided for industrial purposes in areas of high unemployment. Such expenditure could be written off in full in one year, an idea[132] which the Opposition had put forward in debate more than once. This was a most significant use of capital allowances not only selectively,[133] but for a specific purpose which had hardly been attempted before except in a modified form in the cases of shipping, scientific research expenditure and fuel saving equipment.

The Opposition's main line of attack was not directed against the Budget proposals themselves: 'the reductions of the Chancellor are in the right places. How could I say anything else? We proposed them.'[134] It was concentrated on the fact that there was no serious inquest on what had happened last year, the events of which had been dismissed by the Chancellor in a summary of six hundred words or

---

[124] Hansard 11/IV/62 (Jenkins).   [125] Lloyd to Robin Day 9/IV/62.
[126] Maudling's first Budget: Hansard 3/IV/63.   [127] Hansard 10/IV/62.
[128] S. 12, ss. 1–8, F.A. 1963.   [129] S. 13, F.A. 1963.
[130] S.S. 14–32, F.A. 1963 and associated Schedules.
[131] S.38, ss. 1–8, F.A. 1963.
[132] See, for example, Hansard 18/IV/61 (Wilson) or 12/IV/62 (Diamond)
[133] See S. 38, ss. 8.   [134] Hansard 4/IV/65 (Callaghan).

so. If expansion was the correct policy now, why was it not in 1962? The current validity of the Budget was, in effect, being used to demonstrate that 'the traditional Conservative and indeed Treasury policy, that cutting exports and domestic expenditure is a cure for balance of payments without inflation, is disastrously wrong'.[135]

There was certainly a non-partisan case to be made for saying that expansion and the Maudling régime itself had come too late; for in his second Budget,[136] the bold taxation conceptions of 1963 were absent; he was making the transition from 'rapid expansion' to 'smooth progress', and the measures proposed consisted of the clawing back of £100 millions of purchasing power by means of indirect taxation which was the quickest and simplest method of securing the amount of restriction generally considered to be desirable.

The development of income tax under the long period of Conservative rule in the 'fifties and 'sixties is often tangled and confused. Sometimes the legislation proposed is in the interest of social justice, sometimes for purely economic motives and sometimes for sheer administrative convenience; moreover the motives may well be obscure or mixed. But whatever motives were predominant in any one Budget, every Chancellor had found it necessary to include in his proposals some measure of anti-avoidance. For the ten years, particularly, from 1954 to 1963 were the golden age of borderline capital profits and elaborate avoidance schemes in which many of the greatest experts on taxation were engaged.

Since the middle 'thirties' (see p. 191), when Chamberlain had legislated against avoidance and sternly threatened retrospective legislation, avoidance had remained an art rather than become an industry. During the war, the anti-avoidance measures built into E.P.T. were reasonably effective (see p. 198); and in the days of austerity and E.P.L. there was little anti-avoidance legislation and even less discussion about the problem either in the House or the Press generally.

The question was first raised again as a matter of national importance by a Lancashire M.P.[137] in the debate on the 1953 Budget. He had observed that a number of cotton concerns were artificially ceasing and then re-starting;[138] this procedure, under the rules governing Schedule D assessment, could be contrived to secure the non-assessment of considerable profits. Somerset House was, in fact, aware of this technique before it was brought to the notice of the House and eventually legislation put a provisional stop to it in 1954.

This seemed a comparatively simple piece of legislation to meet a

[135] Hansard 4/IV/63 (Crosland).   [136] Hansard 14/IV/64.
[137] Hansard 17/IV/53 (Rhodes).
[138] See now S. 17, F.A. 1954 and Board's Report to 31/III/55, p. 29, para. 71.

comparatively simple situation; and so it was at the time, although now it redounds more to the disadvantage of the Revenue. Far different and far more complex was the device known as 'dividend stripping'[139] which involves a relationship between a trading company and a finance house whereby the reserves of the former are extracted by means of a special dividend the tax on which is made available for relief. Legislation in 1955 contained this device in its original form, but within three years 'the moles of the tax avoidance industry had burrowed beneath the barricades',[140] and further legislation was needed in 1958,[141] which was, very unusually, made retrospective[142] since the operators had had ample warning, and again in 1960.

'Bond-washing'[143] was a further, perhaps the oldest, device, against which there had been pre-war legislation (see p. 191). It consists basically of selling securities 'cum dividend' and their repurchase 'ex dividend' on terms which relieve the holder of surtax and often a considerable amount of income tax also. Variations on this theme have proved so ingenious that it was still necessary to include sections aimed at this device in the 1960 Finance Act.[144]

Indeed by that date, avoidance mechanisms had become so sophisticated that the Budget of that year was labelled a Somerset House Budget since it proposed the most technical Finance Bill, possibly, in the whole history of income tax. It represented the high water mark of avoidance legislation; and besides dealing with such complex stratagems as sales of shares in an investment company to a company dealing in securities, land or buildings where both companies are controlled by the same person, or sales of certain shares again where a building company was involved which could enable the profit on sale of a new erection to escape taxation, it also closed more obvious loopholes. These included hobby farming,[145] the refusal of relief for farming losses unless the activity was carried on commercially, post cessation receipts[146] which could now be generally assessed, and the taxing of compensation for loss of office in excess of £5,000.[147] Not content with this, and partly as the result of a recent tax case,[148] the penalty provisions were also revised and replaced by classified general provisions.[149] Finally, after consultations with the City, Amory,

---

[139] See Final Radcliffe Report (*op. cit.*), pp. 368–71 and D. C. Potter (*British Tax Review*), July–August, 1960, p. 248; F.A. (No. 2) 1955, S. 4; Board's Report to 31/III/56, p. 28, para. 71.

[140] Hansard 18/IV/56 (Wilson).   [141] Ss. 18–19, F.A. 1958; S. 31, F.A. 1960.

[142] See *British Tax Review*, 1959, pp. 412–26.   [143] S. 27, F.A. 1960.

[144] See Ss. 21, 22, 23, 25 and 26.

[145] S. 20, F.A. 1960; see also S. 20 (8) regarding cancelling of the old Rule 13.

[146] Ss. 32–6, F.A. 1960.   [147] Ss. 37 and 38 and 4th Schecule, F.A. 1960.

[148] Hinchy *v.* C.I.R., 38 T.C., p. 625.

[149] Ss. 44–63, 6th and 8th Schedules, F.A. 1960.

who was then Chancellor, brought in three general avoidance sections.[150] 'Specific provisions having failed to keep pace with these new devices, I have had to propose a more general power . . . if it is to be effective for the purpose of stopping these blatant devices.'[151]

Parliament and public, apart from the specialists, may well have wondered why general power had not been taken before, instead of using what appeared to be the technique of bolting the stable door. 'One series of operations is enough to bring huge gains and when the legislation comes along, it does not catch that particular series of operations,'[152] as the Chancellor himself complained. The idea was not new; 'effective general powers'[153] and the writing into law of 'an omnibus protection of the Revenue'[154] had already been suggested. It was, however, tried in Australia where its arbitrary nature inevitably aroused the professional hostility of the Courts.[155] The traditional dislike of the British Parliament for such legislation also was well expressed in the 1960 Budget debate. 'I would prefer to see a small degree of tax avoidance and protect the freedom of the individual rather than to allow administration by diktat.'[156] There was clearly a danger suspected of government by decree spreading beyond the sphere of taxation.

Between piecemeal and possibly tardy legislation, and discretionary bureaucratic powers there was emerging, however, a possibly more acceptable middle course. This stemmed, to take it back no further, from the minority report of the Radcliffe Committee (see p. 226). As can be gathered from the previous summary of avoidance devices, a good deal of them arose basically from the manipulation of years of assessment, or the conversion of apparently taxable into capital profits. Both these escape routes, the signatories of the minority report considered, could well be blocked by the imposition of a corporation profits tax, where assessing year and accounting year would coincide, and a capital gains tax respectively; both these suggested reforms appear time and again in the annual Budget debates, especially after the passing of the 1960 Finance Act.

The question of a corporation profits tax was under active consideration by Somerset House at the beginning of the 'sixties. Selwyn Lloyd had 'wanted to have one system of taxation instead of two'[157] but had been deterred by the adverse recommendation of the Radcliffe Committee; nevertheless before the end of his regime he had been looking at a 'possible scheme' the Inland Revenue draft of which had been, he said, prepared on the usual 'controversial basis';

[150] Ss. 28–30.   [151] Hansard 7/IV/60 (Amory).
[152] Hansard 3/V/60 (Amory).   [153] Hansard 8/IV/59 (Wilson).
[154] Hansard 8/IV/59 (Houghton).   [155] *British Tax Review*, 1961, p. 247.
[156] Hansard 4/IV/60 (Glover).   [157] Hansard 17/IV/61 (Lloyd).

this possibly Freudian slip of the tongue caused some amusement and he hastily amended it to 'confidential'. Maudling had yet another scheme for the fusion of Income and Profits Tax presented to him, but it was 'not satisfactory' and he showed little enthusiasm for it;[158] he did reconsider the idea during his second term, but found it still 'not adequate', although it was during his tenure that the White Paper on an accounts year basis for Schedule D[159] was published; 'more time' was needed, he thought, for considering this projected change.

A capital gains tax, on the other hand, had never been popular with the Government, with the possible exception of Macmillan (see p. 231), but was mainly a Labour-sponsored idea. Gaitskell,[160] Wilson[161] and Callaghan[162] had frequently suggested its introduction, although it was Selwyn Lloyd, as already mentioned (see p. 235), who actually introduced the first capital gains tax. Despite the ease with which it could be avoided, accounting for its comparatively small yield of roughly £1 million in the first full year, its importance was that it did represent a major breakthrough in the principles of income taxation.

Clearly reforms on these two major fronts were, pending the election, imminent, with alternative plans for their implementation in temporary cold storage; it was not to be the responsibility of the Conservative Party, however, to carry them through. For in the autumn it was Labour by a slender majority which inherited the new thinking in direct taxation, and even when full allowance has been made for the very definite elements of continuity, October, 1964 marks the end of a well-identified era in direct taxation extending back to its origins in 1799.

[158] Hansard 3/IV/63 and 14/IV/64.
[159] A scheme for an Accounts Basis for Income Tax on Company Profits, Cmnd. 2347.
[160] Gaitskell and Capital Gains: Hansard 17/IV/61.
[161] Wilson and Capital Gains: Hansard 18/IV/61, Hansard 26/VII/62.
[162] Callaghan and Capital Gains: Hansard 10/IV/63.

CHAPTER XV

Today, Yesterday and Tomorrow

LIKE so many autumn Budgets, the reason for the fiscal measures of November, 1964[1] was the balance of payments situation which led to the 15% surcharge on 'substantially all imports'. As far as the radical reforms of taxing capital gains and corporation profits were concerned which (see pp. 239–40) had been for some years under active discussion in Parliament, press, Somerset House and the City, these would have to wait until the coming April. Meanwhile, in view of the 'inequities of the tax system', its occasional effect as a 'stumbling block to economic progress' and the possibility of making 'the profit motive do the work of planning' by selective tax concessions, the new Chancellor, Callaghan, who, like Snowden, had once worked in an income tax district, gave notice that he would, in the spring Budget, propose both a capital gains tax and a corporation profits tax.

The Opposition[2] complained that he had talked more about a future Budget than about the one he was presenting to the House, and there were certain press comments that he had shaken the confidence of the City and Zurich by his hazy references to the new taxes; but there would have been a considerable outcry if no reference had been made to them before a sudden imposition in April. More telling was the criticism that none of the measures increased the efficiency of British industry and that even if a corporation tax were workable, which it so far had been found not to be, company reserves would now present a standing invitation to Chancellors to raid them if their taxation was separated from individual taxation.[3]

Certainly the proposals generally had aroused an interest in taxation which had not been seen for many years, possibly ever since 1910. Press cutting services found there were now ten times the number of references to fiscal matters than there had been at the beginning of the decade and the Government was encouraged by

[1] Callaghan's first Budget: Hansard 11/XI/64.
[2] Hansard 11/XI/64 (Douglas-Home). See also the *Accountant's Journal*, Dec., 1964, p. 458.
[3] Hansard 12/XI/64 (Maudling).

some theoretical Liberal support since their report 'Taxation'[4] had advocated a single tax combining income and profits tax. A hundred and more companies 'went public' to establish a realistic value for their assets and earning power before Budget Day.

The Budget speech of April, 1965,[5] lasting over two hours, declared its purpose at the very outset. 'First, I intend to reduce the net out-flow of long-term capital from this country by at least £100 million a year. Second, I intend to decrease the pressure on our resources, through lower public expenditure and higher taxation, by £250 million.' To achieve these ends required over fifty separate tax decisions. Combined with the measures of November, 1964 the overall result should be to cut home demand by more than £500 millions in 1965–6, or more than twice the squeeze of Lloyd in his famous deflation of 1961, which netted a mere £210 millions.

The minor direct taxation proposals included the disallowance of business entertaining except in relation to overseas customers, the revision of double taxation and unilateral reliefs, the raising of the exemption limit for income tax to £390 for single and £625 for married persons and of single person's allowance, married allowance and the maximum of wife's earned income allowance by £20. The initial allowance for business cars was to be abolished which merely meant the spread of their cost over a longer period; this proposal was followed by the disallowance of surtax on covenants.

The major taxation changes were the long heralded capital gains tax and corporation tax on which two White Papers were published.[6] The former charges short-term gains (one year on all assets) to full income tax and surtax, and longer term gains at 30%. For companies the rate will be as for corporation tax. Owner occupied houses and goods realizing under £1,000 are, however, exempt. The corporation tax, 'the most fundamental of the tax reforms in this Budget', replaces the combination of income and profits tax on which companies were previously assessed and 'there is every likelihood that the rate will not exceed 40%'. These two landmarks in tax reform put Britain in an unenviable position at the top of the international league in the severity of taxation on the rewards of financial investment and resulted in a Finance Act more complex and more lengthy than that of 1960, with 271 pages, 97 Clauses and 22 Schedules.

'But perhaps the most radical of the reforms was the new Schedule F charge on dividends and other company distributions. Hitherto,

[4] This was published in 1962 by a committee presided over by Professor G. S. A. Wheatcroft.

[5] Callaghan's second Budget: Hansard 6/IV/65.

[6] Two White Papers: Cmd. 2645 (Capital Gains) and Cmd. 2646 (Corporation Tax).

the British system had been based on the proposition that a dividend was, as its name implies, a share of the profits of the company, and that as these profits have been subject to tax when made by the company, they could not be taxed a second time, except to surtax. The assessment in the company had been regarded as substantially an assessment on the underlying shareholders.

It had become increasingly evident in recent years however that this proposition would have to be abandoned because of the avoidance possibilities where the commercial profits and the tax profits diverged. This divergence arose through differences between commercial depreciation and capital allowances for income tax and profits tax particularly as regards investment allowance, as the Exchequer and Audit Department had pointed out, and through manipulation of the basis period rules.

Press comment ranged from '. . . a brave Budget. He (Mr Callaghan) has got his priorities right,'[7] to the accusation that he was treading 'a path strewn with the follies and wreckage of previous Labour delusions'.[8] Parliamentary comment, when wholly party arguments were not being aired, concentrated on the lack of extra incentive for export and the penalisation of private (renamed 'close') companies; indeed, the two main innovations militated directly against productive enterprise; in addition, there was no compensation for the devaluation of investment allowances by the lower rate of corporation tax and no differentiation in the capital gains tax as between the capital appreciation derived as a result of building up a business and that accruing to a mere beneficial owner of land. All these criticisms may yet be answered; for instance a tax credit system for capital expenditure is already under active discussion and in any case it is far too early to attempt a fiscal evaluation of the effects of the 1965 Budget. The new taxes will not begin to bite for many months and it may be years before their full significance can be calculated. One purely historical comment may be in order: all the six Chancellors since the war who ultimately increased taxation considerably, ceased to be Chancellor within a year or less.[9] This may be an omen for Callaghan; although he seems bent on proving an exception.

And yet, although the crystallization of the new conceptions and new mechanisms, which had already been manifest for the nine years following the Radcliffe Committee's Report, had produced a Budget of apparently radical changes, there was no alteration in the basic

---

[7] 'A brave Budget . . .': *Guardian* 7/IV/65.

[8] 'A path strewn . . .': *Daily Express.*

[9] 'All the six Chancellors . . .', namely Dalton, Gaitskell, Butler, Amory, Lloyd and Maudling. Cripps also raised taxation, but by a mere £49 million. See also the *Economist* 10/IV/65, p. 149.

aims of direct taxation. Equity and efficiency were, as they always had been, the constant preoccupations of the legislature and the Chancellor, and constituted the underlying motives which emerge more and more clearly as income tax developed from a simple money-raising mechanism to one of the principal regulators of the economy.

In the eighteenth century, the days of the earliest direct taxes, both equity and efficiency were lacking except, perhaps, in the Window Tax which was administered by the Surveyor; even this was recognized by contemporaries as being imperfect and when the Inhabited House Duty was introduced in 1778, Parliament was clearly taking the view that annual rent was a fairer criterion of ability to pay than the number of hearths or windows. Lord North freely admitted the intricacy of imposing a wholly equitable tax, but at least 'the taxes on coaches, on servants and on houses were proper and eligible as they were visible signs of ability to pay them'.[10]

Rough and ready fiscal justice might well have been secured originally by the expenditure taxes which were eventually massed under the title of the Assessed Taxes; soon, however, as Pitt himself confessed, more than once, they became 'unequal in application and liable to great evasion in practice'. It was of no avail, therefore, to centralize administration under the Commissioners for the Affairs of Taxes if the duties themselves were fiscally unsound, if, for instance, they did not even cover the whole of luxury expenditure. In fact, the exigencies of war finance forced the imposition of income tax which, although 'not free from the objection of inequality' was at least not open to the abuse and evasion which had characterized the Assessed Taxes and the Triple Assessment.

From the beginning of this new era in British taxation policy, there is a clear intention expressed in parliamentary debates and contemporary writings that the imposition of income tax should not cause any fiscal injustice. The reason for the levy of a flat rate of 2s in the £ was so that 'by taxing all in the same proportion' the deduction 'leaves the different sorts of income in the same relative state in which it found them'.[11] Any sort of graduation, which had considerable advocates including Tom Paine,[12] would result in a measure of redistribution and 'the object of the Bill is not to regulate incomes but to tax them'. There was, however, a basic minimum level of income below which the tax should not reach, secured by the system of exemption and abatement. In addition, the permissive deduction of such items as repairs did produce a certain measure of taxation

[10] 'The taxes on coaches . . .': Quoted by Shehab (*op. cit.*), p. 35.
[11] 'By taxing all . . .': Lord Liverpool; quoted by Shehab (*op. cit.*), p. 48.
[12] Tom Paine: See 'Rights of Man'.

of net income. It was Addington who imported a further degree of efficiency by his twin refinements of the system of schedules and deduction of tax at source. Add to this legislative framework the administrative competence of a well-organized bureaucracy and the sum was a thoroughly workmanlike scheme, to some extent the victim of its own success for it aroused the understandable suspicion that the intrusion of the government into the citizen's private affairs might be the precursor of a new despotism.

This was probably the basic reason why Parliament and the country insisted on the Government redeeming its implied promise to repeal income tax which had been granted for the duration of the war 'and no longer', although, to a certain extent, the agitation for repeal was a put-up job. For instance, as is common with petitions, the number of signatures was probably grossly overstated; and there were even some petitions in favour of retaining the tax. In addition, the Government allowed itself to be out-manoeuvred by the Whigs who had seized on the issue as a means of making political capital. It would have been better if Vansittart, the Chancellor, had taken his cue from the feeling for its retention among the progressive politicians and the more enlightened economists.

This feeling continued unabated after the actual abolition, but the hard fact which any Chancellor had to face was that income tax could never be revived without a complete reappraisal of the whole fiscal problem. The raising of loans and the taxing of necessaries, those two old standbys of classical financial policy, only served to perpetuate the adverse balances which could have been remedied by a solution no Chancellor dared propose. The cause of fiscal justice was clearly not being served by a system of exclusively indirect taxation; nor, more important, was the progress of commercial prosperity.

No conception of fairness of incidence troubled Peel's calculations when he reimposed income tax in 1842 although, admittedly, the exemption limit was increased to £150. In his mathematical mind he was simply substituting one tax for another which would be no trouble to administer since the machinery was already there. In any case the tax was 'for a time to be limited'. It seems a curious commentary on Peel's fiscal and financial thinking that, presumably, he contemplated the extinction of income tax when tariff reform had sufficiently swelled the national revenue, despite the fact that if there was no unanimous support for retaining the tax, there was certainly none for a tax structure consisting wholly of duties on commodities. Perhaps his main objection was to its 'inquisitorial' nature especially if regarded as a permanent fact of the fiscal scene, while admitting its value on its current *ad hoc* basis.

No changes of principle were made in the income tax code as it stood in 1842 for a decade, even when the Whigs took over, despite the fact that from its reintroduction, the critics both inside and outside the House were coming round to the opinion that some differentiation should be made between 'permanent and precarious incomes'. The current opinions on income tax, generally, were well ventilated during the sessions of the Hume Committee, but it proved impossible to agree a unanimous report. The sense of the evidence was that income tax was susceptible of improvement in assessment and collection but the general administration worked well. Equity would be better served by differentiation, but not by graduation. Practically speaking, it was a fiscal expedient which had been used, firstly to finance a war and then a free trade policy; but there was, as yet, no whisper of its adoption as an integral part of the revenue.

Gladstone's attitude towards income tax is far less easy to define than that of Peel, partly because he was a far more complex character. At first he saw himself as the inheritor of his master's policy of using income tax for a specific purpose and of his conviction, which the Hume Committee showed was quite generally held, that it was neither suited nor intended to be a permanent part of the revenue. Subsequently he developed a curious ambivalence towards the tax; he was quite willing to use it as an elastic element in the Budget, an innovation he first practised in 1859, while still denying its possible permanency and stubbornly opposing the introduction of any differentiation. The Hubbard Committee, which met during his period of office, came to no concusion and there was more than a suspicion that Gladstone himself had engineered this miscarriage. The reformers' campaign for a more equitable tax refined by differentiation, seemed as far away from success as ever.

With the resignation of the Whig Government in 1866, the history of income tax entered a sort of limbo. The question of the equity of the tax, which had been a live issue for the past twenty years, began to lose its appeal when rates were low, the yield small and the mass of wage earners exempt. Indeed, for a time, differentiation was advocated, not on the grounds of fairness, but because it was thought that thereby the amount of evasion would be diminished, surely the zenith of the *laissez-faire* argument, as applied to taxation. Most of the topics of tax reform inevitably seemed to have a merely academic significance in this period as income tax itself, with its inconsiderable yield, was on the brink of total repeal, and survived almost, as has been suggested, in a fit of parliamentary absence of mind.

Meanwhile the administrative machine had been developing steadily, as mirrored in the Board's reports, which had started in 1857; and of equal and parallel importance was the innovation of income tax Case Law, when in 1874 the right of appeal from a decision of the General or Special Commissioners to the High Court on a point of law was granted to both taxpayer and the Crown. This meant, in the first place, the opportunity, especially when a contentious point of law had been decided by the General Commissioners, of having the decision thoroughly and publicly tested by the Judicature. It also meant the beginning of a whole corpus of reported cases, now in their forty-second volume, which have been decided for or against the taxpayer in the High Court, the Court of Appeal, the House of Lords, the Scottish Court of Session and even the Privy Council. These various Courts during the past three generations or so 'have been forced, not only to seek out the principles inherent in the stark words of the Income Tax Acts, but also to deduce those principles which, though unexpressed, be behind the whole scheme of the Act'.[13]

For there is a surprising lack of definition in the Income Tax Acts, starting with the remarkable fact that nowhere in those Acts is the word 'income' defined, although the Courts have now established that once a source has been allocated to its appropriate schedule, the same income cannot be assessed to another schedule; that is the schedules are mutually exclusive. 'Specific income must be assessed under its specific Schedule, while Schedule D is a residual Schedule so drawn that its various Cases may carry out the object, so far as possible, of sweeping in profits not otherwise taxed.'[14] As a corollary to this, if an alleged profit or gain cannot be brought within the ambit of any of the rules of the various schedules, then, not being related to a source, it is not assessable income.

As for 'profits and gains', there is a long series of tax cases dealing with whether these had arisen from the sale of capital assets taxable as the profits of a trade, or whether they represented mere realizations of capital, which would not be liable. A side issue is that of deciding whether an isolated transaction[15] can be regarded as income. One of the main criteria here has been to discover whether such a transaction, seemingly on its own, could amount to a trade in itself. The casual label 'isolated transaction' does not provide an infallible talisman against assessability.

The Acts are equally reticent on the question of deductions;[16] it was a major problem that, read literally, the Act seemed to produce

---

[13] A. Farnsworth: *Income Tax Case Law*, Preface, p. vii.
[14] Salisbury Estates Ltd *v.* Fry, 15 T.C., pp. 318–19 (Tomlin).
[15] See e.g. Martin *v.* Lowry, 11 T.C., p. 297.
[16] See S. 126 and S. 511, F.A. 1952.

a result which, the Courts concluded, was not intended; for it was stated that no deductions should be allowed other than those 'expressly enumerated' by the Act; no enumeration of allowable deductions in fact exists, merely the prohibition of certain specified deductions.[17] The Courts, therefore, made a very early ruling that 'where a deduction is proper and necessary to be made in order to ascertain the profits and gains it ought to be allowed notwithstanding anything in (the prohibiting sections) provided there is no prohibition against such an allowance in any of the subsequent rules'.[18] 'Proper and necessary' was later defined as meaning, 'according to the ordinary rules of accountancy',[19] which would preclude the allowance of capital as opposed to revenue. The definition, however, did need modification to the extent that what is a proper deduction on normal commercial principles may not, in fact, have been expended for the purpose of carrying on the trade.

Founded on precedents accumulating from judgments on such basic questions as 'What is income?' 'What are profits?' or 'What constitutes an allowable deduction?' gradually emerged the principles which have vitalized the bare bones of Statute Law. But quite apart from deciding cases which have become fundamental to 'the scheme of the Income Tax Acts', the Courts have considered cases of technical and specialized interest some of which have passed into common currency. It is now well known that a punter is not assessable, but an illegal transaction may well be; that a footballer is assessable on his benefit but a county cricketer is not; that a parson pays tax on his Easter offerings, but a schoolmaster does not on board and lodgings in kind.

A somewhat different problem with which the Courts have been presented is the extent to which their freedom of decision may be restricted by the provision that the Commissioners' determination may only be upset if erroneous in point of law; for the borderline between a finding of fact and of law is ill-defined. Certainly the Courts have steadfastly refused to interfere with a decision of the Commissioners if they had sufficient evidence to come to the conclusion they did, even if the Courts, on the same facts, would not have reached the same conclusion.

But although there are variations of the standard problems which have exercised the Courts since the first recorded case in 1875 still arising, one of their most important functions has been, in effect, to keep Statute Law in line with changing social and economic patterns in the modern world. From the earliest, simple cases of wasting assets[20] to the current sophisticated avoidance schemes of dividend

[17] S. 137, F.A. 1952. [18] Lord Parker, 6 T.C., p. 429.
[19] 14 T.C., p. 239. [20] Cf. Coltness Iron Co. *v.* Black, 1 T.C., p. 287.

stripping,[21] the Courts still stand as the impartial interpreters of the Legislature's intentions.

This digression has run ahead, historically, of the development of equity and efficiency in direct taxation, although it is quite clearly part of the former. The often repeated, 'There is no room for equity in a taxing act' does not mean no room for fairness, but no room for anything but a strict interpretation of the relevant statutory words, which is a very different matter. In any case, this steady development of case law is one of the more notable features of the period from 1874 to 1907 which saw a continuation of the battle for differentiation ultimately, after a hard struggle, agreed unanimously to be a desirable amendment and the gradual intensification of that for graduation which was not to be realized until after World War I. The difference between these two projected reforms, each with a comparatively long history, is of great significance. The former was a general modification which would benefit all taxpayers proportionately to their income. The latter would have far greater distributional effects and was linked very clearly to the new and radical conception of taxation as a social instrument. But to consider reform at all, meant that income tax had now finally secured its place as a normal peacetime tax, not an emergency war measure.

It took another Parliamentary Report, the first for forty years, and a Liberal Government to implement its unanimous recommendation, differentiation between earned and unearned income by means of a lower rate for the former; and it took a constitutional crisis and Lloyd George as Chancellor to bring in the first phase of graduation of which the most spectacular feature was supertax. But the strongest stimulus to the law and practice of direct taxation, was the four-year period between 1914 and 1918. With the reforms of the pre-war period and their subsequent gearing to produce seventeen times the pre-war yield, income tax at the outset of the 'twenties was unrecognizable as the diffident child of tariff reform. The Board of Inland Revenue too, having shed its excise responsibilities in 1908, had successfully, for the time, overcome staff shortages and was now in possession of an executive machine dealing with most of the collection and all of the assessing of nearly £600 millions of direct taxation, including the complex E.P.D.; and it was beginning to bypass a good deal of the original local administration, a process which in 1964 resulted finally in all assessing powers being transferred to the Inspector while the Commissioners retained their all-important appellate functions.[22]

One of the casualties of war was the comparative immunity of the

---

[21] Cf. Petrotim Securities *v.* Ayres, 41 T.C., p. 389 or Ridge Securities *v.* C.I.R (L. 2086).

[22] Taxes Management Act, 1964.

wage earner from direct taxation; and this novel and not altogether gratifying situation, together with the rise of the Labour Party, imported a third element into budgetary considerations. To the purely fiscal motive of the nineteenth century had been added the social of the early twentieth century; now political standards were beginning to be used as a yardstick. The 1920 Commission, which had an immense effect on fiscal legislation for at least the subsequent generation, was much concerned with both equity and efficiency; and the series of reforms which it inspired, such as the increase in personal allowances, damped down the initial impact of purely political considerations on financial planning.

It was just as well, since it cannot be said that budgetary policy in the 'twenties and the 'thirties did anything either for the falling export market or the unemployment problem. It was, of course, by no means accepted that the Budget ought to play a leading role in the regulation of the economy; there were still plenty of advocates of the old idea of a balanced Budget, of the Chancellor presenting an annual account of his stewardship. The party arguments turned principally on the proportion of direct to indirect taxation in the Budget, a bias towards the former being regarded as being traditionally Labour policy as a bias towards the latter was traditionally Conservative; and, considering the state of the parties, there had naturally been a shift back towards the pre-war relationship between the two types of taxation.

The war period from 1939 to 1945 for a second time in a generation demonstrated the essential flexibility of income tax administration. For it absorbed a new business tax in E.P.T., a new mode of collecting and assessing tax under Schedule E in the P.A.Y.E. system and finally a radically changed capital allowances procedure which gave industry an immediate opportunity of meeting the challenge of postwar competition which marks the first considered attempt to use taxation reliefs as an incentive to re-equipment expenditure and indirectly as a means of increasing production.

This novel policy of budgetary incentives tied in with the now generally accepted duty of the government to regulate the economy, a duty traceable back to the Budget of 1941, and which has been the constant theme of all post-war Chancellors of both parties; it was in fact Cripps who inaugurated the current practice of debating the economic situation along with the Budget proposals, a practice which can make the speeches somewhat discursive. This regulation briefly consists of making adjustments for both inflation and deflation, maintaining the balance of payments, promoting economic growth, especially in relation to export industries, and encouraging technical research and progress. Both parties have often agreed on the appropriate size of Budget surpluses or deficiencies; division arises when the order of priorities or the methods used come to be decided.

It would be dangerous to over simplify the post-war period except by saying that, in general, the Conservative Party has tended to provide incentives by relieving industry and the surtax payer, while the Labour Party has thought this end best achieved by favouring the individual on lower rates of tax. But there never has been any inevitable correspondence between conservatism in politics and in finance; for instance, Maudling's first Budget was regarded as far more heretical and expansionary than Callaghan's recent orthodox and deflationary measures. For the Budget depends finally on the economic situation and in the end, as Lloyd remarked (see p. 236), the Chancellor is the repository of the nation's financial integrity. 'When the Chancellor is certain what he wants to do and how to do it, then the Treasury will carry it out. When he is unsure and muddled he will be borne along by that mysterious tide called 'the Treasury View'.[23]

The Chancellor in the first place is subject to the collective responsibility of the Cabinet which means that the broad outline of his policy must be acceptable to the party. But as well as political considerations, he must take account of suggestions and pressures from outside the House. Advice pours in from such bodies as the Confederation of British Industries, the T.U.C. and the various professional associations, some of it, Chancellors have complained, tending to be somewhat stereotyped and predictable. This barrage intensifies at the beginning of the year, along with the usual godsibbological[24] speculations. Long before this, however, in the previous summer, the Treasury and such advisers as the Chairmen of the Boards of Inland Revenue and Customs and Excise will have met to begin the talks on measures which may become part of the Budget in the following April; and parallel with this programmed activity, the Chancellor may very often be in touch with the Treasury, the two Boards and their experts not only about legislation which he has decided should be introduced but also about fiscal ideas, possibly arising from some pressure group or sectional interest, which he is considering; he will also have to take a view on suggested technical legislation which the Board of Inland Revenue may have put up on, say, some new aspect of avoidance. Major discussions are kept on a highly confidential basis as between

[23] *Anatomy of Britain* by Anthony Sampson, p. 288.
[24] Godsibbology: This is a word used by Professor Ely Devons; indeed it may have been invented by him, to indicate that new branch of political economy and sociology which bases its analysis on a plausible mixture of fact, esoteric jargon, half-truth, rumour, gossip and anonymous ministerial and ex-ministerial statement.

251

the Chancellor and his various departments; only he knows the total details; the Board of Inland Revenue will not be cognizant of any purchase tax changes; the Board of Customs and Excise will be unaware of any income tax amendments. Throughout this elaborate process the Prime Minister is privy and may be consulted by the Chancellor at any stage, but as far as the rest of the Cabinet is concerned, Maudling, for instance, and Dalton before him, only disclosed full details the night before the Budget Speech.

The Chancellor's position in post-war Britain has been one of peculiar difficulty.[25] In depression he can only hope for small economies in expenditure which the fall in yield from taxation on declining incomes and profits will more than exceed. He may then wish to release more purchasing power by reductions in taxation, but immediately he does he is open to the charge of ignoring equitable considerations; for such a move cannot benefit those who pay little or no tax; large tax reductions can only help those with large personal incomes. His task is no easier in boom periods when tax yield tends to outrun liabilities since direct taxation is often not sensitive or quick enough to control such a movement in time. He may attempt restriction by, say, the increased taxation of company profits, which is popular with wage earners; this, or the threat of it, may reduce company saving too much and possibly output in the vital export industries. He is perpetually faced with the dilemma of imposing taxes with an economic purpose only to find they confound some social purpose, or vice versa. 'Though the duty of regulation is accepted, the science of regulation is still imperfectly known.'[26]

It has also been argued that,[27] whatever the Chancellor may intend, the apparently egalitarian direction of taxation in recent years towards redistribution of income, to which the Board itself draw attention,[28] is only a facade behind which retirement benefits, expenses, the activities of tax planners and the whole apparatus of avoidance give a remarkable immunity to some classes of income. There is not sufficient evidence to say how far this is true even in the light of the Board's statistics which now go far beyond the original administrative records and extend to a very detailed analysis of personal income data. Certainly, as far as fringe benefits are concerned, they may occur both in the directors' dining room and the subsidized canteen. Avoidance is still, as always, a running battle

---

[25] Budgetary regulation: *British Tax Review*, 1959, p. 175. 'The Regulating Power of Taxation.' (Professor C. F. Carter.)

[26] Ibid., p. 180.

[27] See *Income Distribution and Social Change*, R. M. Titmuss.

[28] 'to which the Board itself': Board's Report for the year ended 31/III/49, p. 86.

between the experts on both sides; but it would certainly seem that the cause of equity and efficiency alike may be well served by the new capital gains and corporation taxes. The former could become a major weapon against avoidance and the latter, when it settles down, gains from the fact that it is one tax in the place of two, despite a current movement among the Six for the present British system of a separate income and profits tax. And these two reforms, as the Chancellor stated, are only part of a grand design yet to be unfolded. With regard to Schedule F this, in conjunction with corporation tax, should plug the tax leak (see p. 242) arising from heavy capital allowances and manipulation of basis periods, although these taxes also involve the disappearance of the right of the shareholder to any credit for the tax (whether U.K. or overseas) borne by a Company.

Besides the future plans of the present Government, two general trends are clear. The local administration of income tax, the local General Commissioners and the Surveyor's district, was the direct result of a comparatively elementary transport system. Increasing centralization of income tax administration followed improvements in communications; and the recent experiment of dealing with metropolitan Schedule E liabilities in provincial towns is a striking success. With the advent of the computer this tendency can only increase. The Chancellor was asked in Parliament[29] recently when he hoped to introduce a mechanized accounting system for collection of P.A.Y.E. 'in Scotland, the London area, the North of England, the Midlands and other convenient areas of the United Kingdom respectively'. The reply was that 'a mechanized accounting system will operate from April 1966 for employers in Scotland and the London area. Mechanized accounting will be extended to the rest of the country but the dates have not yet been fixed.'

One of the dangers may be the comparative disappearance of the personal link between taxpayer and the Inspector, but some compensation may be derived from the improvement and increase in statistical evidence. Very little real research has been done on such problems as the effect of taxation as an incentive, as a deterrent, the effect of a slower rate of saving through taxation on the types and number of persons willing to do public work, or the possibility of speeding up the effect of direct taxation in boom and slump periods. It should, before long, be far easier to tackle these semi-sociological questions.

Beyond these immediate points, now that income and profits tax are being combined, it might be possible to amalgamate income tax and surtax; and since there will be a new basis of assessment for companies, a logical consequence would be to assess all liabilities on

[29] Hansard 8/II/65.

Bibliography

Arndt, H. W. *Economic Lessons of the Nineteen Thirties*, London, Cass 1963.

Ashworth, W. *Economic History of England 1870–1939*, London, Methuen, 1960.

Aspinall, A. *Lord Brougham and the Whig Party*, University of Manchester, 1927.

Bagehot, W. *Biographical Studies*, London, Longmans, 1881.

Bastable, C. F. *Public Finance London*, London, Macmillan, 1892.

Bowman, Winifred M. *England in Ashton-under-Lyne*, London, Sherratt, 1960.

Brittan, S. *The Treasury under the Tories*, London, Penguin, 1964.

Buxton, Sydney C. *Finance and Politics* (2 Vols), London, Murray, 1888.

Chamberlain, Austen, *Politics from the Inside*, London, Cassell, 1936.

Churchill, W. S. *Lord Randolph Churchill* (2 Vols), London, Macmillan, 1906.

Clapham, Sir J. *An Economic History of Modern Britain* (3 Vols), Cambridge University Press, 1930–8.

Clark, G. Kitson. *Making of Victorian England*, London, Methuen, 1962.

Coffield, J. *The Tax Gatherers*, London, Hutchinson, 1960.

Connell, B. *Regina* v. *Palmerston*, London, Evans, 1962.

Cook, Colin. *Life of Richard Stafford Cripps*, London, Hodder & Stoughton, 1957.

Dalton, Hugh. *High Tide and After* (Vol. III of his *Memoirs*), London, Muller, 1962.

Dowell, S. *History of Taxation and Taxes in England* (4 Vols), London, Longmans, 1888.

Ensor, R. C. K. *England 1870–1914*, Oxford University Press, 1936.

Farnsworth, A. *Addington, Author of the Modern Income Tax*, London, Stevens, 1951.

Farnsworth, A. *Income Tax Case Law*, London, Stevens, 1947.

Fay, C. R. *Great Britain from Adam Smith to the Present Day*, London, Longmans, 1928.

Fay, C. R. *Huskisson and his Age*, London, Longmans, 1951.

Feiling, K. G. *A History of England*, London, Macmillan, 1950.

Feiling, K. G. *Neville Chamberlain*, London, Macmillan, 1946.

Freemantle, A. F. *England in the Nineteenth Century* (2 Vols), London, Allen & Unwin, 1930.

Gardiner, A. G. *Life of Sir William Harcourt*, London, Constable, 1923.

Garvin, J. L. *Life of Joseph Chamberlain*, London, Macmillan, 1932.

Gash, N. *Mr Secretary Peel*, London, Longmans, 1959.

Gash, N. *Politics in the Age of Peel*, London, Longmans, 1953.

Gillespie, F. E. *Labour and Politics in England 1850–1867*, Durham (U.S.A.), Duke University Press, 1927.

Grampp, W. D. *The Manchester School of Economics*, London, Oxford University Press, 1960.

Griffith, Wyn. *A Hundred Years: The Board of Inland Revenue 1849–1949*, London, Somerset House, 1949.

Halévy, E. *A History of the English People in the Nineteenth Century* (5 Vols), London, Benn, 1952.

Hammond, J. L., and Foot, M. R. D. *Gladstone and Liberalism*, London, English Universities Press, 1952.

Harris, R. W. *Not so Humdrum*, London, Lane, 1939.

Harris, Ralph. *Politics without Prejudice*, London, Staples, 1956.

Harrod, Roy. *The British Economy*, London, McGraw-Hill, 1963.

Hicks, J. R., Hicks, U. K., and Rostas, L. *The Taxation of War Wealth*, Oxford, Clarendon, 1942.

Hicks, U. K. *The Finance of British Government, 1920–1936*, London, Oxford University Press, 1938.

Hope-Jones, A. *Income Tax in the Napoleonic Wars*, Cambridge University Press, 1939.

Hopkins, Harry. *The New Look*, London, Secker & Warburg, 1963.

James, R. R. *Rosebery*, London, Weidenfeld & Nicolson, 1963.

Jouvenal, Bertrand de. *The Ethics of Redistribution*, Cambridge University Press, 1951.

Kennedy, W. *English Taxation 1640–1799*, London School of Economics, 1896.

Keynes, J. M. *How to Pay for the War*, London, Macmillan, 1940.

Keynes, J. M. *The General Theory of Employment Interest and Money*, London, Macmillan, 1936.

Keynes, J. M. *The Economic Consequences of Mr Churchill*, London, L. & V. Woolf, 1925.

Lipson, E. *Economic History of England* (3 Vols), London, Black, 1947.

Longford, Elizabeth. *Victoria R.I.*, London, Weidenfeld & Nicolson, 1964.

Lyman, R. W. *The First Labour Government*, London, Chapman & Hall, 1957.

Lynch, Thomas D. *The History of Income Tax* (Reprint of a Paper), Scottish Chartered Accountants Society, 1965.

Maccoby, S. *English Radicalism, 1832–1852*, London, Allen & Unwin, 1935.

Macleod, Iain, *Neville Chamberlain*, London, Muller, 1961.

Magnus, P. *Gladstone*, London, Murray, 1954.

Mallet, Sir B. *British Budgets* I, London, Macmillan, 1913.

Mallet, Sir B., and George, C. O. *British Budgets* II and III, London, Macmillan, 1929 and 1933.

Marriott, J. A. R. *England since Waterloo*, London, Methuen, 1954.

Miliband, Ralph. *Parliamentary Socialism: a study in the Politics of Labour*, London, Allen & Unwin, 1961.

Mitchell, Joan. *Crisis in Britain, 1951*, London, Secker & Warburg, 1963.

Monypenny, W. F., and Buckle, G. E. *Disraeli* (2 Vols), London, Murray, 1929.

Morley, Lord, *Life of Gladstone*, London, Hodder & Stoughton, 1927.

Mowat, C. L. *Britain Between the Wars, 1918–1940*, London, Methuen, 1955.

Northcote, Sir Stafford. *Twenty-five years of Financial Policy*, London, Saunders-Otley, 1862.

Norway, A. H. *The Government Official*, 1887.

Pigou, A. C. *A Study of Public Finance*, London, Macmillan, 1947.

Pitt, Wm. *Speeches of . . .* (Ed. Hathaway), 4 Vols, London, 1806.

Pollard, S. *The Development of the British Economy, 1914–1950*, London, Arnold, 1962.

Pritt, D. N. *The Labour Government, 1945–1951*, London, Lawrence & Wishart, 1963.

Ramsey, A. A. W. *Sir Robert Peel*, London, Constable, 1928.

Rees, J. F. *A Short Fiscal and Financial History of England*, London, Methuen, 1921.

Rubner, Alex. *Fringe Benefits*, London, Macmillan, 1962.

Sampson, Anthony. *Anatomy of Britain*, London, Hodder & Stoughton, 1962.

Seligman, E. R. A. *The Income Tax*, New York, Macmillan, 1914.

Seligman, E. R. A. *Essays in Taxation*, New York, Macmillan, 1895.

Shehab, F. *Progressive Taxation*, Oxford, Clarendon Press, 1953.

Simon, Viscount. *Retrospect*, London, Hutchinson, 1952.

Snowden, Philip, *Autobiography* (2 Vols), London, Nicholson & Watson, 1934.

Spender, J. A., and Asquith, C. *Life of Henry Asquith* (2 Vols), London, Hutchinson, 1932.

Stamp, J. C. *British Incomes and Property*, London School of Economics, 1896.

Stamp, J. C. *The Fundamental Principles of Taxation*, London, Macmillan, 1921.

Tayler, William. *A History of Taxation in England*, London, Hope, 1853.

Thomson, David. *England in the Twentieth Century*, London, Cape, 1962.

Thomson, David. *England in the Nineteenth Century*, London, Cape, 1964.

Titmuss, R. M. *Income Distribution and Social Change*, London, Allen & Unwin, 1962.

Trevelyan, G. M. *British History in the Nineteenth Century*, London, Longmans, 1922.

West, J. *A History of the Chartist Movement*, London, Constable, 1920.

Wilson, H. *Purpose in Politics*, London, Weidenfeld & Nicolson, 1964.

White, R. J. *Waterloo to Peterloo*, London, Heinemann, 1957.

Williams, Alan. *Public Finance and Budgetary Policy*, London, Allen & Unwin, 1962.

Woodward, E. L. *The Age of Reform*, Oxford University Press, 1938.

Worswick, G. N. D., and Ady, P. H. (Ed.). *The British Economy in the Nineteen-Fifties*, Oxford University Press, 1952.

ORIGINAL SOURCES

Hansard: Budget Debates, etc.
Parliamentary Reports:
  The Hume Committee's Report.
  The Hubbard Committee's Report.
  The Ritchie Committee's Report.
  The Dilke Committee's Report.
  The Colwyn Committee's Report.
  The Tucker Committee's Report.
  The First and Second Radcliffe Committee's Reports.
Reports of the Commissioners of Inland Revenue from the year ended
    31/III/57 to date.
The Income Tax and Finance Acts from 1799 to date.

Newspapers

The daily newspapers mainly used have been *The Times*, the *Guardian* and the *Financial Times* which all have extremely well considered and authoritative fiscal and financial comment.

With regard to Sunday newspapers, the *Sunday Times* and the *Observer* have been invaluable, not only for giving a summary of a week's reactions but for opinions which are not under the immediate pressure of publication.

The surprising feature of all these papers is that while their opinions on current taxation are naturally on a day to day or week to week basis, their forecasts are often astonishingly accurate.

Political periodicals

Principally the *Economist* and the *New Statesman* have been used. The latter's opinions are often somewhat slanted, but both are extremely informative, thorough and responsible in their fiscal pages.

Technical periodicals

The three most useful have been the *Accountant*, *Taxation* and the *British Tax Review*. All three are invariably well informed, lucid and accurate. They are also thoroughly reliable. The latter has rather more theoretical and academic articles, while the first two are naturally more practical, but all have a professional and scholarly outlook.

CONTEMPORARY LITERATURE IN CHRONOLOGICAL ORDER

Date	Author	Title
1799	Friend, W.	*Principles of Taxation.*
1814	Anon.	*Strong Reasons for the Continuance of the Property Tax by a Friend of his Country.*
1822–33	Anon.	Letter addressed to the late Earl of Liverpool, showing that Unjust Taxation is the cause of the evils complained of, with a suggested just system and preliminary observations.
1832	Parnell, Sir H.	*On Financial Reform.*
1833	Sayer, B.	*An attempt to show the Justice and Expediency of substituting an Income Tax for the Present Taxes.*
1844	Buchanan, D.	*An enquiry into the Taxation and Commercial Policy of Great Britain.*
1845	McCulloch, J. R.	*Treatise on the Principles and Practical Influence of Taxation and the Funding System.*
1848	Babbage, C.	*Thoughts on the Principles of Taxation with reference to a Property Tax and its Exceptions.*
1849	Macleod, Sir J. M.	*Remarks on some Popular Objections to the Income Tax.*
1852	Hemming, G. W.	*Just Income Tax, How Possible:* Being a Review of the Evidence Reported by the Income Tax Committee and an Inquiry into the True Principle of Taxation.
1853	Anon.	*A Guide to the Income Tax Acts* (so far as they are applicable to Ireland).
1853	Kingsmill, Sir J.	*Taxation in Ireland.*
1857–60	Hewitt, W.	*Penny Taxation.*
1861	Anon.	*Papers on Taxation:* Direct and Indirect (National Association for the Promotion of Social Science).
1863	Peto, Sir S. M.	*Taxation, its Levy and Expenditure, past and future:* Being an Enquiry into our Financial Policy.
1880	Wells, D. A.	*The Commission of a Discriminating Income Tax.*
1885	Hubbard, J. G.	*Discussion on Income Tax.*
1890	Wells, D. A.	*Principles of Taxation.*

Date	Author	Title
1891	Robinson, F. L.	'Some opinions on certain recently revised propositions suggested with a view to a More Equal Incidence of the Income Tax.'
1892	Blunden, G. H.	'The Position and Function of the Income Tax in the British Fiscal System.'
1893	Seligman, E. R. A.	*The Theory of Progressive Taxation.*
1896	Burns, J.	'A Graduated Income Tax'.
1904	Anon.	*Income Tax*—Wasting Assets.
1904	Anon.	*Income Tax*—Evasion and Fraudulent Returns.
1905	Scarff, A. M.	'The Income Tax Problem' (*Magazine of Commerce*).
1907	Whittaker, Sir T. P.	The New Income Tax Basis and various letters from the *Financial Review of Reviews*.
1909	Leake, P. D.	*Income Tax on Capital.*
1909	Zorn, J. C. L.	*The Incidence of the Income Tax.*
1912	Kolthammer, F. W.	*Some Notes on the Incidence of Taxation on the Working class Family.*
1913	Meuriot, M. P.	'Quinze Ans d'Income Tax' (*Journal de la Société de Statistique de Paris*).
1914	Hobson, J. A.	*The Reconstruction of the Income Tax.*
1914	Williams, E. H.	*Graduated Income Taxes.*
1919	Samuel, H.	*The Taxation of the Various Classes of People.*
1924	Seligman, E. R. A.	*Comparative Tax Burdens in the Twentieth Century.*
1925	Edgeworth, F. Y.	*Papers Relating to Political Economy.*
1930	Anon.	*Report on the Effect of Taxes upon Prices.*
1934	Wootton, B. (Ed.)	*Taxation under Capitalism.*
1935	Laufenburger, Dr H.	*The Interplay of Taxation and Economic Fluctuations.*
1942	Moult, F. G.	*The Economic Consequences of Excess Profits Tax.*

Index